Quantitative Techniques in Foreign Policy Analysis and Forecasting

Michael K. O'Leary
William D. Coplin

The Praeger Special Studies program—utilizing the most modern and efficient book production techniques and a selective worldwide distribution network—makes available to the academic, government, and business communities significant, timely research in U.S. and international economic, social, and political development.

Quantitative Techniques in Foreign Policy Analysis and Forecasting

PRAEGER SPECIAL STUDIES IN INTERNATIONAL POLITICS AND GOVERNMENT

Praeger Publishers New York Washington London

Library of Congress Cataloging in Publication Data

O'Leary, Michael Kent.
   Quantitative techniques in foreign policy analysis
and forecasting.

   (Praeger special studies in international politics
and government)
   Bibliography: p.
   1. International relations—Research.   I. Coplin,
William D., joint author.   II. Title.
JX1291.05   327'.01'84   74-32341
ISBN 0-275-05630-9

PRAEGER PUBLISHERS
111 Fourth Avenue, New York, N.Y. 10003, U.S.A.
5, Cromwell Place, London SW7 2JL, England

Published in the United States of America in 1975
by Praeger Publishers, Inc.

This study is one of a number done by academic and other research institutions for the U.S. Department of State as part of its external research program. The program is designed to supplement the department's own in-house research capabilities and provide independent, expert views to policy officers and analysts on questions with important policy implications.

In recent years the Office of External Research has reviewed many examples of quantitative studies dealing with international and foreign affairs. However, in the judgment of many department officers, much of the academic work in quantitative analysis seemed too methodologically complex, too inconclusive, and often too removed from the practical concerns of government officials to appeal to agencies with policy and operational responsibilities in foreign affairs. Such agencies, including the Department of State, rely mainly on more traditional and qualitative modes of analysis.

The general problem addressed in this project was whether this gap in research styles could and should be bridged--whether some of the methods of social scientists intent on making their work more scientifically rigorous could be applied, with advantage, by government analysts intent on preserving or increasing the more or less immediate usefulness of their work.

The detailed terms of reference for the study were developed by a working group including William J. Trainor, Pio D. Uliassi, and Howard M. Wiedemann of the Bureau of Intelligence and Research; Daniel H. Daniels and Susan T. Tait of the Methods Staff of the Deputy Undersecretary for Management; and John W. Bowling and Paul M. Kattenburg of the Foreign Service Institute. Uliassi served as chairman of the working group and overall monitor of the project.

The External Research Program is planned and coordinated by the Department of State Research Council and managed by the Office of External Research

E. Raymond Platig, Director
Office of External Research
Department of State

CONTENTS

LIST OF TABLES

LIST OF FIGURES

This book presents the results of a study designed to show some of the potentials and limitations that quantitative studies of comparative politics and international relations have for the actual makers of foreign policy. The study, known as Project Quest, was undertaken by the authors and their collaborators under a contract with the Office of External Research of the U.S. Department of State.

Many books and articles have been written on the subject of what functions social science can play in the policy process.[1] We believe, however, that this study is different from most others in several respects.

First, the research on which this book is based received the fullest cooperation of officials in the Department of State. Foreign policy officials are often much too harried by their daily tasks to be able to stop and discuss with an outsider the question, "Are there any ways in which social science might be able to help you do your job better?" In this case, however, officials in the State Department made the decision that they wanted to do just that. Therefore they arranged to have a group of scholars --the authors of this book--serve as special outside investigators into the possible uses of social science in the work of intelligence and analysis of the Department of State. The authors were to be particularly attuned to the possible applications of quantitative data and quantitative techniques to foreign affairs analysis. The institutional commitment made a tremendous difference in the access the scholars received as they pursued their various topics of investigation. Not only did a panel of officials from the Bureau of Intelligence and Research regularly meet with the scholars to give general advice on topics to be studied and to react to the progress being made but also many officials in the department who were working on topics that became part of the project contributed their time and expertise to help the particular scholars involved. To the

This research was supported by the Office of External Research, Department of State, under Contract #1722-220056. Views or conclusions contained in this study should not be interpreted as representing the opinions of the Department of State.

extent that cooperation and responsiveness on the part of
analysts is a necessary part of a study dealing with how
the analyst can be assisted to do his job better, we feel
that this project was on especially firm ground.

A second unique feature of this investigation was that
the first stage of the work involved taking a careful look
at what, in fact, the intelligence analysts actually did.
Many previous recommendations by scholars about how they
could help have been innocent of much detailed knowledge
of the nature of the work they were going to improve upon.
In our case, however, we had both the inclination and the
opportunity to study this work carefully.

Another notable feature of this book is that the demonstration of how quantitative techniques can be used is
cast in a middle level of generalization. We do not talk
about how a specific decision might have been made better
if social science techniques had been used. Nor do we
engage in broad generalizations about how the use of social
science might radically reform the policy-making process.
Our focus is midpoint between these two extremes. Having
identified the major areas of effort in which the department analysts concern themselves, we have attempted to demonstrate how a variety of quantitative techniques might be
employed in these major areas of effort.

This book is divided into three parts. Part I consists of only one chapter, in which we present a report of
our systematic analysis of the type of work produced by
the Bureau of Intelligence and Research. This summary is
based on the coding of 545 documents produced by the bureau
during fiscal year 1972 (July 1, 1971 to June 30, 1972).
The documents were coded by content analysis into several
categories. In brief, we were asking the question: how
does the work of the Bureau of Intelligence and Research
(INR) look from the perspective of social science analysis?
In the second part of the chapter we discuss the implications of our findings for the utility of social science as
an aid to the foreign policy analyst. Part II consists of
the six case studies we used to demonstrate the usefulness
of a variety of social science techniques. These case
studies cover instability in African politics, voting in
Western Europe, the politics of bargaining between North
and South Korea, military expenditures in Latin America,
monitoring and predicting violence in the Middle East, and
the politics of global oil flows. Part III consists of
our analysis of the overall utility of social science techniques for a variety of tasks performed by foreign affairs
analysts. Our recommendations to the State Department as

to actions it might take to make prudent applications of social science to foreign affairs analysis are presented in Appendix C.

We have incurred many debts in the preparation of this study. Above all, we must thank the members of the State Department's working group who were the overseers and co-ordinators of the project. The members of this group, of which Pio D. Uliassi was the chairman, are mentioned in the Foreword. Many other persons within and outside the INR in the State Department contributed to various aspects of the project, and we offer them sincere, collective thanks.

There were many members of the "production team" to whom we are in debt. The graphics are the work of Syracuse University's Center for Instructional Development and also of Miss Beth Maier. Typing was expertly done by Mrs. Diane Wallace and Mrs. Leonore Skurk. The entire study was put together by Mrs. Cathy Lopez. We thank them all.

Finally, we must attribute work on the various chapters of this book to a number of different people. Howard B. Shapiro and Dale Dean conducted the content analysis of documents in the INR that was the basis of our description of the current activities of the INR in Chapter 1 and was also the basis of the entire project in the sense that we had to determine where State Department analysts were before we could make suggestions on where they could go. In addition, Dale Dean was our "liaison" man in the State Department, performing a wide variety of activities for all aspects of the project. The writing of Chapter 1 and Appendix A was a collective effort of Dale Dean, Howard B. Shapiro, William D. Coplin, and Michael K. O'Leary.

Data collection and data analysis for each of the six case studies, Chapters 2 through 7, were undertaken by the following persons:

Chapter 2: Patrick J. McGowan (also the principal author of this chapter)
Chapter 3: John H. Hodgson (also the principal author of this chapter)
Chapter 4: George A. Lopez
Chapter 5: Young W. Kihl
Chapter 6: John R. Handelman
Chapter 7: Gary Brey and Gloria J. Tripolone

Chapter 8 and Appendix C were written by William D. Coplin, Michael K. O'Leary, and Howard B. Shapiro. Appendix B was prepared by Young W. Kihl.

NOTE

1. Among the most recent and representative analyses
of the contribution of social science to foreign affairs
analysis are the papers contained in Raymond Tanter and
Richard H. Ullman, eds., Theory and Policy in International
Politics (Princeton, N.J.: Princeton University Press,
1972). Other works include: Max Milliken, "Inquiry and
Policy: The Relation of Knowledge to Action," in Daniel
Lerner, ed., The Human Meaning of the Social Sciences (New
York: Meridian Books, 1959); E. Raymond Platig, "Foreign
Affairs Analysis: Some Thoughts on Expanding Competence,"
International Studies Quarterly 13 (March 1969): 19-30; E.
Raymond Platig, "Research and Analysis," Annals of the Amer-
ican Academy of Political Science 380 (November 1968): 50-
59; John Gange, ed., "The New Intelligence Requirements,"
Background 9 (November 1965): entire; and Robert L. Roth-
stein, Planning, Prediction, and Policy-Making in Foreign
Affairs (Boston: Little, Brown, 1972). See also several
papers given at an annual convention of the American Polit-
ical Science Association, Chicago, 1971, among them Charles
F. Hermann, "The Knowledge Gap: The Exchange of Information
Between the Academic and the Foreign Policy Communities";
David B. Bobrow, "Analysis and Foreign Policy Choice:
Some Lessons and Initiatives"; and Raymond Tanter, "The
Policy Relevance of Model Building in World Politics." The
most well-known studies of the intelligence process itself
are Sherman Kent, Strategic Intelligence for American World
Policy (Princeton, N.J.: Princeton University Press, 1949);
Harry H. Ransom, The Intelligence Establishment (Cambridge,
Mass.: Harvard University Press, 1970); Roger Hilsman,
Strategic Intelligence and National Decisions (Glencoe,
Ill.: Free Press, 1956); Klaus Knorr, "Failures in Na-
tional Intelligence Estimates: The Case of the Cuban Mis-
siles," World Politics 16 (April 1964): 455-67; and Harold
L. Wilensky, Organizational Intelligence: Knowledge and
Policy in Government and Industry (New York: Basic Books,
1967).

THE USE OF
SOCIAL SCIENCE IN
FOREIGN AFFAIRS
ANALYSIS

QUANTITATIVE TECHNIQUES
IN STATE DEPARTMENT
RESEARCH

One major difference between this study and others
that examine the relationship between scholars and policy
makers is that we have conducted an intensive study of the
activities of a government agency intimately involved in
foreign policy making, the Bureau of Intelligence and Research (INR) in the U.S. Department of State. Essentially
we have conducted a case study whose results, though certainly not generalizable to all activities of all government agencies involved in foreign policy, may be pertinent
to aspects of foreign policy analysis throughout the government.

The major purpose of this chapter is to present the
results of our analysis of the activities of the INR, with
particular attention to the use of quantitative data and
techniques by INR analysts. After presenting this overview,
we will evaluate the relevance of current academic research
in comparative politics and international relations to the
activities of foreign affairs analysts. The chapter con-
cludes with a summary of the case studies that are presented
in Part II, with an emphasis on how the case studies correspond to the types of analyses undertaken by government
analysts.

OVERVIEW OF CURRENT ACTIVITIES
OF THE INR ANALYST

As outsiders, we were faced with no small problem in
attempting to summarize the work and products of the INR.
To get a feel for the work performed in the bureau, we
chose to study, as our measure of output, three sets of

relatively formal written documents: Research Studies, Intelligence Notes, and Miscellaneous Memoranda. Research Studies are the most formal and generally the longest documents; Miscellaneous Memoranda are the least formal and generally the shortest documents. We studied all such documents produced in fiscal year 1972 that were classified no higher than "Secret." We were able to identify 545 of these documents. The sample should not be considered as representative of all of INR's output, for the following reasons:

1. Documents classified higher than "Secret" were not analyzed; therefore, many political and military issues are underrepresented.
2. We did not survey less-formal oral and written presentations made by analysts to INR users; some analysts pointed out that these briefings contained a good bit of quantitative data because they were responses to current events and presented data on elections, ship movements, and so on.
3. Documents that were interagency reports (classified as "controlled dissemination") were not surveyed; this has its greatest effect in reports on Western Europe.

In spite of these limitations on the coverage of INR output, we feel that the 545 documents surveyed represent an accurate sampling of an important component of both the amount and type of work performed by the INR.* Thus we feel that our analysis of these documents constitutes a sufficient basis for discussing the potential role of the quantitative research of international relations and comparative politics scholars.

In attempting to summarize the INR product, we conducted a content analysis of INR documents to abstract information on INR methods relevant to the use of quantitative data and quantitative techniques. The "coding scheme"

---

*In the data presented throughout this book there are some variables in which there are 545 cases and some in which there are 504. The documents were analyzed at two different times for different variables. On the second pass through the documents, we were not able to retrieve 41 of the original documents, mostly Miscellaneous Memoranda. It was the consensus of both the consultants and the INR analysts that the exclusion of these 41 documents would not substantially affect the analysis.

is presented in Appendix A. The scheme yielded an average of .90 intercoder reliability across all categories. That is, in the tests to determine whether the coding scheme produced data that reflected the coding rules and not the idiosyncracies of coders, the coders agreed on their coding decisions almost all of the time. This reliability score is above the norm for most social science research, and we are convinced that the scheme gave us a reliable summary of the documents.

The first step was primarily designed to help us learn about the INR product. However, some of the findings we generated are of general interest to the overall purpose of the project and will be discussed here briefly. We were particularly attuned to three aspects of the findings: (1) the use of quantitative data, (2) the patterns of forecasting, and (3) the complexity of the focus.

Use of Quantitative Data

Tables 1.1 and 1.2 and Figure 1.1 give a picture of the type and use of quantitative data employed in the documents. Table 1.1 shows that 26 percent of the 504 documents employed quantitative data, with political and economic indicators receiving equal attention. Table 1.2 shows that the INR analyst does not usually identify the sources of his information (64 percent unidentified sources). In many cases this comes from his general background knowledge of a situation, based on newspapers, cables, verbal exchanges, and other general sources. Where the data source is identified, it is usually a government document.

Concerning the presentation of data, Figure 1.1 shows that of the 148 documents (out of 545) that used quantitative data, 57 percent presented that data in the text, with no tables or other visual displays of the data. In all cases but one, data was in raw form, that is, the data was trade figures, percentage of votes, and so on. In only one document was the data in transformed or statistical form, that is, in a form that used a statistic to show the relationship between two factors or variables. And that statistic was a citation of work found in a scholarly publication, and not something the INR analyst had computed. This is not to say that there is no verbal use of association, for there is much of this, but there is no use of the correlational statistics that summarize associations between variables.

5

TABLE 1.1

Amount and Type of Quantative Data Used

Data Type	Fre-quency of Use	Per-cent-age
Political	63	48.1
Troop and arms strength ✓	14	10.7
Number of diplomats or diplomatic missions	12	9.2
Voting figures	12	9.2
Military aid	9	6.9
Economic aid	4	3.1
Persons or areas under government control	2	1.5
Balance of seats in legislature	2	1.5
Intensity of military activity	2	1.5
Number or worth of foreign firms national-ized	2	1.5
Number of government executive personnel	1	0.8
Public opinion data collected privately	1	0.8
Public opinion data collected by government	1	0.8
Membership in regional organizations	1	0.8
Economic	62	47.3
Trade and balance of payments	32	24.4
Internal production of goods	12	9.2
GNP and other development indicators	8	6.1
Monetary flows between nations	7	5.3
Budget data	3	2.3
Social	6	4.6
Population size and growth	2	1.5
Emigration-immigration-refugee movements	2	1.5
Cultural and educational exchanges	1	0.8
Tourist flows	1	0.8
Total documents using quantitative data	131	
No quantitative data used	373	
	504	

Note: Percentages are computed on the basis of the 131 documents that use quantitative data.

6

TABLE 1.2

Data Sources of the INR Analyst

Type	Number of Documents	Per-centage
Government documents of country studied	23	4.6
U.S. government documents	24	4.8
U.S. government documents of overseas missions	11	2.2
Other INR publications	6	1.2
Documents of intergovernmental organizations	19	3.8
Newspapers	21	4.2
Statements of leaders, communiques, and the like	79	15.7
Unidentified sources including reports based on analyst's general background knowledge	321	63.7
Total	504	

FIGURE 1.1

Method of Presenting Quantitative Data
(number of documents = 148)

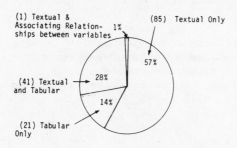

(1) Textual & Associating Relationships between variables 1%

(85) Textual Only

57%

(41) Textual and Tabular   28%

14%

(21) Tabular Only

7

Patterns of Forecasting

Figures 1.2 through 1.7 represent some interesting aspects of the types of predictions made by the INR analyst. Figure 1.2 shows the types of analysis of the documents and indicates that only about 40 percent of the documents are current intelligence, meaning that they are responses to recent events or predictions for the immediate future.* Almost 300 documents are longer range (Reference), in that they attempt to provide background information.

FIGURE 1.2

Type of Analysis
(number of documents = 504)

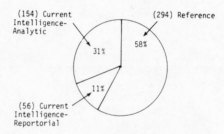

(154) Current Intelligence-Analytic

(294) Reference

31%

58%

11%

(56) Current Intelligence-Reportorial

Figure 1.3 shows the purpose of the analyst in writing a document. Analysts include no forecasts in slightly more than half of the documents (287 out of 545). Also, they are much more concerned with explaining events (328 documents) than with merely describing or predicting them

---

*Among the reports that are classified current intelligence, reportorial documents are merely descriptions of a situation, while analytic documents provide explanations of a situation or discuss the possible consequences of a situation. These distinctions are elaborated in the coding scheme (Appendix A).

FIGURE 1.3

Purpose of the Analysis
(number of documents = 504)

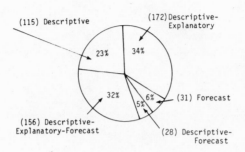

them (174 documents), although such explanations carry
predictive implications in many cases.

Table 1.3 presents a cross tabulation of the type of
document against the purpose of the document. This cross
tabulation shows that Intelligence Notes are most likely
to contain forecasts and Miscellaneous Memoranda least
likely, and that Memoranda are most likely to be descriptive and/or explanatory and Intelligence Notes least likely.

TABLE 1.3

Type of Document and Purpose of the Analysis

	RS		IN		MM	
	Num-	Per-	Num-	Per-	Num-	Per-
	ber	cent	ber	cent	ber	cent
Descriptive and/or ex-						
planatory	157	56	58	50	73	67
Contains some forecast	121	44	59	50	36	33

Note: For the type of document, RS refers to Research Studies, IN to Intelligence Notes, and MM to Miscellaneous Memoranda.

9

FIGURE 1.4

Reference to a Future Date
(number of documents = 504)

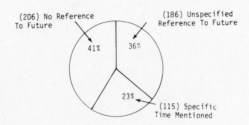

(206) No Reference
To Future

(186) Unspecified
Reference To Future

41%   36%

23%

(115) Specific
Time Mentioned

Figure 1.4 presents a breakdown of the documents in terms of whether or not they refer to the future and, if they do make such a reference, whether or not a specific date is referred to. A substantial number of documents make either no reference or a completely unspecified reference to the future.

FIGURE 1.5

Time Frame of References to the Past
(number of documents = 476)

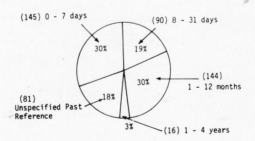

(145) 0 - 7 days

(90) 8 - 31 days

30%   19%

30%

(144)
1 - 12 months

(81)
Unspecified Past
Reference

18%

3%

(16) 1 - 4 years

10

Figures 1.5 and 1.6 show the time dimension contained in the reports. We look at two aspects of this dimension, the reference to past events and the reference to possible future conditions. As Figure 1.5 illustrates, the INR analysts most frequently refer to events in the four weeks prior to the date of the document (235 documents); of these, 145 are references to the week prior to the document. In addition, 114 documents refer to events that occurred between one and six months prior to the writing of the document.

In dealing with the future, INR analysts are not nearly so specific as in dealing with the past. This is understandable in light of the verbal and qualified forecasts made in reports. Figure 1.6 shows that of the 298 documents that make any reference to the future, 183 (62 percent) of these references are unspecified. Thirty-three references (11 percent) are made to the week following the date of the document, and 49 references (16 percent) are made to the month following the date of the document. Another 38 documents (13 percent) have as their nearest future reference the period from one to six months after the document was written.

FIGURE 1.6

Time Frame of References to the Future
(number of documents = 298)

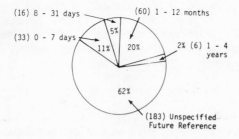

(16) 8 - 31 days   (60) 1 - 12 months

(33) 0 - 7 days   5%

                 11%   20%   2% (6) 1 - 4 years

              62%

              (183) Unspecified
              Future Reference

TABLE 1.4

Number of Countries and Topics Analyzed in a Document

Number	Countries	Topics
1	389	295
2	120	169
3	29	51
4 or more	7	30

Complexity of the Focus

Our purpose with Tables 1.4 through 1.7 is to illustrate the substantial amount of complexity contained in the documents. Although Table 1.4 indicates that a majority of documents referred to one country and one general issue, a substantial number of documents contained references to more than one of each. Many of the one-country studies are analyses of internal phenomena. If these are excluded, a larger percentage of the documents on international phenomena would focus on two or more countries.

The range of countries discussed is substantial. Each of 86 countries was analyzed at least once in the documents. In addition, the various regions of the world as a whole were frequently examined. Table 1.5 presents the 10 most frequent subjects of analysis, and Table 1.6 shows the number of times each of the regions of the world was represented in the analysis.

The range of topics was also substantial. Table 1.7 presents the 12 most-discussed issues.

The information on the countries and topics of issues examined in this set of documents shows, if nothing else, the complexity of the INR's work. The combination of countries and topics covered runs into the thousands. It is therefore reasonable to conclude that foreign affairs analysts are covering such a variety and number of topics that any tools to ease their burden would be welcomed.

In brief, our conclusions are as follows:

1. Quantitative techniques are used in a small percentage of documents and in quite traditional ways (for example, reporting economic growth or social patterns).

2. Forecasts or predictions are frequently made by the INR analyst, but they tend either to be very short-

12

TABLE 1.5

Most-Frequent Subjects of Analysis ✓

Subject	Number of Times Analyzed	Per-centage
Soviet Union	120	29.9
United States	54	13.5
Worldwide	54	13.5
People's Republic of China	52	13.0
North Vietnam	25	6.2
Latin America as a whole	25	6.2
Western Europe as a whole	19	4.7
Chile	19	4.7
South Vietnam	18	4.5
Japan	15	3.7
Total	401	

TABLE 1.6

Subject of Analysis by Region of the World

Subject	Number of Times Analyzed	Per-centage
Americas (excluding the United States	57	17.1
Western Europe (non-Warsaw Pact countries)	51	15.3
Eastern Europe (excluding the USSR)	55	16.5
Africa	21	6.3
Middle East	37	11.1
Far East (excluding People's Republic of China)	55	16.5
South and Southeast Asia (excluding Vietnams)	58	17.4
Total	334	

TABLE 1.7

Most Frequently Analyzed Documents

Issue	Number of Times Analyzed	Per- centage
Trade	87	16.1
Elite character and maneuvering	73	13.5
Attempts at unity or détente be- tween nations	70	13.0
Use of troops, bases, or arms	66	12.2
Military aid and arms sales	42	7.8
Internal economics of a country	38	7.0
Political unrest in a country	31	5.7
Financial problems between nations	30	5.6
Diplomatic exchanges and relations	27	5.0
Proposals for peace	27	5.0
Elections in a country	26	4.8
Economic and technical aid	23	4.3
Total	540	

term or to leave the time frame of the forecast unspecified.
3. The analyst attempts to deal with a substantial amount of complexity in terms of the topics and countries covered.

COMPARISON OF THE WORK OF THE FOREIGN AFFAIRS ANALYST WITH THE QUANTITATIVE LITERATURE OF POLITICAL SCIENTISTS

The purpose of this section is to explore the degree to which the analytic tasks of the foreign affairs analyst could be directly aided by the quantitative techniques now employed by scholars. By "directly," we mean the use of existing data sets, theoretical concepts, and analytical methods <u>as they are now employed by the quantitative schol-ar</u>. The quantitative works that we have surveyed in writing this section are drawn from the fields of international relations and comparative politics, since our data suggests that there are many documents on internal conditions in foreign states in addition to those on relations among

TABLE 1.8

Variables Used to Draw the Sample of Documents

Variable	Codebook Number*
Type of document	3
Classification	4
Office of origin	5
Purpose	8
Subject or region	10
Topic of analysis	11
International setting	12
Type of data used	13a
Organization of data	13b
Past time referred to	9a
Future time projected	9b

*See Appendix A.

states.* Fortunately, some recently published works provide a relatively systematic survey of the use of quantitative techniques in the fields of international relations and comparative politics, and we have based our generalizations about the scholarly literature on those works.[1]

To compare this scholarly work with the analysis and forecasting done by the INR, we selected a sample of 54 of the 545 documents representing the range of analytic tasks undertaken by the bureau.

We used our initial study of the 545 INR documents to draw a sample. The purpose of the sample was to maximize the variety of documents covered on the criteria, listed in Table 1.8, used to classify documents. Our procedure was to choose documents so that every possible value of each variable listed in Table 1.8 occurred in the sample.

---

*In coding issues discussed in the documents, we found 732 discrete issues, of which 210 were internal and the rest external. Of the 131 documents that used quantitative data (see Table 1.1), 57 are measures of internal phenomena and 74 are measures of interactions among nations. Thus, while 29 percent of the issues analyzed were internal, 44 percent of the quantitative data used were measures of internal phenomena.

For example, the sample contains at least one document from each office, and so on. We are concerned not with how representative the sample was of the proportion of dimensions in the 545 documents, but rather with the degree to which every possible category of each variable and type of prediction was included.

The documents chosen were categorized according to three types of analytical dimensions:

1. The units of analysis employed in the document.
2. The types of variables used.
3. The forms of analysis used.

The following section briefly compares the analysis in the sampled documents with the academic literature.

Units of Analysis

The term "unit of analysis" refers to the entity--a person, group, institution, society, social force, or any other unit--that the analyst or scholar is studying. In the case of forecasting, for example, the unit of analysis is the entity whose behavior or future condition the analyst is trying to predict. In the area of international relations and foreign policy, units of analysis may be official decision makers, nations, subnational groups, or transnational institutions.

We must point out a highly significant fact found in the survey of units studied by the INR analysts. The range of units of analysis is most formidable. INR studies on questions of economics deal with the economy as a whole, and with special economic interest groups such as labor unions. In the political realm, they deal with the entire electorate, with political parties and other factional groups, with governments, and with divisive groups within governing coalitions. They deal with specific governments and their agreement and disagreement with others.

The point is that the units of analysis range widely from the very aggregated to the very specific. These topics include matters dealing with entire societies, such as the performance of the economy or the voting intentions of the electorate, down to quite specific topics such as the activities of specific groups or individuals.

This point is most significant because it bears directly on the possible utility of scholarly quantitative work as an aid to the INR analyst. The scholarly litera-

16

ture in both international and comparative studies does
not demonstrate such a wide range. On the contrary, quantitative scholars have confined themselves almost exclusively to the most general and highly aggregated units of
analysis--the international system, the nation, and the
political system. To the extent that INR analysts address
themselves to such highly aggregated topics as a nation's
overall economic development, national population growth
rates, national elections, and general levels of cooperation and conflict between governments, there is some chance
that scholarly work may be relevant and helpful. But to
the extent that analysis and forecasting deal with more
specific and particular units, such as individual businesses,
political parties, or the role of the diplomatic mission of
one country, existing scholarly literature will be of no
direct help.

Types of Variables

As might be expected from the above discussion, we
have found that the types of variables used by the INR
analyst are much more concrete than are the variables
studied by the quantitative scholar. It might be useful
at this point to discuss what we mean by the term "variable." Generally speaking, INR analyses do not contain the
term "variable." This is no doubt true for many reasons,
not the least of which is the stylistic inadequacy of the
term. It imparts a certain degree of formalism and "scien-
tificness" to writing that is generally considered to be
interpretive in purpose. Hence, terms like "causes," "factors," "conditions," and "events" appear instead of the
term "variable" in INR documents. Acknowledging that word
usage is a matter of preference and custom more than anything else, we have used the single word "variable" in
place of the many different words and phrases that appear
in the INR documents we have studied.*

---

*The purpose of this discussion is to prevent the kind
of unpleasant surprise evidenced by Dean Acheson when he
found himself listed as a "variable" in a study of the
American decision to resist aggression in Korea. Social
scientists usually mean no disrespect in listing individuals as variables; however, it is generally more compli-
mentary to be listed as an independent variable rather
than a dependent variable.

We surveyed the 54 documents in our sample to identify
the kinds of variables the INR analyst deals with. We
were interested in discovering the kinds of behavior and
attributes of the units of analysis whose behavior the
analyst was attempting to predict. Once again, the differences between INR analyses and scholarly works are striking.
The documents contain a wide array of variables ranging
from the general to the specific. One is struck by the difference in the level of specificity between the INR documents on the one hand and the academic studies on the other.
The INR analyst looks for variation in such relatively
specific variables as visa actions by governments, the
production of critically important types of weapon, and
the percentage of unemployment among students. The scholar,
for his part, typically looks at the urbanization of a nation, general levels of military spending, and nationwide
frequencies of unemployment. Although these latter variables may occasionally be used by the analyst, they appear
in most cases to be too general to serve his purposes.

The difference between the groups might be just a matter of level of abstraction and not a matter of basic differences in research purpose. Both groups, for example,
may be interested in the political stability of regimes or
the basic ideological orientations of nations and still
deal with variables at different levels of specificity.
However, our comparison suggests that on the whole this is
not the case. The quantitative scholar is interested in
discovering regularities across cases, whereas the INR
analyst is interested in identifying when and how conditions might arise that could affect American interests.
Although each group has some interest in the general purposes of the other, the differences in variables considered
is generally an indication of a major difference in purpose.

Second, the differences can be attributed to differences in data sources for the two groups. The scholar depends in most cases on published statistics, on content
analysis of public documents like newspapers, on voting in
the United Nations, and on public opinion or elite surveys.
In contrast, the INR analyst appears not only to depend
upon published statistics but also to draw upon different
sources of information. He frequently employs "content
analysis" of either public or private documents and rarely
cites public opinion or elite surveys. As Table 1.2 shows,
the principal data sources of the analyst appear to be
written or oral information that he receives through reports
as well as official communications among government officials.

Finally, the difference may be attributed to the types
of causal factors examined by the two groups. The scholar
wants to produce theoretically satisfying and parsimonious
explanations, and may therefore employ whatever variables
provide this. But the INR analyst is interested in the
factors that can be "manipulated" to change a situation.
This may require completely different variables than those
used by the academic.[2]

Because of their different settings, the scholars and
the INR analysts not only have different data bases, they
also view data in a radically different manner. The scholar
who uses quantitative techniques is forced to consciously
treat his information search procedures as data-making activities. Because he is aware of the difficulties in assessing the validity of the data (that is, does it represent reality), he develops formal methods to check its reliability (that is, is it accurately gathered). Hence, a
certain amount of formalism is characteristic of the scholar's approach to the acquisition of information.

In contrast, the INR analyst views information search-
ing not as data making, but rather as the act of himself
becoming informed. He meticulously surveys the written
and oral material that comes to him, looking for reliability
·and validity, through the process of logically placing the
pieces of the puzzle of reality together. He sees his re-
sponsibility not in terms of developing formal evidence of
the reliability of his information, but rather in terms of
making his own subjective evaluation of whether or not the
information is valid. The process of acquiring information is therefore not one of data making, but is one of
determining according to his own standards the validity of
his information.

Whether the contrast in the styles of the two sets of
individuals is a product of their backgrounds and training
or is a product of the kinds of information received and
the intellectual tasks performed, is an open but very important question. If it is a product of background and
training, then the solution is simply one of education.
However, if the problem is inherent in the kinds of information sources that are available to them, then even the
most extensive training in quantitative methods will not
result in the extensive use of quantitative techniques by
the INR (assuming the information sources remain the same).
If the problem is a function of the interaction of both
factors--different styles and different data-bases--then
change will have to take place in both areas.

Forms of Analysis

Those activities that the intelligence officer calls analysis, forecasting, or estimating, the social scientist calls positing a relationship between two or more variables and drawing a conclusion from that relationship. If we think of intelligence analysis in terms of studying the relationship between variables, five major questions can be asked of any analysis in order to classify it.

1. What are the dependent and independent variables? Example: "The perennial dispute between [X] and [Y] parties over [issue Z] is threatening to topple the seven-month-old coalition government."[3]

2. Does the analysis consist of bivariate (two-variable), or multivariate (many-variable), statements? Example of bivariate: See Number 1 above. Example of multivariate: "[Opposition Party X's] absolute majority in a local election and the resignation the same day of a deputy from [Party Y] (a member of the ruling coalition) have placed the ruling coalition under further strain."

3. Are the independent and dependent variables employed in the analysis continuous variables (measuring more or less of the phenomenon), or discrete variables (measuring only the category into which a phenomenon fits)? Example of continuous variable: economic growth. Example of discrete variable: breakup of ruling coalition.

4. Are the relationships between the variables linear, or nonlinear? Example of linear: "The parliamentary majority is shrinking to the peril point as the crucial votes on ratification of the proposed treaties draw nearer." Example of nonlinear: "Economic growth has been uneven, favoring the urban areas and the upper-income groups."

5. Are the variables related at the same point in time (unlagged), or at two or more points in time (lagged)? Example of unlagged relationship: See example of nonlinear relationship in number 4 above. Example of lagged relationship: "Now that [country X] has decided to permit its currency to float, speculative pressure against [country Y's] currency may mount, calling into question how long [country Y] will be able to maintain the parity rate for trade and related transactions."

An important point about these questions is that the answers given indicate how difficult and demanding the analysis will be. Generally speaking, bivariate analysis is simpler and less demanding than multivariate analysis. Continuous variables are less demanding than discrete var-

iables, since it is usually simpler to deal with marginal
increases or decreases of a quantity, which is the case
with continuous variables, than to deal with the presence
or absence of a condition or event, which is the case with
discrete variables. It is less demanding to analyze linear,
as opposed to nonlinear, relationships. And it is less demanding to analyze simultaneous relationships than to deal
with time lags between variables.

Social scientists, in conducting quantitative research
in international relations and comparative politics, show
a strong inclination to engage in work that is less demanding. That is, they deal with continuous variables and assume linear, simultaneous relationships among them. (They
do frequently employ multivariate, as opposed to bivariate,
analysis.) By contrast, analysis found in the INR documents tends to be of the most demanding kinds, involving
multivariate analyses with many discrete variables, in
which the relationships are frequently nonlinear and involve
important time lags. As a matter of fact, the kinds of relationships found in the great majority of INR analyses
represent such complexity that no single quantitative work
in the social sciences could even begin to test their validity. To illustrate this point, consider the following
quotation from an INR document:

> Adoption of an openly "hard line" policy toward
> . . . countries in which actual or potential in-
> vestment disputes exist would not generally be
> in the best interests of [country Y]. Such a
> policy would create more problems than it would
> solve, by giving a rallying cause to ultra-na-
> tionalists . . . by raising issues in countries
> where no investment disputes exist, and by jeop-
> ardizing company positions where settlements are
> being sought.

Making the simplest assumptions possible about this
statement (linear relationships and no time lags), we still
are presented with an extremely complex set of variable relationships. Let us symbolize "hard-line policy" as I_1;
"rallying cause to ultranationalists" as D_1; "raising issues
in other countries" as D_2; and "jeopardizing company positions" as D_3. (Note that these are all discrete variables.)
If we draw an arrow indicating the relationships that are
stated or implied between the variables, we have this representation:

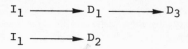

$$I_1 \longrightarrow D_1 \longrightarrow D_3$$

$$I_1 \longrightarrow D_2$$

Or consider this statement: "[Ruling party X's] chances for maintaining themselves in power are increased both by the divisions and disarray that continues to mark much of the opposition, and by the existence of a well-entrenched Communist party that helps neutralize a large portion of the political spectrum." This statement must be predicated on at least some time lag, so that even if we presume linear relationships we are presented with the following symbolic summary. ("The majority party's chances for maintaining themselves in power" we will call D_2; "division in the opposition" we will call I_1; "a well-entrenched Communist party" we will call I_2; and "neutralize a large portion of the political spectrum" we will call D_1.)

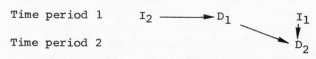

Time period 1 $I_2 \longrightarrow D_1$ I_1

Time period 2 D_2

In spite of more frequent and sustained attempts to deal with these analytical complexities, the quantitative scholar in comparative politics and international relations has not made sufficient progress at this time to be of use to the foreign affairs analyst. The tools that some day may make these analytical problems more tractable have not been thoroughly developed and tested. Consequently, the predominant quantitative literature still deals with linear and continuous relationships with little or no attempt to handle lagged and/or discrete relationships. Like the treatment of units of analysis and variables, there is a substantial degree of difference between the analytical work of the quantitative scholar and that of the INR analyst with respect to the treatment of estimating relationships among variables.

THE SELECTION OF CASE STUDIES APPLYING
QUANTITATIVE TECHNIQUES TO
FOREIGN AFFAIRS ANALYSIS

Given our analysis of the type of work currently being done by the foreign affairs analyst, and the limited applicability of quantitative research in international relations and comparative politics, we devised six case studies that would show where quantitative techniques were and were not relevant to foreign affairs analysis. Our case studies use some procedures that are employed by scholars and some that we have created. They focus on improving the three general tasks of the foreign affairs analyst as described below. This section will present the reasoning behind the selection of the case studies and the characteristics of the case studies that reflect the INR documents we studied.

The first of the foreign affairs analyst's tasks we identified is information gathering. The analyst collects information on a wide range of complex topics. The sources of this information are largely written reports, cables, verbal exchanges, and general background knowledge. There is virtually no use of quantitative techniques for collecting, storing, and presenting information. One of the primary uses of quantitative techniques is the handling of complex information more efficiently, especially the organization of information into clear and efficient formats. Thus the first purpose of the case studies was to deal with the question of the extent to which quantitative techniques could aid the INR analyst in a variety of information-gathering tasks.

The second of the foreign affairs analyst's tasks that we identified is descriptive analysis. Many of the documents we surveyed did not deal with forecasting, but were designed to provide background information and general explanations of conditions. From a social science perspective this is essentially a hypothesis-testing function: certain factors or "variables" are used to account for certain phenomena. Thus our second purpose in the case studies was to determine which quantitative techniques are relevant to testing the explanations and assumptions of foreign affairs analysts.

The third task that we felt was suggested by the INR documents was forecasting. Forecasting is one of the chief purposes of intelligence. And indeed over one-half of the documents did contain forecasts. Thus the third purpose of our case studies was to show how quantitative methods can be used by INR analysts to generate useful forecasting estimates.

These three tasks--information gathering, descriptive analysis, and forecasting--are interrelated. Nevertheless it is possible to examine how various techniques can contribute to each of the tasks separately. Before we present the case studies in the next six chapters, we want to provide some summary information on them. In particular, we want to demonstrate how the range of subjects covered matches the range of work undertaken by INR analysts. The title and a brief description of each of the six cases appears below:

PREDICTING POLITICAL INSTABILITY IN TROPICAL AFRICA

Coverage:

Nations: 32 black African nations
Time period: 1960-69

Principal Topics Analyzed:

Communal instability; elite instability (coups d'etat)

Data: Events data and data on socioeconomic and political attributes from public sources

Quantitative Techniques: Time-lagged correlations; regression analysis; discriminant function analysis

Results: The study successfully tests a predictive model of political instability in Africa based on an index of how prone each state is to coups d'etat.

ESTIMATING RESULTS AND CONSEQUENCES OF ELECTIONS IN ITALY, FRANCE, AND FINLAND

Coverage:

Nations: Italy, France, and Finland
Time period: Post-World War II to present

Principal Topics Analyzed: Percentage of vote won by incumbents; percentage of vote won by Communists

Data: Voting data and data on voter turnout; unemployment; inflation; major events from public sources; quick-assessment questionnaire

Quantitative Techniques: Scatterplots, correlation

Results: The results are fair to poor in testing the assumption of INR analysts about the effect of economic and political conditions on elections. A quick-estimation questionnaire to tap the views of experts provided accurate predictions of election results.

24

EXPLAINING MILITARY EXPENDITURES IN LATIN AMERICA

Coverage:

> Nations: 19 Latin American nations; emphasis on Argentina, Brazil, Chile, Colombia, Peru, and Venezuela
> Time period: 1960-70

Principal Topic Analyzed: Arms expenditures

Data: Arms expenditure data from Department of State (Gertrude E. Hare, 1971); events data from Latin American Military Behavior Project at Syracuse University; attribute data from World Handbook of Political and Social Indicators

Quantitative Techniques: Scatterplots, correlation, cross tabulations, Markov chain processes, National Profile Scoresheet

Results: Assumptions about arms expenditures were not supported for all countries, but a National Profile Scoresheet was successful in predicting changes in expenditures in certain countries.

EXPERT-GENERATED DATA IN NORTH-SOUTH KOREAN BARGAINING

Coverage:

> Nations: North Korea and South Korea
> Time period: 1973

Principal Topics Analyzed: Policy positions of states; the estimated likelihood of the resolution of issues

Data: Expert-generated data on five issue-related variables collected by systematically surveying experts from the State Department and universities

Quantitative Technique: Computer simulation

Results: Concerned mainly with a technique for generating information, this study showed that experts could be systematically questioned to give quantitative estimates on variables and that substantial agreement on these estimates could be obtained. A computer simulation was used to generate forecasts of estimated disposition of issues.

PROJECTING VIOLENCE IN THE MIDDLE EAST

Coverage:

Nations: Israel, Egypt, Syria, and Jordan
Time period: January 1965–January 1969

Principal Topic Analyzed: Level of violence in the Middle East

Data: Events data on violent acts in the Middle East from Edward Azar's Conflict and Peace Data Bank

Quantitative Techniques: Running means and standard deviations; correlation

Results: A measure of violent interaction was generated using foreign policy events data. Successful forecasts were generated of the probability of violence between pairs of states.

MEASURING AND MODELING COALITIONS IN GLOBAL OIL POLITICS

Coverage:

Nations: 34 principal oil-consuming and oil-producing states
Time period: 1964-70

Principal Topic Analyzed: Bloc cohesion

Data: Cohesion and disarray in oil politics measured by indexes of oil flows, trade, UN voting, and oil-related foreign policy events

Quantitative Techniques: Gini index of concentration; relative agreement scores; formal modeling

Results: Data were tested in alternative formal models to show how different viewpoints could be efficiently presented and tested using nonverbal symbols; available data disconfirmed several hypotheses about national behavior.

FIGURE 1.7

Case Study Coverage of the Most-Frequent Topics of Analysis

Case Studies

Topics	African Insta-bility	Mid-Eastern Violence	West European Elections	Korean Issues	Latin American Expenditures	Global Oil Politics
1 Trade	x					x
2 Elite character and maneuvering	x					
3 Attempts at unity or détente			x	x	x	x
4 Uses of troops, bases, or arms						
5 Military aid and arms sales		x			x	
6 Internal economics	x		x		x	x
7 Political unrest	x		x		x	
8 International financial problems	x				x	x
9 Diplomatic exchanges and relations				x		
10 Proposals for peace				x		
11 National elections	x		x			
12 Economic and technical aid	x					

FIGURE 1.8

Case Study Coverage of Time Periods in Forecasts

Time Periods	Case Studies					
	African Instability	Mid-Eastern Violence	West European Elections	Korean Issues	Latin American Expenditures	Global Oil Politics
1 week		x		p		
1 month		x		x		
3 months	p	p		p	p	p
1 year	x	p	p	p	x	x
Greater than a year	p	p	x	p	p	p

Note: x = actual time period used in the study.
      p = potential time period that could be used.

FIGURE 1.9

Case Study Coverage of Types of Data

Types of Data	Case Studies					
	African Instability	Mid-Eastern Violence	West European Elections	Korean Issues	Latin American Expenditures	Global Oil Politics
Governmental statistics	x		x		x	x
Voting records			x			
Trade	x				x	x
Content analysis	x	x			x	x
Expert-generated			x	x		

FIGURE 1.10

Case Study Coverage of Analytical Techniques

Analytical Technique	Case Studies					
	African Insta-bility	Mid-Eastern Violence	West European Elections	Korean Issues	Latin American Expenditures	Global Oil Politics
Displays of one variable						
Time series		x	x		x	x
Cross-sectional distributions	x	x	x		x	x
Indexes	x	x	x	x	x	x
Relationships between two variables						
Cross-tabulations	x	x	x		x	
Correlation	x	x	x		x	
Regression	x					
Analysis of variance						
Scatterplots	x		x	x	x	
Relationships between more than two variables						
Regression	x					
Causal modeling	x					
Factor analysis				x		
Discriminant function analysis	x					
Analytical models						
Probability models				x	x	x
Simulation models		x				
Flowcharts		x				x
Graph theory						x

Let us turn now to some systematic comparisons of the six studies. First we will consider the extent to which the studies include topics of interest to foreign affairs analysts. Figure 1.7 lists the 12 most frequently analyzed topics in INR documents (previously displayed in Table 1.7) and indicates the coverage of these topics by the case studies. In all but two instances each major INR topic was dealt with at least twice in the six case studies.

Second, the case studies tried to reflect the time frame of INR analyses. Of those forecasts in INR documents that specified a future date, the majority were predictions about the very near future. Consequently, we sought to design case studies in which relatively short time frames were employed. This was not always possible, since data sometimes is available for only longer time periods--frequently on an annual basis. Figure 1.8 shows both the time periods actually used in the case studies and also the time periods that could potentially be used if more intensive data-gathering techniques were used. Note that the quantitative analyses of the African, Latin American, and Oil Politics studies could not be conducted for time periods shorter than three months because they depended on aggregate data normally available only on an annual or semiannual basis.

A third purpose of the case studies was to illustrate the different types of data that might be used in the INR's work. Figure 1.9 shows which case studies employed various categories of data. As noted above, the INR analysts make rather infrequent use of quantitative data. Therefore our purpose in the case studies was primarily to sample the work of social scientists with an eye to both actual and potential uses by INR analysts.

Finally, we wanted to illustrate a wide variety of quantitative techniques of analysis in the case studies. The techniques listed in Figure 1.10 are all relevant to one or more of the three tasks of the INR analyst--information gathering, descriptive analysis, and forecasting. They range from the relatively simple, such as visual inspection of graphs, to the more complex techniques of simulation and graph theory.

NOTES

1. For our literature survey, we used Susan B. Jones and J. David Singer, <u>Beyond Conjecture in International Politics: Abstracts of Data-Based Research</u> (Itaca, Ill.:

Peacock, 1972); Patrick J. McGowan and Howard B. Shapiro, The Comparative Study of Foreign Policy: A Survey of Scientific Findings (Beverly Hills, Calif.: Sage Publications, 1973); John Gillespie and Betty Nesvold, eds., Macro-Quantitative Analysis: Conflict, Development and Democratization (Beverly Hills, Calif.: Sage Publications, 1971); Ted R. Gurr, Polimetrics: An Introduction to Quantitative Macropolitics (Englewood Cliffs, N.J.: Prentice-Hall, 1972); and Robert B. Burrowes, "Theory Si, Data No! A Decade of Cross-National Research," World Politics 25 (October 1972): 120-45.

2. For this argument, see Philip M. Burgess, "On Putting Our Oars in the Water: A Clinical Perspective on the Design and Analysis of Foreign Policy" (Paper presented at the Foreign Policy Research Conference, Lake Cumberland, Ky., 1973).

3. These and subsequent quotations are taken from INR documents. The names of countries and actors have been masked to prevent identification.

2

PREDICTING POLITICAL INSTABILITY IN TROPICAL AFRICA

The purpose of the first case study is to demonstrate how quantitative tools might be used by INR analysts to predict the occurrence of political instability in tropical Africa. In addition to demonstrating a quantitative method for making such forecasts, this study examines the current approach of INR analysts to estimating political instability in Africa. It also attempts to demonstrate that a sufficient theoretical basis presently exists upon which to make predictions using quantitative techniques.

Political instability in Africa is widespread. From the point of view of the United States, coups d'etat have removed from office "unfriendly" governments (the Nkrumah regime in Ghana in 1966) and "friendly" governments (the Busia regime in Ghana in 1972). It would therefore be difficult to make a case that it is in the interests of the United States to consistently support or oppose irregular governmental change in independent black Africa. It is quite clear, however, that a key factor in changing the foreign policies of African states toward the United States and other countries is a change in African regimes. The foreign policies of General Amin, for example, are not those of former President Obote. Analysts in the INR are therefore legitimately concerned with forecasting political instability in tropical Africa. Whether specialists in quantitative international politics should help INR analysts accomplish this forecasting function is a more debatable question, given the present (1974) broad outlines of American foreign policy toward Africa, and southern Africa in particular. It is the present author's belief that if the State Department's Bureau of African Affairs and the INR's African Division had a greater voice in shaping U.S.

policy toward Africa, these policies would then be more in the interests of the African states and the United States. Techniques that may help the bureau and the division succeed in making their views heard ought therefore to be made available. This case study illustrates one such set of tools for foreign affairs analysis.

The report of this case study is divided into the following sections:

The Views of INR Analysts
The Theoretical Basis for Making Quantitative Estimates
  Some Methodological Considerations
  Defining and Measuring Political Instability
  Descriptive Analysis
  Explanatory Analysis
Predicting Coups d'Etat in Tropical Africa
Utility of the Techniques to Foreign Affairs Analysts

THE VIEWS OF INR ANALYSTS

In preparing this case study, an effort was made to assess the views of the African affairs analysts in the INR concerning the occurrence of African political instability. These viewpoints were surveyed in part by analyzing the contents of available Research Studies, Intelligence Reports, and Miscellaneous Memoranda classified no higher than "Secret," and in part by interviewing five analysts who have dealt with African affairs in INR. No claim, therefore, can be made that what follows is representative of the thinking of every member of the State Department or INR on this topic. Nevertheless, what the analysts write and say does produce a consistent picture that probably represents widespread beliefs among those who deal with African affairs.

The first point of interest is that the analysts' views are also widely held in the academic community. Their analyses are not at all dissimilar to much professional academic writing. For example, most INR analysts would agree with the analysis of African instability presented by Aristide R. Zolberg of the University of Chicago:

The incidence of coups appears to be independent of the quantitative or qualitative variables normally used to differentiate among African states. . . . Whether or not a coup occurs in a given African country at a particular time is related to

specific and circumstantial features of that
country's current political and economic situation, rather than to any fundamental and lasting
characteristics which differentiate that country
from others on the continent.[1]

This is only a more convoluted way of saying what one
senior analyst argued, that "anything can happen at anytime,
anywhere" (interview, January 15, 1973).

Notably characteristic of the cultural milieu of the
Department of State, and thus of INR analysts, is a case-
by-case approach and a concern with only the most current
of events. One of the findings of the project, reported
in Chapter 1, was that, out of 545 Research Memoranda and
Intelligence Reports produced in 1972, 389 (or 71 percent)
dealt with only one country. This focus on the affairs of
a single state was also manifest in the INR studies for
the present case study. Each of the documents dealing with
African political instability treated only one country.
In interviews, analysts were able to discuss the features
of each instance of instability, but they would not or
could not make comparisons among African states on a sustained basis.

This case-by-case approach is so ingrained in the department's normative and intellectual environment and bureaucratic structure that analysts simply do not think in
comparative terms. When one analyst was asked to pick out,
from among the 14 states his office deals with, the country that was most likely to experience a coup in 1973, he
was forced by his methodology to present as a response a
20-minute, country-by-country description of current politics in each country. When asked by this interviewer to
pick the one state that was most likely for whatever reason to have a coup in 1973, he refused, saying that it was
impossible to make such predictions. There are a number
of explanations for this type of response, possibly including the interviewer's failure to make clear what he wanted.
However, in the context of the other interviews and the
written work, one is drawn to the conclusion that the prac-
tice of treating each country as separate and distinct has
limited the willingness and ability of the analyst to make
the kinds of generalizations necessary to answer the question.

A concern with the most current events is equally
evident in the materials examined for this case study. In
Chapter 1 we reported that, out of the 395 Memoranda and
Reports that did contain a specific reference to past

events, 235 (or 60 percent) dealt with events occurring no earlier than the previous month. In a similar fashion all of the African documents read for the present case study dealt with very recent instability events or current rumors of such events. This is not to say, however, that analysts are ignorant of history and past events. On the contrary, frequent references to these topics were made in the oral interviews conducted in the preparation of this case study. It is to say, however, that this knowledge of history, and the relevance of the past to an analysis of the present, does not usually appear in the written analyses of African political instability, perhaps because of the historical sophistication of consumers of INR reports.

In spite of these tendencies, the analysts did make forecasts and did attempt to explain coups and other related forms of instability in Africa. For that reason, an attempt was made to uncover the implicit theory that seemed to be operating in the thinking of the analysts. Factors used in the written documents and in the oral interviews were classified into the following broad topic headings: (1) individual characteristics of the top leader; (2) features of the government elite as a whole; (3) political structures and processes; (4) economic factors; (5) sociological characteristics of the African society; and (6) external influences upon a given state from other African states or elsewhere.

The explanations used by analysts for the occurrence of coups and instability repeatedly fall into one or more of these categories. This means that although the analysts normally concern themselves with a single country and a short time frame, they do engage in what social scientists call "theorizing." The analyst is likely to speak of a "persistent factor" or "conditions that make a coup likely," rather than of the social scientists' "variables," "models," and "theories." But these are more differences in semantics than in substance. The analysts use their (implicit) theories in an effort to predict and explain instability in particular countries at a particular time. Social scientists use their (somewhat more explicit) theories to generalize across a larger number of countries and over a longer time frame.

Furthermore, there is a decided pattern in the types of factors the analysts cite as being important in African instability. They generally play down (at least by implication) the importance of social factors in explaining instability. Thus, little attention is paid to a common allegation of nongovernmental students of African affairs that instability is partly caused by the fact that national elites are more closely linked to elites of the former metropole than to their own countrymen, that is, the general problem of dependence. The analysts also play down an economic interpretation of African instability. They do often cite a "stagnating economy" as a background factor associated with coups d'etat, but this is about all.

Political factors are given the most emphasis by the analysts, being cited almost twice as frequently as any other factors. Their political analyses are not, however, related to current comparative political "theories" such as systems analysis or structural-functional analysis. Instead, INR explanations tend to take on the ad hoc and post hoc character of some scholarly explanations such as this argument advanced by Zolberg:

> If the incidence of coups appears random, this is not true of the manner in which they develop. The atmosphere within which a coup is likely to occur can be created by almost any type of conflict situation, originating almost anywhere in the social structure, within the ruling elite or outside it. . . . The government has to be threatened, which means that the initiators of the coup must be able to deploy force in the capital. Hence, successful coups usually involve two bodies of manpower; trade unions and the formal bearers of force, and Army and police.[2]

Similarly, in an analysis of a coup in one African state, the INR analyst pointed out that the deposed regime had been popular with the majority of the population, and with the rural sector that was benefiting from the regime's rural development projects, but that a dissatisfied urban minority--the army and trade unions--had the capacity to act, and thus overthrew the government.

In discussing political factors, analysts stress the importance of inept and unpopular government policies, implying that there is a feedback between government action on the one hand and government support and legitimacy on the other. Analysts also emphasize the importance of key interest groups with a capacity to act against a government, especially those which are urban based or well armed, such as the army and police; youth; students and intellectuals; labor unions; civil servants; traders; the church hierarchy; and "urban dwellers" in general. It would seem that what is implied is an interest-group theory of African politics. Important characteristics of these groups are their cohesion or fragmentation.

Certain general characteristics of the political system are also sometimes mentioned as being important. The existence of institutionalized procedures for change in leadership and the presence of a strong national political party are considered as decreasing the likelihood of coups and other forms of instability. Finally, the presence of widespread corruption in the system and a past history of instability are said to promote instability both in the present and the future.

Other factors, which might be called background factors, appear to the analysts as less important (as judged by the infrequency with which they are cited) but nevertheless as conditioning the likelihood of instability. A stagnating economy, which can have a number of manifestations such as inflation, unemployment, and single-crop dependency, is the principal economic factor cited. The chief sociological factor mentioned is the ethnic pluralism of the state and a history of ethnic rivalries in the military forces and in society at large. External factors receive little attention as factors leading to instability. One exception is that some analyses discuss the special situation of the former French colonies. Many analysts, but not all, are prepared to argue that France's position is often crucial in francophone Africa. Certain regimes, such as those in Senegal, the Ivory Coast, Niger, and Cameroon, where France is heavily involved and close to the head of state, are less likely to manifest instability than states believed to be less important to the French economic and political elite. The analysts do give some weight to the political skill and physical health of the African president or prime minister as being barriers to antiregime instability. Finally, the relative cohesion or fragmentation of the elite is seen in some cases to be important. If an elite sector, or interest group, is cohesive, and if its institutional autonomy is threatened by inept governmental policies, then it may move against the government. This is often cited as a factor promoting military interventions in politics in Africa.

All in all, the INR analyses of African instability present an ambiguous picture. On the conscious and direct level of analysis, analysts seem to agree with scholars such as Zolberg who argue that there are no systematic factors associated with instability and that these phenomena occur randomly throughout Africa. In short, no general explanations of African political instability are possible.

The best one can do is to offer ad hoc and post hoc explanations, once a coup has occurred in a given country. This
apparent randomness probably derives from the case-by-case
approach of INR analysts. But, on an implicit and indirect
level (one might almost say unconscious level), the analysts
appear to rely on what can be called an interest-group
theory of political instability in Africa.

This theory argues that African governments have very
limited resources that they can use to obtain compliance
from masses and elites. Moreover, these limited resources
of money, power, and legitimacy have often been ineffectively
used because of inept and unpopular governmental policies.
These two factors have led to increased political activity
by ethnic and interest groups in society. The government
is increasingly faced with demands from the ethnic interest
groups in the rural sector and the occupational interest
groups in the urban areas. With limited resources, power,
and authority, the government increasingly relies upon
force, which leads to direct or indirect military intervention and communal violence. In the next part of this chapter we will use quantitative data to test both the explicit
conception that coups and instability are random and the
implicit interest-group-based theory of the analysts.

Any analysis, whether it uses the quantitative techniques of this case study or the qualitative case-by-case
approach of the INR analysts, should not be designed just
to explain African political instability. Analysis should
help us to forecast or anticipate the occurrence of the
problem in question. INR analysts generally deny that the
occurrence of instability can be predicted with a useful
degree of accuracy. Insofar as they deny the impossibility
of predicting discrete events in particular countries,
there can hardly be any doubt that they are correct. Even
the most optimistic social scientist would also agree that
such precise prediction is impossible at present. However,
many social scientists--and some analysts--would agree that
probabilities can be attached to the likelihood of instability in a given country and that probabilistic predictions
can be made about the frequency and level of instability
phenomena in Africa for a given time period. These types
of predictions are the only ones that can be made from
statistical generalizations and thus the only ones ever
made by social scientists. We cannot predict how a particular individual will vote, but we can predict quite well
what proportion of people with a given set of characteristics will vote Republican, or Democrat.

Nevertheless, many State Department analysts doubt
the possibility of making useful probabilistic predictions,
in addition to denying the possibility of predicting discrete
events. This view is quite understandable in light of the
analytic procedures normally employed in the department.
The case-by-case and day-to-day approach leads analysts to
respond to the question of how can you predict a coup by
saying, "If you could, what you would want to do is psycho-
analyze the five or ten key people and see what their
breaking point is. Then you could say when a coup might
occur." (Interview, January 15, 1973.) The day-to-day and
case-by-case approach quite naturally leads analysts to
deny the relevance of academic research to their interests.
    Not surprisingly, the case-by-case and day-to-day
technique leads to only the most cautious predictions, such
as the following:

> In the absence of an identifiable group strong
> enough to challenge [General X], it would be pre-
> mature to predict his early overthrow by a coup.
> But the present power structure within the army
> is unstable enough to make a coup an ever-present
> danger, and it would not be surprising to see
> [General X] replaced by another army leader or
> group--thereby creating an even more unstable re-
> gime (INR report, January 1972).

Is a coup d'etat against General X likely, or unlikely?
This quotation merely illustrates our previous point--with
which social scientists and INR analysts would agree. With
rare exceptions, it is not possible to make useful predictions about specific events. And, as the quotation demonstrates, an attempt to do so is likely to result in ambiguous generalizations about the situation in question.
    Since INR analysts do not work with explicit theories
(but, unavoidably, with implicit ones), their bases of
prediction are past experience and a general "feel" for
the problem. This is illustrated by the predictive technique of the next quotation, on a different situation:

> [President Y] would undoubtedly rush back to
> [the capital] if he believed he faced real trou-
> ble, but, after all, he is not infallible.
> Frightened army officers could take preemptive
> security measures in his absence against their
> rivals. Such a limited move could quickly set
> off a chain reaction over which [President Y]

might lose control. <u>If previous experience is any guide</u>, this probably will not happen, but [President Y] will have to defuse the mounting fears and frustations within the military on his return to [the capital] if coup rumors are not to become reality. (INR report, February 1972, emphasis added.)

What is striking about this analysis is the failure to mention any factors other than past experience that might help one anticipate whether a coup is going to occur. It is probably true that in the absence of any explicit theory, past experience is the best guide we have for making anticipatory statements. However, a combination of explicit theory and social science techniques can be used to make much firmer predictions than those we have quoted. A demonstration of this point will be presented in the rest of this chapter.

THE THEORETICAL BASIS FOR MAKING QUANTITATIVE ESTIMATES

The purpose of this section is to demonstrate that a comparative study of political instability in tropical Africa can yield theoretical relationships sufficiently strong to build a system for statistical forecasts. In the next section of the case study we will identify the specific statistical forecasting method we think would best fit the purpose. However, before we can do that we must deal with the question of whether the only way that coups and civil wars in Africa can be explained is after the fact and with reference to each particular case.

Some Methodological Considerations

When we use the term "sufficiently strong theoretical relationships," a particular viewpoint of social science methodology is assumed that requires further discussion. Basically, we feel that the most critical factor in developing useful and valid social science knowledge is the development of conceptual definitions. Although many individuals, including academics and members of the intelligence community, feel that the social sciences are jargonistic, it is absolutely necessary that care be taken with definitions if "sufficiently strong theoretical relationships" are to be discovered and if they are to mean anything.

If careful scientific definitions are the absolute prerequisite for quantitative analysis, then the most important place to start the process is with the phenomena one is seeking to describe, explain, and ultimately anticipate. The technical term used for the phenomenon under such scrutiny is "dependent variable." In this particular case study, the dependent variable is political stability in tropical Africa.

Before we define this concept, however, three comments are in order about the process of concept definition. First, there is no such thing as a right or wrong scientific definition, only a definition that is more or less useful. Whatever instability "really" is, this question is not the concern of social science. Thus, the definitions we will soon present are stipulative definitions, nothing more than rules for the use of words like "coups," "communal instability," and "elite instability." Second, the test of the usefulness of a scientific definition is the extent to which concepts so defined can enter into general sentences that explain the phenomenon in question. For example, "race" is a scientifically useless concept, for although it can be clearly defined by reference to genetic structures and blood types, race is not related to anything else. If you know only a person's race, you cannot predict anything else about the person without additional information. By this criterion, our definitions can be evaluated only after empirical research has been undertaken. Other than the following, there are no a priori criteria for evaluating scientific definitions. Third, every definition must stipulate at least one empirical referent so that we can observe the presence or absence of the defined trait in the real world. "Race" has this characteristic, and so will our definitions of political instability. Our definitions therefore stipulate rules for language usage, nothing more. They should not be vague or ambiguous, and they should have real-world or empirical referents.

This brief digression into the philosophy of concept formation is necessitated by the imprecision with which terms like instability, turmoil, conflict, and violence have been used in scholarly writing and in analyses by government researchers. A fundamental application of social science methods to foreign affairs analysis would be the clear-cut and consistent use of words to refer to various foreign affairs phenomena.

Defining and Measuring Political
Instability

We are concerned in this case with <u>political insta-</u>
<u>bility</u>, which is a characteristic of <u>governments</u>. By "gov-
ernments" we mean those institutions and activities in societies that determine who gets what, when, and how, or
whereby valued things are allocated in the society. The
members of the United Nations all have governments that
perform this allocative activity more or less well, and
membership in the United Nations will thus be our empirical
indicator of the existence of a government. All of the independent African states are members of the United Nations
and thus meet this operational definition of having governments. "Politics," given our definition of governments,
refers to the activities of decision makers to get compliance for allocative decisions. Governments get compliance
for their decisions by the use of influence, authority,
and coercive power. "Political instability," therefore,
is a condition affecting governments in which the established patterns of authority break down, and the expected
compliance to the government is replaced by political violence. Instead of complying with government decisions out
of habit, belief, or loyalty, individuals and groups in
society engage in behavior characterized by the physical
injury or subjection of persons or property with the intent
to bring about an alteration in the structure of the government; this is political violence.

Having defined political instability in Africa in
terms of violence between political actors in conflict
over the decisions governing the distribution of rewards
in society, we must now specify the empirical referents of
such behavior. Previous comparative empirical research on
African political instability indicates that there are two
basic and statistically unrelated types that can be called
(1) elite instability and (2) communal instability.[3] By
basic we mean that these types are conceptually distinct,
and by statistically unrelated we mean that instances of
each type of instability do not occur together at the same
time in the same countries.

"Elite instability" refers to events in which members
of the political elite, or some alternative elite such as
the military, use violent action or the threat of violence
to remove persons from their command positions in the na-

tional government. Operationally, three distinct types of
behavior represent empirical manifestations of elite instability in Africa.

Coups d'etat are events in which the existing political regime is suddenly and illegally displaced by the action of relatively small elite groups without an overt mass
participation in the event. The change in regime may vary
from the wholesale replacement of decision makers to a dis-
solution of the constitutional relationships without large-
scale personnel replacement. Coups may be organized by
the governing elite or by an alternate elite like the military. The aims are varied and personal injury can range
from negligible to very great.

Attempted coups are unsuccessful coups in which it is
known that some combination of the following occurred:
(1) the assassination, attempted assassination, or arrest
of some members of the governing elite, (2) a disruption,
interruption, or takeover of government facilities that
is temporary (less than one week), and (3) the sudden muti-
ny, mobilization of, or action by armed forces explicitly
aimed at the takeover of government.

Plots are events in which an announcement or admission
is made by the governing elite that a plot to overthrow
the government has been discovered. Whether it was a
"real" coup plot can never be absolutely determined; the
official statement that plotting existed is regarded as itself a significant instance of elite instability.

The incidence of events such as these for the states
of Africa can be recorded from public sources such as Africa Digest, Africa Report, Africa Diary, African Research
Bulletin, Europa Yearbook, Middle East Journal, Deadline
Data, New York Times Index, and scholarly monographs on
the countries in question. Coders can then be trained and
set to work abstracting, coding, and key-punching these
events. If the rules used by the coders are sufficiently
specific, a high degree of intercoder agreement can be
generated in the identification and coding of instability
events from the sources. As in the case of any type of
document-based research, events data collections are only
as good as the original sources. African events data is
likely to be more reliable for big, English-speaking states
than for small, French-speaking countries, and it is unreliable prior to 1962. Still, the three types of event
just defined--coups, attempted coups, and plots--are all
very "newsworthy" and likely to be picked up by the press.

Once every identifiable instance of elite instability
behavior has been recorded, it is then necessary to create

some sort of scale of elite instability on which each African country can be placed. Many methods of scale construction are used in the social sciences. One of the simplest
methods is to add up the instances of elite instability
for each state. If one considers each type of behavior
qualitatively different, then weights can be attached prior
to summation. If we give coups a weight of 5, attempted
coups a weight of 3, and plots a weight of 1, we produce
the scale of elite instability in Table 2.1.
     Similar procedures can be applied to defining and mea-
suring communal instability. "Communal instability" refers
to events in which members of communal groups--that is,
groups whose members share ascribed characteristics of
ethnicity, language, religion, or territory--use violence
to change the distribution of authority among communal
groups within the general population or between the government and the group. Operationally, four distinct types of
behavior represent empirical instances of communal instability in Africa.
     Civil war is an event in which an identifiable com-
munal group attempts by secession to form a new government
based on boundaries of ethnic community, or by takeover to
monopolize political power for the communal group within
the existing political system. We will give such an event
a weight of 5.
     Rebellions are events in which an identifiable com-
munal group seeks to gain increased autonomy from the national government or attacks supporters or agents of the
government without aiming to secede from or monopolize the
existing polity. A rebellion will be given a weight of 4.
     Irredentism represents an event in which an identifia-
ble communal group seeks to change its political allegiance
from the government of the territorial unit in which it re-
sides to a government, either existing or to be created,
in which the decision makers share the communal identification of the irredentist group concerned. An instance
of an irredentist movement will be scored 3.
     Ethnic violence is an event of short duration in which
members of two identifiable communal groups are antagonists
in violence not designed to secure independence, autonomy,
or political realignment for the groups concerned. Being
less dangerous for the existence of governments, ethnic
violence will be weighted 1.
     When we consult the same sources used to gather data
on elite instability and when we multiply the score for
each event by the number of years in which it was reported
for any country (in order to weight for the duration of

47

TABLE 2.1

Scales of Elite and Communal Political Instability for 32
Independent Black African States, from the Date of
Independence to December 1969

	Elite Instability			Communal Instability	
Rank	Country	Value	Rank	Country	Value
1.	Dahomey	26	1.	Sudan	38
2.	Sudan	22	2.	Ethiopia	30
3.5	Zaire	20	3.5	Zaire	27
3.5	Togo	20	3.5	Nigeria	27
5.	Congo, B.	17	5.	Chad	17
6.	Burundi	16	6.	Rwanda	15
7.	Ghana	13	7.	Kenya	14
8.	Nigeria	12	8.	Uganda	12
9.	Sierra Leone	11	9.	Mali	6
11.	CAR	8	11.	Burundi	5
11.	Somalia	8	11.	Ghana	5
11.	Uganda	8	11.	Ivory Coast	5
13.5	Mali	7	13.	Congo, B.	4
13.5	Upper Volta	7	14.5	Somalia	3
15.5	Liberia	6	14.5	Zambia	3
15.5	Senegal	6	16.	Mauritania	2
17.	Chad	5	18.	Cameroon	1
18.5	Ethiopia	4	18.	Dahomey	1
18.5	Guinea	4	18.	Sierra Leone	1
20.	Gabon	3	26.	Botswana	0
21.	Ivory Coast	2	26.	CAR	0
24.	Cameroon	1	26.	Gabon	0
24.	Kenya	1	26.	Gambia	0
24.	Lesotho	1	26.	Guinea	0
24.	Malawi	1	26.	Lesotho	0
24.	Niger	1	26.	Liberia	0
29.5	Botswana	0	26.	Malawi	0
29.5	Gambia	0	26.	Niger	0
29.5	Mauritania	0	26.	Senegal	0
29.5	Rwanda	0	26.	Tanzania	0
29.5	Tanzania	0	26.	Togo	0
29.5	Zambia	0	26.	Upper Volta	0

Average value	7.19		6.75
Coefficient of varia-bility	102.09		151.56
Standard deviation	7.34		10.23

Note: Date of independence for Liberia and Ethiopia set at
1956 to agree with the independence of Sudan.

Source: D. G. Morrison, R. C. Mitchell, J. N. Paden, and
H. M. Stevenson, Black Africa: A Comparative Handbook (New York:
Free Press, 1972), pp. 128-29.

communal instability behavior) and then sum the resulting products, we get the scale of communal instability that is also reported in Table 2.1.

The object of conceptual definition, operational definition, data gathering, and scale construction is to measure reliably and validly complex social phenomena such as African elite and communal instability. No measurement operation is perfect in any scientific enterprise, whatever the field of inquiry. On the other hand, one cannot ask and attempt to answer scientific questions without measurement procedures. Thus, in the application of quantitative techniques to the study of foreign affairs problems, we must continually ask if our measurement operations have produced scales and indexes of the phenomena in question that are "good enough" to serve as the basis for research and possibly for policy recommendation. The "good enough" question is another way to talk about the related issues of reliability and validity.

In constructing scales such as those presented in Table 2.1, the major sources of measurement error and thus low reliability are the coders and the data sources. Tests of intercoder agreement can be undertaken to check one source of error, and in this case the coders can be shown to have had no difficulty in identifying and accurately coding the events.[4] Source reliability is a more difficult aspect of reliability to evaluate, and there is no absolute criterion one can use to estimate it. It should be noted, however, that the object of the exercise we have just completed is not to collect and code every instance of such behavior that ever happened in each of these 32 African states. It would be nice to do this if one could, but it would be foolish to think that one had ever completed such a task, given real-world constraints of time, energy, and money. Rather, one aims to identify and code every such event reported in a comprehensive but workable set of sources. Some actual events may not be represented in the resulting scales. As long as there is no evidence of systematic error or bias in the scales, such as French-speaking states having low scores because only English-language sources were used, such error may be considered random and therefore unlikely (under the assumptions of probability theory) to materially effect the results of analysis. There does not appear to be any such systematic bias in these two scales, so we will therefore consider them acceptably accurate (but not "perfect") measures of elite and communal instability in Africa for these states during this period of time.

While apparently reliable, do these scales measure
what we defined above as communal and elite instability?
This is the vexatious question of the validity of our measures, for which, again, there is not an absolute answer.
There are, however, four types of validity questions that
can be asked of scales such as these, and if the answers
are all favorable, then this constitutes convergent evidence
that we have measured what we set out to measure. First
we can ask, "What is the face validity of these scales;
that is, do the resulting scores and rank orders agree
with what expert opinion would expect? Do they look about
right?" This is obviously a rather weak and very judgmental
method for assessing validity, but all validity assessments
are contingent and judgmental anyway. As foreign affairs
experts, the readers of this case study are as well placed
as its authors to make face judgments about the validity
of our measures. We must remember, however, that expert
opinion can be wrong, as medical doctors and investment
analysts illustrate every day. Therefore, more rigorous
techniques for assessing validity have been developed by
social scientists.

Content validity refers to the representativeness of
the items or, in this case, types of events, that have been
included in the scales. Do the event types of coup, attempted coup, and plot capture the main features of African elite instability? Do civil wars, rebellions, irredentist movements, and ethnic conflicts get at the typical
features of African communal conflict? Again, answers to
these questions rely very heavily upon expert opinion.
As before, it is not the object of the exercise to include
in the operational definition of each type of instability
every possible type of event relating to each pattern.
Rather, are the included event types a "representative sample" of elite and communal instability? In this case they
do appear to meet this judgmental test; moreover, statistical analyses of this data (via factor analysis) have
shown that the types of events included in the operational
definitions of elite and communal instability are associated with each other.[5]

Construct validity directly asks whether we have in
fact measured what we started out to measure. The answer
to this question is looked for in the degree to which our
attempt to measure instability is correlated with other
persons' independent attempts to measure the same phenomenon using different indicators. If independently created
scales M and M' are in close agreement, it is inferred
that they have validly measured X, the concept or construct

they claim to represent empirically. The social scientists
who created our two scales report a strong correlation
($r = .72$) between their scale of communal instability and
Gurr's measure of internal war.[6] However, there is no relation between our measure of elite instability and Gurr's
measure of conspiracy. Thus, there is some evidence for
the construct validity of the communal instability scale,
but none for the elite instability scale. It should be
pointed out that it is possible to compare these results
only with Gurr, for he is the only other social scientist
who has so far tried to measure these phenomena for tropical Africa.[7] As so often happens, only when more independent attempts to measure instability in Africa are undertaken can we begin to say anything definite on the construct validity of these scales.

The final validity question we can ask of these scales
is their <u>criterion validity</u>. Often theories and hypotheses
tell us how scales should be related if they are each valid
measures of their related concepts. All other things being equal, a valid scale of intelligence should be positively correlated with a valid scale of academic achieve-
ment. If the two scales are so associated, we then infer
that they validly measure what they claim to measure. If
this sounds like circular reasoning, it is, but it is not
illogical as long as our theoretical expectation is stated
<u>prior</u> to looking at the correlations. Alas, this is not
always the case. We cannot, at this stage of the case
study, assess the criterion validity of our two scales,
but we will return to this topic in the final section of
this chapter.

It cannot be stressed too strongly that by attempting
to measure validly and reliably the phenomenon of African
political instability, we have described the phenomenon.
For the social scientist, measurement and description are
almost synonymous. Moreover, by measuring elite and communal instability for 32 states we have engaged in a form
of <u>comparative description</u>. Comparative description allows
us to begin the task that must follow the development of
adequate definitions and measurement--descriptive analysis
that can ultimately lead us to the discovery of strong
theoretical relationships.

Descriptive Analysis

In this section, we will discuss the kinds of simple
descriptive analyses that can be undertaken once one has

constructed scientific definitions and measures. Although
it will be clear that many of the descriptive analyses presented below could be of some use to the foreign affairs
analyst in his attempts to make forecasts, we will not discuss the predictive use of this form of descriptive analysis. Other case studies present the role of simple descriptive statistics as part of quantitative forecasting procedures. Our intention at this point is to show how simple
forms of univariate and bivariate descriptive analyses can
be used in developing theoretical relationships.

By looking at each of the two scales we have developed
separately, we are engaged in univariate descriptive analysis and can ask three types of questions. First, where do
particular cases fall along the scale? Does Kenya manifest
much elite instability? In comparison with other African
states through the end of 1969, the answer from Figure 2.1
is clearly no. In terms of communal instability, arising
from the Somali irredentist movement and ethnic conflict
within Kenya, it is a comparatively high-ranking state.
If scales like these were constructed every year, one
could then trace the upward or downward movement of a given
state. These might be termed instability "fever charts."
Sharp upward shifts in the absolute and comparative levels
of instability could provide evidence for anticipatory action by the U.S. government.

It is important to stress the comparative nature of
such assessments. Suppose communal instability is becoming
more frequent everywhere in Africa, including the state of
interest, say Kenya. If one looked just at Kenya, one
might issue unwarranted early warnings based on an absolute increase in communal instability in Kenya. But, when
a comparative dimension is introduced, the "dangerous" absolute increase of communal instability in Kenya, in the
context of a continent-wide increase, might in fact lower
Kenya's rank order. Alarmist speculation would then be
more difficult.

This leads us to the two other types of questions one
can ask in doing univariate comparisons. We may be concerned with the general level of instability in Africa at
a given point in time. This requires measures of central
tendency such as the averages given in Figure 2.1 and other
such statistics as the mode and median. In the case of
these two scales the average value (the mean) is fairly
close for both types of instability. The median values
are quite different, however. The median is the score
that divides the scale at its midpoint into two equal
groups of 16 states each. The median scores are: elite

instability, 5.5; and communal instability, 1.5. The communal instability scale is highly "skewed," indicating that elite instability is more widespread than communal.

Finally, one can ask descriptive questions about differences among African states in terms of their patterns of instability. It is sometimes argued that quantitative measures and statistical analysis should in fact highlight such differences if they exist. Thus, the standard deviations and coefficients of variation reported in Figure 2.1 show that elite instability is more uniformly distributed among African states than is the more variable phenomenon of communal instability. Also, the range in scores (the magnitude of the difference between the lowest and the highest value) is half again as great for communal instability as it is for elite instability (38 as compared with 26).

Perhaps the most effective way to highlight both similarities and differences in behavior is the scattergram. Scattergrams (or scatterplots) are a form of bivariate analysis where each point in two-dimensional space represents the scores of a country on the two variables considered. In Figure 2.1 we have plotted the 32 African states according to their scores on communal instability (horizontal axis) and elite instability (vertical axis). It is immediately apparent that there is little relationship between these two types of political instability in black Africa, for if there were a stronger relationship, the states would be closer to the diagonal regression line. Indeed, these two scales are correlated quite weakly ($r = .33$).

The scattergram contains much other interesting evidence. Clearly, only three countries--Sudan, Zaire, and Nigeria--have witnessed relatively high levels of both communal and elite instability. What other characteristics do these apparently different states also share? Also clustering together are 19 African states that have had little elite or communal conflict (the lower-left "box"). What socioeconomic and political features do they have in common that have caused them to be relatively free of instability phenomena? How has Dahomey been able to experience such extensive elite instability and yet keep it from spilling over into communal conflict among its three main regional ethnic groups? Scatterplots such as Figure 2.1 seldom answer difficult questions, but they obviously help us highlight similarities and differences and they help us ask potentially fruitful questions, questions we might never have considered without the aid of such relatively simple quantitative devices for displaying data.

FIGURE 2.1

Scattergram of Elite and Communal Instabilities

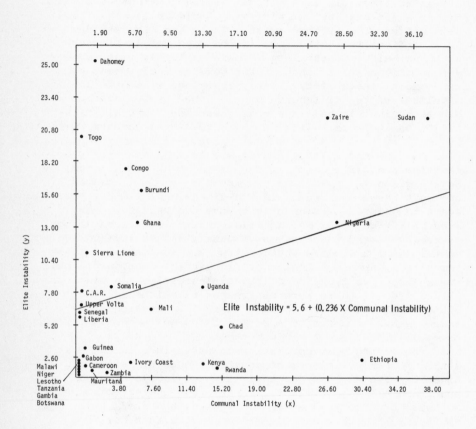

54

When one has data for two scales, as we do, one can ask a number of interesting descriptive questions concerning the relationships of the two scales. First, how closely are they associated? As we have seen in Figure 2.1 and in the correlation of r = .33, the answer is, not very much. This is useful information, for it tells us that these are essentially independent political phenomena, and that policies designed to prevent elite instability need have no impact on communal instability, and vice versa.

Second, we can ask what relationship there is between the two measures over time or at different points in time. Figure 2.2 presents what are called cross-lagged correlations between our two measures at two different periods in time, 1960 to 1964 and 1965 to 1969. The diagonal presents the correlation of each scale with itself at a later time period. Elite instability in 1960-64 is almost perfectly related to elite instability in the following half decade (r = .97). This represents empirical, comparative evidence for one of the few generalizations INR analysts were willing to make about coups d'etat in Africa, that once they occur in a country they are much more likely to recur. The incidence of communal instability in one period is likewise related to the incidence of the same type of instability in a following period (r = .47). These correla-

FIGURE 2.2

Relationships Between Types of Political Instability in Africa: Cross-Lagged Correlations

	1965 to 1969	
	Elite Instability	Communal Instability
1960 to 1964		
Elite instability	.97	.40
Communal instability	.16	.47

Source: D. G. Morrison and H. M. Stevenson, "Political Instability in Independent Black Africa: More Dimensions of Conflict Behavior Within Nations," Journal of Conflict Resolution 15 (September 1971): 365.

tions represent the influence of recent <u>history</u> on current behavior. It is often said that quantitative methods of analysis cannot deal with historical factors. This is just not true. The correlations we have just discussed represent the relationship between events happening in one country at one period of time and similar events occurring there at a later period of time. The relationships among events over time is surely part of history, which, as this case obviously shows, can be dealt with by quantitative techniques to some extent.

The very strong correlation between elite instability at two different periods of time is of some interest.* We do not always have to have a sophisticated theory in order to be able to predict events. We are sure that in the near future the United States will continue to have the highest standard of living in the world, in fact we are willing to wager considerable money on it, even though we do not know the sociological and economic theories that would account for this prediction. What we are doing is projecting from a linear trend. This is often sufficient for decision making. What the correlation of .97 tells us is that until a good theory of African coups d'etat is developed, the best bet is to predict that the more elite instability a country has had in the past, the more likely it will have the same in the future. The empirical bases for such predictions must be continually reexamined as new data become available, but the point to stress is that when used with caution and merely <u>as an aid to informed judgment</u>, such empirical correlations can be of help to the analyst and decision maker.

The other correlations in Figure 2.2 are also of interest. They permit us to infer developmental relations between the two types of political instability phenomena.** It would appear that communal instability does not lead to subsequent elite instability, which is not what one might have expected ($r = .16$). On the other hand, there is a moderate relationship between elite instability and following communal instability ($r = .40$). This suggests that communal instability in Africa is in part a response by communal groupings to elite instability that either fails

---

*For the statistically literate reader, it is in part caused by the distorting effects of outliers on the product-moment correlation.

**That is, these correlations suggest plausible explanations that would then have to be checked out in a subsequent research study.

to bring about a desired change in ethnic representation
in government or effects too radical a change. This post
hoc interpretation leads us into the causal analysis of
political instability in Africa, and we should therefore
turn to the views of the foreign affairs professionals on
this matter before we continue with our quantitative analysis of behavior.

Explanatory Analysis

Having completed the detailed tasks of specifying concepts, constructing variables, and conducting simple forms
of descriptive analysis, we are now ready to deal with the
critical question of whether explanatory theory, that is,
strong theoretical relationships, can be identified. To
develop our explanatory reasoning, which as we have already
mentioned is necessary to construct the predictive technique to be discussed in the next section of this chapter,
let us return once more to the contention of many intelligence analysts as well as scholars that it is impossible
to explain coups and civil wars in Africa except after the
fact and with reference to each particular case. Are instances of elite and communal instability distributed randomly in Africa? Do they not have measurable and theoretically comprehensible correlates? The quantitative methods
currently employed in international relations and cross-
national political research are appropriate for investigating these questions.

An appropriate statistical method for assessing the
truth content of alternative causal explanations of political and economic phenomena is regression analysis. This
technique has been developed extensively by econometricians
and geneticists. With this approach we have a dependent
variable (Y) that varies across a number of cases. In our
case study, we have two such dependent variables--the scores
of the 32 African states on elite and on communal instability given in Table 2.1. Each set of scores has a variance, which is the square of the standard deviations reported at the bottom of Table 2.1. These are 55.577 for
elite instability and 108.064 for communal instability.
In doing regression analysis we seek out a set of theoretically and/or policy-relevant variables that co-vary with
our dependent variable. By analyzing the pattern of co-
variance between our dependent variable and our set of independent variables we establish a regression equation.
In the case of two variables, such as those in Figure 2.1,

the equation takes the form: elite instability = 5.6 + (0.236 × communal instability) + error. This equation tells us that an African state's score on elite instability is the sum of a constant term (5.6, which is the level of elite instability to be expected in the absence of any communal instability) and the product of the country's score on communal instability and the regression coefficient 0.236 (the slope of the regression line in Figure 2.1) plus an error term.

In evaluating a regression analysis we first want to know the amount of variance in the dependent variable that is accounted for by our independent variable(s). In Figure 2.1 we do not have a satisfactory regression result because we are accounting for only 11 percent of the variance in elite instability. In this section, however, we will present regression analyses of elite and communal instability in Africa that account for 72 percent and 76 percent, respectively, of the variance in these two dependent variables. This is a very good level of "explained" variance. When one has achieved such high levels of explained variance the next step in regression analysis is to compare and contrast the influence of each independent variable on the dependent variable.

To do this implies that one has done multiple regression analysis, in which a set of independent variables (two or more) have been used. Multiple regression equations have the form:

$$Y = a + b_1X_1 + b_2X_2 + b_3X_3 + \ldots + b_nX_n + e$$

where Y represents the dependent variable, a represents the constant term, and b_1 to b_n represent the partial regression coefficients (slopes) associated with each of the X_1 to X_n independent variables, and where e again represents an error term.

There is a problem, however, with this type of analysis. Since each independent variable has been measured in different units--percentages, dollars, number of people-- their associated slopes or partial regression coefficients are not directly comparable because unit changes in the independent variables represent different quantities--men, dollars, or percentages. Therefore, if one wishes to compare the impacts of different independent variables, given that one has accounted for an important proportion of the variance in the dependent variable (Y), one usually transforms the scores into standard units and calculates a regression equation in the form:

$$Y = \beta_1 X_1 + \beta_2 X_2 + \beta_3 X_3 + \ldots + \beta_n X_n + e$$

where the beta weights (β) are standardized partial regression coefficients. Since the beta weights have been calculated on the basis of standardized raw scores, they are directly comparable, that is, a beta of .25 is smaller than a beta of .63 and the difference between betas of .20 and .40 is the same as the difference between betas of .60 and .80.

To summarize, when one has variable phenomena, such as African elite and communal instability, one may try to account for variation in these scores by doing a regression analysis. The idea is to select a set of independent variables that represent explanatory factors that are theoretically relevant and/or open to policy manipulation, such as the per capita amount of foreign aid received. In doing the regression analysis one wants to achieve two things, first to account for as much variance as possible in the phenomenon to be explained (this represents a crude index of the explanatory power of one's theory) and second, to examine the relative impact of each independent variable on the dependent variable (this permits assessments of which factors are most powerfully related to the dependent variable).

We will now proceed to do separate regression analyses of African elite and communal instability. But first, we must select a set of indicators of the independent factors that "cause" instability. The discussion of the views of INR analysts and certain academics contained in the first section of this case study indicated that these students of African affairs consider two broad types of factors as being operative in the African environment. First, certain socioeconomic factors operate as "background factors" or "coincidental factors" that establish an environment in which a coup or other form of instability might take place. The size of the African state may be related to instability because the bigger states have poorer communications systems and more diverse populations to integrate into one national political system. A frequently mentioned background factor is the ethnic pluralism of the state; the greater this pluralism, the more probable instability is thought to be. Implicit in many analysts' explanations of particular coups is the problem of social mobilization, the emergence, because of social change and modernization, of masses of people who have rising expectations and who are making demands on the government. Rapid urbanization is thought to be a destabilizing factor as well. Finally, there is the degree of <u>national integration</u> provided by the national infrastructure and the government's policies. Each of these five socioeconomic factors has been measured by the indicators listed in Table 2.2.

As the correlation (r) scores show, each indicator is related to both measures of instability as expected, except for urbanization. The bigger the country, the more instability of both types, but particularly communal instability. The same holds for ethnic pluralism. Social mobilization is more complex. The percentage of workers in agriculture is an indication of the absence of social mobilization and it should be negatively related to instability, as it is. The proportion of wage earners in the population, on the other hand, is a measure of the extent of mobilization, so it should be, and is, correlated in a positive fashion with both types of instability. <u>The number of commercial vehicles is an index of communications and commercial ties within each African state and thus of national integration.</u> It is, as expected, correlated in a negative direction with instability. Finally, the rate of urbanization between 1955 and 1965 should be correlated positively with both types of instability, but it is not. We will return to this when we discuss the regression analyses. Except for our indicator of urbanization, all our measures correlate with instability in the direction predicted by our explanatory ideas; this is evidence of the criterion validity of our indicators as discussed earlier.

The analysts and some academics also point to a second set of distinctly political factors operating to promote or inhibit African political instability. We have seen that much instability behavior, but particularly elite instability, is thought to be a consequence of the action of interest-occupation groups to protect their collective positions. We have indexed the size of such a key group by measuring the number of men in the armed forces in 1967. Table 2.2 shows that this is positively correlated with instability, as expected. Inept government policies leading to a loss of legitimacy and to an economy that is stagnating are often thought by analysts to promote instability. Measures of positive economic performance should, therefore, be negatively correlated with instability, and they are. In interviews, some analysts mentioned a strong, single party as the best safeguard against political instability. We have measured this by the number of political parties banned or proscribed between 1957 and 1969 in each African state. This index is positively correlated with both measures of instability, more strongly so than

60

TABLE 2.2

Bivariate Correlations of Indicators of Factors Affecting
African Elite and Communal Political Instability
(N = 32)

Factor and Indicator	Elite Insta- bility r	Communal Insta- bility r
I. Size		
1. Population, 1969[a]	.20	.69**
II. Ethnic pluralism		
2. Number of spoken languages, 1967	.35*	.69**
III. Social mobilization		
3. Percent of workers in agriculture, 1968[b]	-.49**	-.11
4. Wage earners as percent of the active population, 1963[a]	.10	.11
IV. Urbanization		
5. Percent increase in percent of population in cities, 1955-65	-.38*	-.35*
V. National integration		
6. Number of commercial vehicles, 1966	-.20	-.37*
VI. Interest-group size		
7. Total armed forces men, 1967	.31	.76**
VII. Government economic performance		
8. Per capita GNP, 1968[a]	-.12	-.24
9. Cumulative balance of trade, 1963-68, as percent of 1967 GNP[b]	-.34*	.00
VIII. Political party unity		
10. Number of illegal parties, 1957-69	.79**	.54**
IX. External support		
11. Average annual per capita aid, 1967-69[a]	-.18	-.41*
12. Aid from ex-metropole per capita, 1969[b]	-.27	-.38*

[a]Used only in the analysis of communal instability.
[b]Used only in the analysis of elite instability.
*Correlation significant at the .05 level.
**Correlation significant at the .01 level.

any other single indicator. Finally, external support as measured by foreign aid per capita is thought by some analysts to be a factor inhibiting instability. We thus expect negative correlations, and that is indeed what we observe. Because all our indicators of political factors correlate with our two measures of instability in the directions expected, we may regard them as reasonably valid measures of our basic factors.

The data used to measure both the independent factors and the dependent instability variables has been taken from a recently published public data source.[8] Original data collection could have been undertaken for this case study, but it was judged more useful to illustrate what can be done with already available data, because analysts usually do not have the time to collect original quantitative data sets.

We shall now attempt to explain African communal and elite political instability by use of the quantitative technique of regression analysis. If many analysts are correct, and if Zolberg is correct, then we should not find any systematic relationship between our factors and the instability measures. That is to say, although each factor may have been operative in some one case, these factors will not relate to instability across all cases. This is what we could call the null hypothesis of no systematic relationships between quantitative independent variables and African political instability. If we find no systematic relationships, then we must conclude that we can explain instability only on a case-by-case and day-to-day basis. On the other hand, if we do find strong relationships (as measured by the percentage of explained variance), we can examine the impact of each factor and offer general explanations of instability.

Figure 2.3 presents the results of our regression analysis of African communal instability between the time of independence and the end of 1969. We are accounting for more than three-quarters of the variance in communal instability (76 percent), which is a very satisfactory proportion of explained variance. This indicates that communal instability is not a random phenomenon. The national incidence of communal instability is related to quantitative variables that distinguish among African states.

The numbers associated with each arrow in Figure 2.3 are the beta weights or standardized partial regression coefficients. They indicate the proportional impact, when all other factors are held constant, of one standard unit change in the independent factor on communal instability.

FIGURE 2.3

Causal Model of Communal Instability in Black Africa

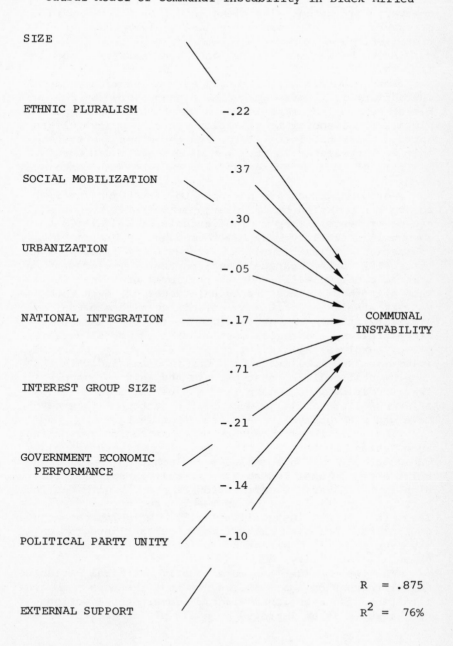

SIZE

ETHNIC PLURALISM   -.22

SOCIAL MOBILIZATION   .37

.30

URBANIZATION

-.05

NATIONAL INTEGRATION ———— -.17 ————————→ COMMUNAL
                                            INSTABILITY

.71

INTEREST GROUP SIZE

-.21

GOVERNMENT ECONOMIC
   PERFORMANCE

-.14

POLITICAL PARTY UNITY   -.10

                                        R = .875
                                        R^2 = 76%
EXTERNAL SUPPORT

Thus, for every increase of one standard deviation unit in the number of commercial vehicles used (national integration), communal instability decreases by .17 standard units. However, this technical explanation of beta weights is not necessary for their use or for their policy-relevant interpretation.

As we have said, beta weights are comparable because they have been standardized. It is therefore clear that the factor that is most strongly associated with communal instability is interest-group size as measured by the number of men in the armed forces. Comparatively, ethnic pluralism and social mobilization are only moderately related to communal instability, and the other factors are only weakly related to it. Let us discuss these results in terms of what a foreign affairs analyst might make of them.

Certain factors are not open to direct and immediate policy manipulation by African governments or by non-African governments. They may, nevertheless, be related to communal instability. We see that ethnic pluralism (+.37) and social mobilization (+.30) increase the likelihood of instability both separately and together. The size of an African country (-.22) reduces the level of instability when all other factors are taken account of, even though a size by itself is positively correlated with communal instability at the r = .69 level. The factors of size, ethnic pluralism, and social mobilization can be affected by policy hardly at all (size) or only slowly and indirectly (pluralism and mobilization). Our findings indicate that governmental policies that promote the shift of people from traditional to modern life-styles increase the risk of communal instability, despite the fact that they may have other advantages to African governments.

The socioeconomic factors of urbanization and national integration are more directly open to governmental policy manipulation. In this analysis urbanization (-.05) is not related to communal instability at all, in spite of its significant bivariate correlation of r = .35 with the latter. National integration is weakly, but negatively, related to communal instability (-.17). This indicates that governmental policies that promote national integration may have some small effect to decrease the incidence of communal instability.

When we consider the more clearly political variables in our regression analysis, we see that there is some confirmation of conventional wisdom. Governmental action that results in an improved economic performance by an Af-

rican government (-.21), or that increases the per capita
foreign aid available to the African regime (-.10), will
tend to decrease the likelihood of communal instability,
but only weakly. Government policies that increase the
size of the military forces in an African state are associated with major increases in communal instability (+.71).
This may be a chicken-or-egg problem, because we do not
know whether increases in military size have the consequence of more frequent communal instability, or frequent
communal instability leads to the governmental reaction of
increasing its armed forces. Our results do show, however,
that where the military is large and presumably influential
there is also a great deal of communal instability. Finally,
while the weakness of the party system is positively related to communal instability in a bivariate fashion
(r = .54), in our multivariate analysis it has a weak negative relationship with communal instability (-.14) when
other factors are controlled.

The picture that emerges from our analysis is that
where African states have large and influential military
forces and extensive ethnic pluralism and social mobilization, there will be extensive communal instability. In
those countries where government policy is achieving some
degree of success in promoting national integration and
economic development, as well as flows of foreign aid to
the state, the likelihood of communal instability is low.
It is up to readers of this book to decide whether this
analysis "makes sense," whether it represents a theoretically and practically satisfying explanation of communal
instability in Africa. We do know that it is a powerful
explanation statistically, for it accounts for more than
three-fourths of the variance in communal instability in
Africa.

Figure 2.4 represents our regression analysis of
elite instability in Africa. We are accounting for a
large degree of the variance in elite instability--just under three-quarters of the variance, or 72 percent. This
is more evidence that instability is not a case-by-case
phenomenon, but rather that it does have important socioeconomic and political correlates.

In this analysis, the factor that most strongly affects the likelihood of elite instability is the weakness
of the political party system (+.73). Social mobilization,
interest-group size, and government economic performance
are moderately related to elite instability, and the other
factors are only weakly related to it.

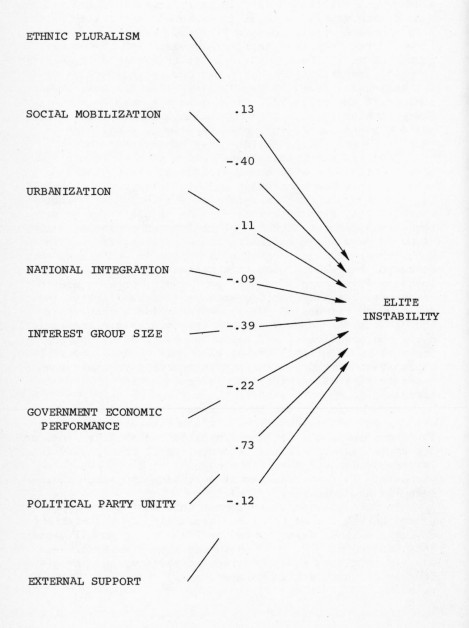

FIGURE 2.4

Causal Model of Elite Instability in Black Africa

ETHNIC PLURALISM

SOCIAL MOBILIZATION   .13

                            -.40

URBANIZATION

                             .11

NATIONAL INTEGRATION   -.09

                                              ELITE
INTEREST GROUP SIZE   -.39   INSTABILITY

                            -.22

GOVERNMENT ECONOMIC
  PERFORMANCE

                             .73

POLITICAL PARTY UNITY   -.12

EXTERNAL SUPPORT

Among the socioeconomic factors that are open only to indirect policy manipulation, we see that the extent of social mobilization makes elite instability more likely. (That the beta weight is negative, -.40, is expected, because the extent of social mobilization is indexed by the proportion of workers in agriculture and the larger this percentage, the less the level of mobilization.) Ethnic pluralism and urbanization increase slightly the chances of elite instability, and the level of national integration slightly decreases its chances. These relationships are all as we expected. We should also note that these socioeconomic factors are less strongly related to elite instability than they are to communal instability, suggesting that it is the more distinctly political factors that account for elite instability, which again makes sense.

A policy message can be obtained from this analysis of the political factors associated with elite instability. Countries that have a fragmented party system have more elite instability; this is the single most important factor operating to create such instability (+.73). Governments that are achieving some degree of success in promoting economic development (-.22) and in securing foreign aid (-.12) have less chance of experiencing elite instability phenomena. Finally, interest-group size is negatively related to elite instability (-.39), which is the one unexpected result in the analysis. Although the size of the armed forces is positively correlated with elite instability ($r = .31$), it is not apparent why in this multivariate analysis it is negatively related to the dependent variable.*

The picture that emerges from this analysis of African elite instability is that an African state that has a fragmented party system and an increasing degree of social mobilization is most likely to experience elite instability. African states that are making some progress in the areas of national integration, economic growth, and foreign assistance flows are less likely to have coups and other related elite instability phenomena. Statistically, this too is a powerful explanation, because it accounts for 72 percent of the variance in the dependent variable.

Our analyses of African elite and communal instability using contemporary quantitative methods show that instabil-

---

*There is a technical statistical reason, multi-collinearity among independent variables. This is present in both regression analyses, but a discussion would go beyond the scope and purposes of this case study.

ity can be explained; that it is not a case-by-case phenomenon best understood by day-to-day methods of analysis.
Certain socioeconomic and political factors within each African state are related to these two types of instability,
but in different manners. Finally, the fact that some of
these factors are open to policy manipulation by African
governments (such as integration and party unity) and by
non-African governments (such as economic performance and
aid per capita) suggests that nonviolent forms of policy intervention are possible to promote or inhibit instability,
depending upon the objectives of the acting governments.

PREDICTING COUPS D'ETAT IN TROPICAL AFRICA

Our discussion in the preceding section was designed
to illustrate that significant theoretical relationships
among variables do exist. The kinds of analysis conducted
in that section might never be seen by the policy maker
and, in fact, might never have to be undertaken by the INR
analyst. They represent the kind of theoretical work that
could be done by scholars and could be used by INR analysts
to inform themselves of what variables to use in building
predictive models. In this section of the case study, we
will demonstrate how the preceding explanatory work could
be used to construct a system for forecasting coup d'etats
and related events in tropical Africa.
We have learned from the foregoing analysis that there
are a number of variables that correlate quite highly with
elite instability. When multiple regression techniques are
employed, an explanatory model that is quite powerful
emerges. With this background in mind, how can we translate our findings into a forecasting model?
One way to anticipate coups d'etat and related events
is to think in terms of types of state, those that are
prone to such events and those that are not. If the country we are interested in can be shown to have a high probability of belonging to the group of states that are not
coup-prone, then we can make the cautious prediction,
based upon this quantitative evidence and other sources of
information, that a coup is unlikely in the state of interest. In order to make such anticipatory statements, we
must use methods that are more systematic than reacting to
the latest cable from the field.
If our objective is to isolate types of African states
--those that are or are not coup-prone--then we must be
explicit in our methods and theory. We have seen in this

case study that, in the absence of theory, the best guide is past experience. Therefore, as a first step we can divide our 32 African states into two categories or classes, those that had at least one successful coup d'etat between the date of independence and the end of 1969 and those states that did not. This gives us a first group of 14 African states that, on the basis of past performance, are likely to have coups in the future and 18 that are unlikely to have coups because they did not have them in the past. Two points are in order about this mode of anticipatory reasoning. First, it is obviously very crude; that is so because explicit theory has not been used except for the generalization (often implicit) that the future will be like the past. Second, in the absence of explicit theory, we can do no better than this type of reasoning, which is why past experience and "seat-of-the-pants" judgment are so often used by INR analysts.

However, we can do better because we now have some general theoretical notions about the correlates of coups d'etat in Africa. In our regression analysis of this dependent variable, elite instability, in Figure 2.4, we found that five factors were related to the incidence of coups d'etat: (1) social mobilization and (2) political party disunity, which promote instability, and (3) interest group size, (4) government economic success, and (5) external support, which inhibit elite instability. If we combine these five quantitative correlates of elite instability with our knowledge of the past performance of each African state, we can apply the statistical technique of discriminant function analysis to the problem of predicting African coups d'etat.

Discriminant function analysis is a statistical routine widely used in the business world, in such areas as the issuing of consumer credit. Banks and loan companies have developed statistical profiles of good and bad credit risks based upon past experience. Representative good credit risks are placed in group A and representative bad credit risks are placed in group B. An applicant for credit fills out a questionnaire giving basic data on himself, and then by use of discriminant function analysis, he is matched against each group and the probability that he is a good risk or a bad risk is calculated. This may seem like a trivial example, but from the point of view of bankers and loan company managers nothing is more vital than determining the credit worthiness of loan applicants, because this affects both profits and the job security of the bankers and managers. Of course, these people do not make their decisions solely on what the computer says, they use their expert judgment, but the technique is reliable enough to be a useful aid to decision making, <u>and this is all any quantitative technique can claim to be.</u>

In our application of discriminant function analysis to the problem of anticipating African coups d'etat, our first step is to group the African states either into the category of having had a successful coup through the end of 1969, which gives 14 cases, or into the category of not having had such a coup d'etat, giving 18 others. The next step is to calculate the group averages and the total average on each variable, and the within-group and between-group variances across all five variables. In a statistical sense, this technique seeks to establish a discriminant function that is a linear combination of the variables that minimizes the variance within each group and maximizes the variance between groups. In simple terms, discriminant function analysis tries to minimize the differences within each group and to maximize the distance between the groups, thus producing homogeneous groups that are "discriminated" from each other as much as possible.*

If we look at the numbers displayed in Table 2.3, we can get a feel for what is going on in this type of analysis. We see that the average value of each variable for the two groups is quite distinct. <u>As a group</u>, countries that have had coups through the end of 1969 have a greater level of social mobilization, larger urban interest groups, a worse government economic performance (stagnating economy), less political party unity, and less metropole foreign aid per capita than do the non-coup countries. This quantitative analysis points to a certain degree of homogeneity among the countries that had coups as compared with those that did not, which is not apparent when we look at their names. Some coup countries are former British colonies, others are former French colonies; some are big, some are small; some are rich by African standards, others by the same standard are poor. On face value, the one thing that groups them together is that they had at least one successful coup up to the end of 1969. However, our preceding regression analysis pointed to systematic factors affecting the frequency of elite instability among all African

---

*Again for the statistically literate, discriminant function analysis is nearly identical to multiple regression analysis when the dependent variable is coded as a dummy (0 or 1) variable.

TABLE 2.3

Group and Total Average Scores on Discriminant Function
Analysis Variables

Factor and Indicator	States with One or More Coups to 1969 (N = 14)	States with No Coups to 1969 (N = 18)	Average Value of All Cases (N = 32)
Social mobilization, percent workers in agriculture, 1968	80.4	87.0	84.1
Interest group size, percent workers in public sector, 1965	36.9	26.1	30.8
Government economic performance, cumulative balance of trade, 1963-68 as percent of 1967 GNP	-7.9	23.7	30.8
Political party unity, number of illegal parties, 1957-69	5.4	0.8	2.8
External support, aid from ex-metropole per capita, 1969, $ U.S.	3.5	7.5	5.8

states, and these quantitative differences show up in this
first stage of our discriminant function analysis.

The second stage of a discriminant function analysis
is to establish a discriminant function and, on the basis
of the weightings assigned by this equation and the score
of each African state on each variable, to assign probabilities of group membership to each state. We will not
discuss the discriminant functions created in our analysis.
We will focus just on the resulting probabilities and what
they have to say about the relevance of quantitative techniques to the problem of forecasting coups.

Table 2.4 lists our resulting probabilities. We have
listed first the 14 African states that had at least one
successful coup through the end of 1969. The second group
represents the 18 states that did not have a successful
coup d'etat. In agreement with the ideas of INR analysts,

TABLE 2.4

Probabilities of Group Membership of Coup-Prone and
Non-Coup-Prone States

Classification	Coup-Prone Group p	Non-Coup-Prone Group p
I. States with one or more coups through 1969		
Nigeria	1.00	.00
Zaire	.99	.01
Sudan[a]	.99	.01
Dahomey[b]	.99	.01
Ghana[b]	.97	.03
Congo, Brazzaville[a]	.95	.05
Togo	.94	.06
.Sierra Leone[a]	.93	.07
Upper Volta	.74	.26
Somalia	.68	.32
Uganda[b]	.56	.44
CAR	.43	.57
Burundi	.41	.59
Mali	.28	.72
II. States with no coups through 1969		
Cameroon	.62	.38
Ethiopia	.34	.66
Chad	.22	.78
Mauritania	.22	.78
Senegal	.21	.79
Gambia	.21	.79
Guinea	.17	.83
Tanzania	.11	.89
Kenya	.10	.90
Niger	.10	.90
Malawi	.09	.91
Lesotho[b]	.07	.93
Rwanda	.04	.96
Ivory Coast	.02	.98
Botswana	.01	.99
Liberia	.01	.99
Zambia	.00	1.00
Gabon	.00	1.00

[a]Countries that experienced a serious coup attempt
between January 1, 1970, and December 31, 1972.

[b]Countries that experienced a successful coup between
January 1, 1970, and December 31, 1972

we can argue that if a country had a coup before 1970, then
it is coup-prone in the period 1970-74, and vice versa.
Our discriminant function then assigns to each case probabilities of membership in the coup-prone and non-coup-
prone groups. Among the 14 states that had coups up to the
end of 1969, 11 most probably belong to the coup-prone
group. Three do not belong to that group, but rather have
better than a fifty-fifty chance of falling into the non-
coup-prone group. During the period of 1970-74 these three
states (Central African Republic, Burundi, and Mali) did
not experience a successful coup or a serious attempted
coup. This is a good prediction. Also note that all of
the states in black Africa that did have a successful
coup [a] or a serious coup attempt [b] between 1970 and
1974 are classified as highly probable members of the coup-
prone group with the exception of Lesotho and Rwanda. In
January 1970, Prime Minister Chief Jonathan of Lesotho,
after losing an election, staged a palace coup to keep himself in power. There was no significant military intervention, unlike all of the other instances of instability in
this period, which were led by the military.

Thus, if one were using this technique to establish
groups of states that were likely to have a coup and then
to anticipate whether a given country is likely to have a
coup, one would find this analysis quite helpful. The 11
countries from Nigeria (1.00) to Uganda (.56) and Cameroon
(.62) can be considered as likely to have a coup between
January 1970 and March 1974. Seven of these 11 states did,
during this period, have a successful coup or a serious
coup attempt with military intervention. Regarding the
members of this group, including Cameroon, which have not
yet experienced coups since 1969, we can justifiably say
that "anything can happen at any time, anywhere." We also
have evidence to suggest that among 20 African states,
coups are unlikely, for each of these states is most probably classified in the non-coup-prone group. In only two
cases out of the 20, Lesotho and Rwanda, did a coup occur.

As before, we must stress what quantitative methods
can and cannot do for the analyst. The probabilities calculated by this discriminant function analysis measure
only the degree to which a given state is similar or dissimilar to states that have or have not had coups in the
period from independence to the end of 1969. It is then
up to the analyst to determine on the basis of this quantitative evidence and other information whether or not a
coup is going to occur in the country he is concerned with.
If Zaire has a probability of .99 of belonging to the coup-

prone group, this is evidence that Zaire fits very closely the class of states in which coups are likely. Rumors of coups in Zaire must then be taken seriously. The Ivory Coast has a .98 probability of belonging to the non-coup-prone group. This is evidence that unusual circumstances must obtain for a coup to become a likely event. In short, statistical methods treat <u>classes</u> of cases like coup-prone and non-coup-prone African states. Individual cases can be fitted into general statistical patterns, and this should be of great help to the intelligent analyst. What will <u>actually happen</u> in a given country cannot be predicted by any methodology presently available or likely to be available in the foreseeable future.

Having an empirically based model such as the one just described to generate probabilities of coup-proneness could be of use to the foreign affairs analyst. Periodic updates of the data on which the analysis is performed could yield probabilities of coup-proneness for the analyst that in turn help him in his role as part of the "early warning system" in the State Department. While the probabilities generated could serve as no more than a set of guidelines for the analyst, they would be an input from a source of data and explanatory reasoning that capitalizes on more generalized factors than are implicitly recognized as important in the occurrence of a coup. In addition, the explanatory work behind the model would help in guiding foreign policy decision making by the department, although more specific details relevant to the context of each country would still play the major role.

UTILITY OF THE TECHNIQUES TO
FOREIGN AFFAIRS ANALYSTS

The best way to judge the general utility of the techniques employed here might be illustrated by presenting a hypothetical report that might be written by an INR analyst on tropical Africa. The report might look something like this:

Title: Signs of Long-Range Instability in Country X

Notwithstanding recent reports from the field, conditions in Country X appear to be increasing the probability of a coup d'etat over the next year. Although there have been few reported events that could be considered significant, changes in certain inter-

74

nal and external patterns of X's foreign policy suggest that the probability of a coup has increased.

A recent quantitative study using statistics to generate probabilities of coups d'etat has shown that the five variables listed below together account for over 70 percent of the factors that determine whether or not a coup takes place over a three-year period. Table A shows those variables and the change over the past twelve months for Country X.

The significant factor concerning the changes reported in Table A is that change has occurred for each of the variables in a direction that contributes to coup-proneness. The overall effect is to alter the coup probability, generated by a model designed for predictive purposes, from .57 to .73. Although we can say that the trend is clearly in a direction of greater probability for a coup, we cannot say when the coup will take place.

TABLE A [2.5]

Country X and Variables Predicting Coups

	Relationship to Coup-Proneness	Level in 1972	Level in 1973
Percent workers in agriculture	Negative	75	65
Percent workers in public sector	Positive	23	27
Cumulative balance of trade	Positive	-7.9	-11.5
Number of illegal parties	Positive	2	4
Aid from ex-metropole per capita	Negative	4.7	3.2

Based on this analysis, it was decided to conduct a thorough study of Country X. Detailed information was requested from Desk Officers and from mission staff on a variety of economic, social, and political questions. The next couple of pages discuss their estimates of the probability of a coup over the

next year and also the consequences of a coup for
U.S. foreign policy.

Whether or not a report written like the sample above
would be of value to INR users or potential users can best
be answered by the analysts and users themselves. Hopefully, the report shows what this particular technique can
and cannot do. More specifically, it can only serve as a
general warning of evolving patterns and cannot pinpoint
the exact time. However, it does serve to provide concrete
evidence on a multivariate basis of trends within a country
or set of countries that in turn provides an early warning
system so that more focused research and policy-making attention can be generated.

As for the costs of such a capability to the INR, two
particular types of costs have to be discussed. The first
is the availability of computer programs to perform the
analysis, and the second is the question of the quantitative skills of the INR analyst.

As far as the computer program is concerned, statistical packages are available that perform the regression
and discriminant analyses on data. Costs for the statistical analysis of the data according to the procedures discussed in this case study would be minimal, since the State
Department's computing center already has the packages that
would be required for the regression analysis routines and
the discriminant function routines.

The computer program and analysis question, however,
also involves the translation of data into computer format
and the manipulation and updating of data files. These
functions would have to be performed by a computer programmer, although less than 10 hours of his time would be
required for this particular study once procedures were developed for any set of analyses.

When we come to the question of the quantitative
skills of the INR analyst, the task of estimating costs is
more difficult. First, let us assume that both the INR
analyst and the potential users of the reports produced by
the analyst understand the notion of assigning a probability of a coup to different countries. The wide use of
probability notions not only in government but throughout
our society (for example, weather predictions) suggests
that this assumption is relatively safe. Accepting this
assumption, the theoretical and forecasting analysis could
be provided on an ongoing basis for a relatively small
amount of money by an outside consulting firm. This solution would also eliminate internal computer costs. Al-

though this would probably be the cheapest solution, it would certainly not be satisfactory. The reason for this is that neither the analyst nor the user would feel comfortable with accepting a single number for each country to indicate probability. The credibility of the figure might increase over time, but there would be an equally strong--if not stronger--chance that the probability estimate would not be considered seriously.

For that reason, we should face the task of training the INR analyst to understand at the very least the statistical technique that generates the prediction as well as the statistical techniques that underlie the theoretical work necessary to choose the variables used in the predictive model. This would require some amount of training in the use and philosophy behind regression and discriminant function analysis. If the training procedures described in Appendix C were employed, we would be talking about a one-week training effort. This assumes that no part of the week has to be spent talking about the utility of quantitative techniques, as well as that a set of training packages is available.

It appears to us that the costs of using this particular procedure would not be substantial. Some training would be required, computer programming services would be required, and availability of the routines would be required. However, to use this particular complex of techniques without others would be costly, since data acquisition and general training is assumed in our estimate. This is discussed in Appendix C.

NOTES

1. Aristide R. Zolberg, "The Structure of Political Conflict in the New States of Tropical Africa," American Political Science Review 62 (March 1968): 78.

2. Ibid.

3. D. G. Morrison and H. M. Stevenson, "Political Instability in Independent Black Africa: More Dimensions of Conflict Behavior Within Nations," Journal of Conflict Resolution 15 (September 1971): 347-68.

4. D. G. Morrison, R. C. Mitchell, J. N. Paden, and H. M. Stevenson, Black Africa: A Comparative Handbook (New York: Free Press, 1972), p. 125.

5. Morrison and Stevenson, op. cit., pp. 362-63.

6. T. R. Gurr, "A Causal Model of Civil Strife: A Comparative Analysis Using New Indices," American Political Science Review 62 (1968): 1104-24.

7. Morrison, et al., op. cit., pp. 124-25.
8. Ibid.

**ESTIMATING RESULTS
AND CONSEQUENCES OF
ELECTIONS IN ITALY,
FRANCE, AND FINLAND**

The purpose of this case study is to explore the utility of applying quantitative techniques to the work of the INR analyst who is concerned with elections in Finland, France, and Italy. Our study is prompted by the fact that scholarly studies of elections have yielded a set of quantitative techniques that are as sophisticated as would be required for analysis of any past problem by INR.

The study is divided into four parts:

Studies by INR Analysts of Elections in Finland,
   France, and Italy and Their Relevance to a Quantitative Study of Elections
Using Quantitative Techniques to Test Assumptions Made
   by INR Analysts
Using Predictive Surveys as a Forecasting Mechanism
Costs and Utility of Quantitative Techniques in Election Studies

STUDIES BY INR ANALYSTS OF ELECTIONS IN ITALY,
FRANCE, AND FINLAND AND THEIR RELEVANCE TO
A QUANTITATIVE STUDY OF ELECTIONS

A review of INR studies of elections in the three European countries under consideration reveals several features that are directly relevant to the use of quantitative techniques.* In discussing these features and the rele-

*The sample of INR election studies consisted of 16 documents drawn from the following years: 1962, 1968 (France), 1966, 1970 (Finland), and 1968, 1972 (Italy).

vance of quantitative techniques to them, we are accepting as given the kinds of analytical tasks now performed by the INR analyst. The purpose of this case study is not to suggest new analytical activities for the INR analyst but to demonstrate how quantitative techniques might help in the tasks now being performed.

The predominant characteristic of INR election studies is the emphasis on description and explanation rather than prediction. This is consistent with the general pattern reported in Chapter 1 (described in Figure 1.3). In general, INR analyses are intended to be descriptive and explanatory rather than predictive, and this was certainly true for our sample of INR studies of elections in Finland, France, and Italy. This is by no means a criticism, but simply a descriptive statement of INR activity based on our analysis of documents.

A second feature of the INR reports surveyed is the obvious concern for elections as both an independent and a dependent variable. By independent variable we mean that the INR analyst frequently attempts to discuss the conse-quences of election results, particularly in terms of the composition of a postelection cabinet and the course of future domestic and foreign policies. Somewhat less fre-quently, elections are treated as a dependent variable; that is, the INR analyst attempts to explain and sometimes predict the outcome of an election.

A third feature of INR election studies is the general absence of quantitative data. To be sure, there are refer-ences to general economic trends, public opinion polls, or aggregate election results. However, there is no attempt either to utilize quantitative indicators in the presenta-tion of trends or to test with quantitative data the assump-tions made about elections. Again, this feature is repre-sentative of the broad pattern in INR efforts for fiscal 1972 that is discussed in Chapter 1. While this pattern can be partly attributed to the general unwillingness of INR analysts to use quantitative analysis, it is also a result of the fact that many analyses focus on coalition formation across various parties and to a certain degree on intraparty politics. In most cases, this focus on spe-cific internal political conditions surrounding an election precludes quantitative analysis, so that we could not simply apply existing studies to INR analyses.

A brief word about existing quantitative studies should clarify the problem. Basically, one can distinguish between two approaches to the use of quantitative techniques in election studies. The first is the approach of the pollsters.[1] Experience with modern polling techniques reveals that the skill of the pollster in predicting election results is in the short term quite high, particularly as one approaches the time of an election. The polls provide little by way of concrete evidence until a few weeks before the actual voting, since conditions that generate the poll results can change radically during the course of a campaign. However, as one approaches election day, one can have more confidence in the predictions of pollsters, although they have been known to make mistakes.

The second approach is the quantitative study of elections and election results usually practiced by the political scientist. This approach is not concerned with predicting election results as much as it is with explaining patterns that emerge from election results. Critical variables like income, religion, occupation, issue orientation, exposure to the media, and party identification are used as independent variables in the search for explanatory theories of electoral behavior.[2] Consequently, the political scientist is usually interested in the shifts in attitudes over a relatively long period of time. By way of contrast to the polling approach, the political scientist is not so concerned with the prediction of election outcomes as he is with the evolution of general public attitudes and/or the process through which patterns of voting behavior are formed.

For the purposes of the INR analyst, the work of pollsters and political scientists should be used as findings to assist his efforts rather than as a set of analytical tasks to be undertaken. Indeed, the results of polls are to some extent utilized by INR analysts in their preelection analyses. However, we will suggest (in a later section of this case study) ways in which the results of polls and other short-range forecasting can be used more systematically. At this point it should be emphasized that the INR would be wasting money if it were to repeat the work of pollsters by conducting its own surveys or even by reanalyzing the data generated by pollsters. The findings generated by polls are already of sufficient quality to be used directly by the INR analyst.

Similarly, the findings of political scientists might be important to the INR analyst in long-range forecasting. Mass and elite surveys of attitudes show broad shifts in

public and elite thinking, and could assist in the general
search for explanations of the causes and consequences of
elections. However, it would not be sensible for the INR
analyst to collect or reanalyze the type of data used by
political scientists because of the substantial costs and
even more important, the marginal gains that would result
from such activities. The reason for only marginal gains
is that the kinds of questions asked by academicians deal
with broad relationships between socioeconomic features of
the electorate and attachment to party loyalties and symbolic identities. Questions of how specific classes of individuals feel about political parties or symbolic statements (for example, social welfare, secular schools, di-
vorce, and union rights) appear too far removed from the
policy-relevant concerns of the user of INR research.

Recognizing that there would be no direct transfer of
quantitative techniques from the pollster or the political
scientist to the INR analyst, we feel it necessary to approach the task of an analyst from the point of view of
how quantitative techniques generally available in the social sciences might be applied to the work of the analyst.
Figure 3.1 indicates the broad categories of work performed
by the INR analyst.

Although we stated above that the bulk of an analyst's
work with respect to elections in the three countries under
study involves description and explanation, some attempt
is made to perform the kinds of tasks indicated in all
nine of the cells in Figure 3.1. At the moment, each of
the activities in the nine cells is performed by the INR
analyst through nonquantitative techniques of analysis.

Quantitative techniques can, however, be suggested
for use in seven of the nine cells. Two of the cells--
description of issues and parties, and description of general policy changes--can be handled primarily through verbal description or through quantitative techniques other
than those in the case study. The INR analyst could use
quantitative techniques to summarize election results for
his users. By the time he had acquired the necessary data,
however, a matter of several weeks or months, there would
probably be little interest among his users in a description of the election.

At the level of explanation, the analyst could use
quantitative techniques in an identification of the factors influencing the outcome of an election. This appears
to be a major concern of the INR analyst, although it is
not one that has resulted in the use of quantitative tech-

FIGURE 3.1

Types of Work Performed by the INR Analyst

	Preelection	Short-Term Postelection	Long-Term Postelection
Description	Issues and major parties	How each party fared in the election	Identification of policy changes
Explanation	Factors that may influence the election	Factors that influenced the election outcome	Explanation of policy shifts
Prediction	Election results; cabinet formation	Cabinet formation; stability of government; short-term policy shifts	Change and stability in governmental policies

niques. In the next section of this case study, we will demonstrate how to perform quantitative analyses of explanatory assumptions regarding the factors that bear on the outcome of an election. Quantitative techniques can also be used to study the impact of elections on the domestic and foreign policies of a given country. However, the techniques for such analysis are discussed in other case studies in this book. We will discuss what kind of activities might be undertaken in the final section of this case study.

At another level, we have already indicated that preelection predictions could be made through use of quantitative techniques now employed by pollsters. However, we also noted that the INR analyst should not attempt to duplicate the efforts of the pollster. We will suggest a different technique—brief expert questionnaires—by means of which an analyst might supplement the work of pollsters in seeking to provide his users with a capacity to anticipate the outcome of an upcoming election. Insofar as the question of cabinet formation is concerned, some political scientists are presently attempting to develop coalition theory, which takes election results and generates predictions about the distribution of cabinet portfolios to members of different parties. The efforts of these scholars are not discussed in this case study because their findings seem to have marginal utility for the INR analyst and his user.

The major quantitative analysis presented in this case study is the testing of explanatory assumptions of INR analysts. A presentation of a brief questionnaire technique is also included to illustrate a different approach to the application of quantitative techniques, an approach that might assist the INR analyst in the making of more precise forecasts.

USING QUANTITATIVE TECHNIQUES TO TEST
ASSUMPTIONS MADE BY INR ANALYSTS

In examining the reports prepared by INR analysts on Finland, France, and Italy, four major explanatory assumptions that can be studied through quantitative techniques were identified as important factors in the determination of election outcomes.* Throughout this study we will de-

_____

*Other factors were studied by INR analysts but are not considered in this case study; among these are person-

84

fine election results in two distinct ways: the percentage
of communist vote and the percentage of the vote of the
prime minister's party. Although election results are defined in a wide variety of ways by INR analysts, these two
measures are representative of their analytical concerns.
Basically, the analysts identify four factors as affecting
either or both, the percentage of the communist vote and
the percentage of the incumbent vote. They are:

Voter turnout
Unemployment
Inflation
Major events

In following pages, we will discuss each of these explanatory factors to see if quantitative techniques can determine the extent to which the assumptions of INR analysts
are valid. We will use data from the post-World War II his-
tories of Finland, France, and Italy for illustrative purposes.[3] A discussion of some of the assumptions implied
in the kinds of quantitative analysis undertaken will also
be provided.

Voter Turnout

Many scholars feel that voter turnout is an important
factor in determining the outcome of elections. This position is also taken in a number of INR reports. Among both
scholars and INR analysts, however, there is some disagreement over the actual impact of voter turnout on the results
of an election. Some observers emphasize that a low turnout increases the strength of the left in European politics
because of the communists' ability to get out the vote even
when turnout is generally low, whereas other commentators
suggest that leftists are the ones who fail most frequently
to cast ballots when turnout is low. There are also assertions that low turnout helps the incumbent party because
it means that the electorate is generally satisfied with
the status quo.

---

ality, the effect of small militant groups, the effect of
the centrists (which are considered "swing" groups), the
discipline of the communists, and the effect of the new
generation of postwar voters.

Voter turnout is an important variable from the perspective of the INR analyst. It is frequently cited in
their pre- and postelection analyses. In addition, since
voter turnout may be affected by major domestic or international events, it is of some interest to see in what way
voter turnout does in fact affect election results.

For these reasons, we have collected data for each of
the three countries under study to see if level of voter
turnout is associated with election results as measured by
the percentage of communist vote and by the percentage of
incumbent vote. Figure 3.2 displays the data in the form
of six scatterplots for the three countries. A scatterplot
is a way of relating two variables to each other. The
points of the plot--indicated by numbers corresponding to
the year of the election--represent the positioning of the
national turnout variable in relationship to the percentage
of either communist or incumbent vote. The correlation
(represented by "r"), ranging between -1 and +1, appears
on each graph to indicate the strength of association between the two variables. A "-1" indicates an inverse re-
lationship--as national turnout percentage goes up, the
percentage of communist vote or incumbent vote goes down.
A "+1" indicates the opposite. A zero correlation indicates no clear-cut relationship between the two variables.
The straight line drawn through the points on each scatterplot visually summarizes the extent to which the two factors go up or down simultaneously. Table 3.1 lists the
correlation results for comparative purposes.*

The correlations differ from one country to another,
showing national differences in how voter turnout affects
elections. The correlations reported for Italy are reasonably high, indicating that as national turnout percentage goes up, both incumbent and communist vote go up. The
correlations reported for Finland and France are quite low,
indicating that there is no strong relationship between
voter turnout percentage and either of the two measures of

---

*In this and other tests, significance levels are not
calculated because we are dealing with the universe of
cases and not making inferences from a sample to a larger
population. Also, in this and other tests, correlation coefficients are not corrected for degrees of freedom, a procedure that would reduce the correlations slightly. (For
presentation of the appropriate procedure to correct for
degrees of freedom, see Carl F. Christ, Econometric Models
and Methods [New York: John Wiley and Sons, 1966], p. 509.)

86

FIGURE 3.2

Scatterplots of Voter Turnout and Percentage Communist and Incumbent Vote

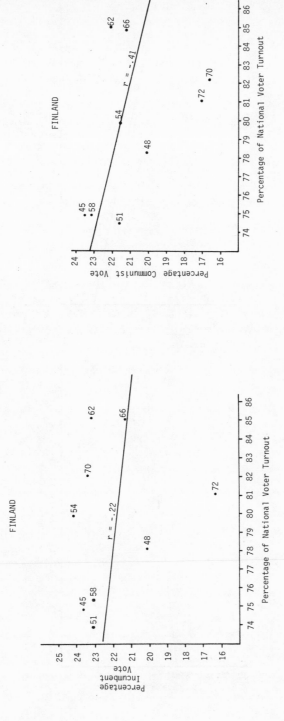

FIGURE 3.2 (continued)

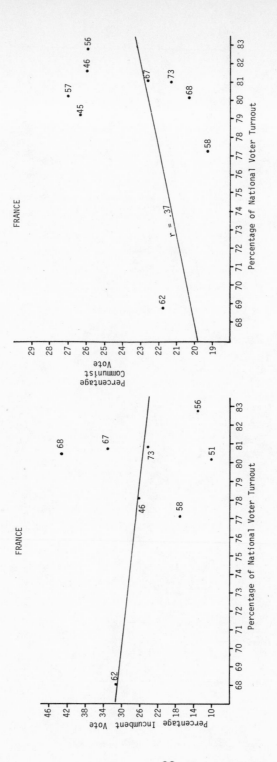

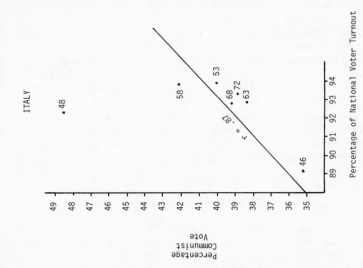

ITALY

Percentage of National Voter Turnout

r = .87

Percentage Communist Vote

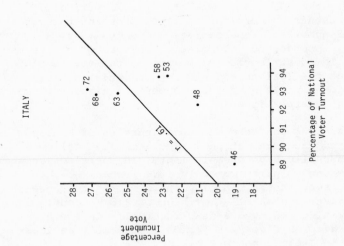

ITALY

Percentage of National Voter Turnout

r = .61

Percentage Incumbent Vote

89

election results. For Finland, the correlations, though not strong, are negative, suggesting that as voter turnout goes up both communist and incumbent vote go down. In general, however, the small number of elections used to calculate each of the correlations suggests that we should not put great confidence in the generalizations. Nevertheless, the scatterplots when taken together with the correlation coefficients are instructive because they allow the analyst to acquire a picture of the patterns of the variables across the three states as well as over time. They also confirm the tendency in INR reports and scholarly literature to see voter turnout as being a contributory, but not determining, factor in election results.

Unemployment

INR analysts are unanimous in considering unemployment as an important factor in determining the outcome of elections. In particular, the level of unemployment is seen as related to the success and failure of Communist parties. But INR analysts, like academic specialists, disagree among themselves as to whether Communist parties gain or suffer at the polls as a result of high unemployment.

To test the relationship between unemployment and the communist vote, we studied Finland and Italy in depth (France was excluded in view of the low level of unemployment among Frenchmen in the post-World War II period). Figure 3.3 presents numbers for mean unemployment between elections and numbers for percentage of communist vote in a scatterplot in order to determine the nature of the relationship. The distribution of points on the scatterplots indicates that the Italian and Finnish Communist parties fare worse at the polls when unemployment is high, with extremely high correlations (-.95 for Italy and -.75 for Finland).

It is striking that the Communist parties of Finland and Italy fared badly in national elections that followed periods of unusually high unemployment. In the election of 1970, the Finnish party won only 16.6 percent of the popular vote, even though unemployment over the four preceding years averaged an all-time high of 2.8 percent. The Italian party also achieved a near-record low in the election of 1958 after a five-year period of the most serious unemployment in Italy's postwar history.

For further analysis of the strong statistical relationship between communist vote and unemployment in Italy,

TABLE 3.1

Correlation Between Voter Turnout and Percentage
Communist and Incumbent Vote

	Percentage Communist Vote	Percentage Incumbent Vote
Finland	-.41	-.22
France	.37	-.23
Italy	.61	.87

we experimented with different ways of representing time
dimensions. We think that the mean for the period between
elections is a good measure, although we would expect the
unemployment factor to be strongest one or two years before an election. To examine these assumptions, we calculated the correlation coefficient for one year and two
years before an election, for the year of the election, and
for the mean between elections. Table 3.2 depicts the results for Italy in five elections (1953, 1958, 1963, 1968,
and 1972). It shows there is a strong tendency for the
communist vote to be high when unemployment is low, and
vice versa. This holds true when considering unemployment
in an election year, in the one or two previous years, and
in the period between elections.

To explore our hypothesis further, we examined Finland at the regional level. Patterns holding at the national level frequently do not hold at the regional or local levels. However, quantitative techniques can be used
at all levels as long as the data is available. Table 3.3
supports the proposition that an increase in unemployment
hurts the communist vote by showing a strong positive correlation between high unemployment and a drop in the percentage of voters who cast their ballots for the Communist
party. Northern Finland had the highest average unemployment between the 1966 and 1970 parliamentary elections, yet
it was precisely in this region that the Communist party
experienced its greatest electoral setback.

On the basis of these figures we would expect evidence
of a consistent association between unemployment and percentage communist vote. Our correlations show that the
association is strong, but due to the small samples, this
finding must be regarded as tentative. Contrary to what
might appear to be a logical and theoretical relationship

91

FIGURE 3.3

Scatterplots of Average Unemployment and Percentage Communist Vote in Finland and Italy

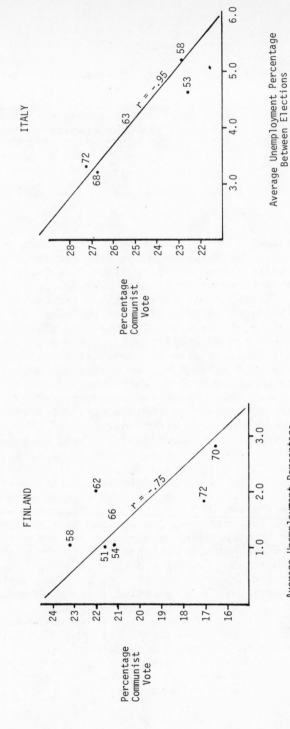

TABLE 3.2

Correlation Between Unemployment and Percentage Communist
Vote in Italy for Different Periods of Time

Two Years Before	One Year Before	Election Year	Mean Between Elections
-.86	-.90	-.78	-.95

Note: For four election years: 1953, 1958, 1963,
and 1972.

between the two variables, which is sometimes expressed in
the writings of INR analysts and in the scholarly literature, we have found that unemployment is clearly not bene-
ficial to the Communist parties in Finnish and Italian
elections.

Turning to the relationship between unemployment and
percentage incumbent vote, one would expect the prime minister's party to lose seats with an increase in unemployment prior to an election. However, a study of the correlation coefficients in Table 3.3 indicates mixed results.
Figure 3.4 shows a very weak negative correlation between
unemployment and an increase in the incumbent vote for Finland, yet a strong positive relationship for Italy. Unlike the relationship between unemployment and the communist vote, which held up for both Finland and Italy, the

TABLE 3.3

Effect of Unemployment on Communist Vote in Finland
by Region

	Average Unemployment Percentage, 1966-70	Percentage Communist Vote		Decrease in Percentage Communist Vote
		1966	1970	
Southern Finland	2.0	19.1	15.3	3.8
Western Finland	2.7	20.0	15.9	4.1
Eastern Finland	3.7	19.9	13.9	6.0
Northern Finland	5.3	32.9	25.7	7.2

FIGURE 3.4

Scatterplots of Average Unemployment and Percentage Incumbent Vote in Finland and Italy

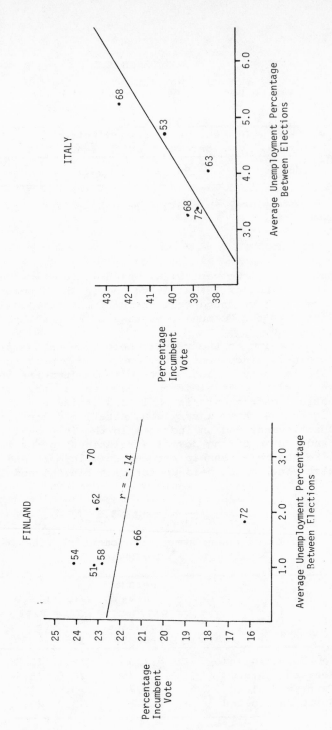

relationship varies for the two states when seen in the context of the incumbent vote.

Inflation

There is agreement among INR analysts that inflation is an important variable in the determination of election outcomes. Inflation is generally viewed as a source of weakness for the incumbent party and a source of strength for the Communist party. In our analysis inflation was measured by a cost-of-living index computed by the International Labor Organization in its annual Yearbook of Labour Statistics. However, a study of the patterns found in the data suggest that such generalizations do not hold up across the three countries. We measured inflation by examining the cost of living for each of the three countries based on data obtained from the International Labor Organization.

Table 3.4 indicates the correlation coefficients for each of the three states relating the change in the cost of living to percentage of the communist and of the incumbent vote. Although the small number of cases precludes any firm conclusion, the numbers show that the patterns for the three countries differ to some extent. The communists appear to suffer much more in Italy than in either France or Finland from an increase in the cost of living. The Italian incumbent appears to gain substantially and consistently from an increase in the cost of living, while incumbents in both France and Finland suffer.

Because of the varying level of correlations for the three states on the relationship between percentage communist vote and cost of living, more detailed information is presented in Figure 3.5. Our scatterplots for each of the three countries reveal a mixed pattern, however.

TABLE 3.4

Correlation Between Cost-of-Living Increase and Percentage of Communist and Incumbent Vote

	Percentage Communist Vote	Percentage Incumbent Vote
Finland	-.21	-.24
France	.52	-.59
Italy	-.49	.87

FIGURE 3.5

Scatterplots of Percentage Communist Vote and Cost-of-
Living Annual Average

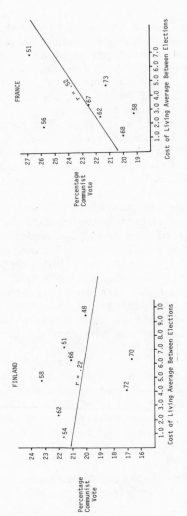

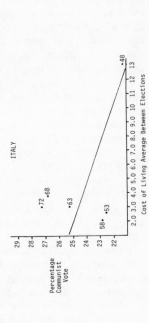

The French Communist party gained its largest postwar percentage of the popular vote in 1951, at which time inflation was also at a peak. The apparent association between high inflation and a strong communist vote is therefore positive in this instance. But one also notices that in the election of 1956, when the communist percentage of seats in the National Assembly was the highest ever in the postwar period, and its percentage of the popular vote was second only to the election results of 1951, inflation was very low. The apparent association between high inflation and a strong communist vote is negative in this instance. However, over the entire time period, the association between high inflation and strong communist vote is positive.

The pattern is also mixed for Italy. In the elections of 1963, 1968, and 1972, which followed periods of considerable inflation, the communists did well at the polls. But the results of the 1948 election are contrary to the latter pattern. Inflation has not been worse in the postwar period, yet the Communist party won its smallest percentage of seats and its smallest percentage of the popular vote in 26 years of electioneering.

The data for Finland tends to support the general negative relationship between cost of living and percentage communist vote. Inflation was at a peak in the period preceding the 1948 election, but the communists fared badly in a relative sense. The communist vote dropped from 23.5 percent in 1945 to 20.0 percent in 1948, and this dip in strength would not be surpassed for 24 years. Moreover, when inflation was lowest (1951-54) the communists did rather well when judged against the results of other postwar elections.

For this analysis of the relationship between percentage communist vote and cost of living over the three countries, it appears that the general notion that inflation will help the communist vote is incorrect. However, it is also clear that the pattern is neither consistent nor strong over time and across the three countries. As in the case of the voter turnout and the unemployment variables, cost of living provides only a partial guide in the search for factors that shape electoral outcomes in Finland, France, and Italy.

The Impact of Events

There seems to be general agreement among both INR analysts and scholars that dramatic external and internal

97

events have an impact on the outcome of elections. In
fact, it is tempting to argue that the low communist vote
in the Italian and Finnish elections of 1948 at a time of
high inflation might be partially explained by a major international event in 1948--the seizure of power in Czecho-
slovakia by the Communist party. The difficulty one en-
counters in testing the degree to which major events affect elections is that such events occur sporadically and
appear to be major from some perspectives but not from
others. Therefore, the attempt to quantify such events is
limited by the multiple conditions that are relevant only
in the specific context of the event.

Recognizing this difficulty, we have nonetheless decided to trace the electoral history of Finland since World
War II in an effort to detect a pattern in which major
events, domestic or international, could have had an impact
on Finnish politics. Because of the problems of collecting
data on events, it is necessary to limit our study to Finland. A list of the major domestic and international
events selected is reported in Figure 3.6.

We have listed the major events that were salient
topics of concern within Finland during the time of each
postwar election. We have classified each one as to its
likely impact--favorable (+), unfavorable (-), or neutral
(0)--on the incumbent party and on the Communist party.
The table also shows how the two fared in each election.
Electoral success or failure is measured by the percentage
points gained or lost from the previous election. As the
table shows, in about half of the elections the results
were consistent with the anticipated impact of the events
listed. Here again we see that an independent variable
has a contributing influence on voting, but does not provide the whole explanation. The next step in research is
to combine the variables so that taken together they can
better account for voting than any of them could individually.

USING PREDICTIVE SURVEYS AS A
FORECASTING MECHANISM

One of the overall conclusions from the quantitative
analysis performed in the preceding section is that there
is no consistent correlational base over time or across
countries to employ conventional multivariate statistics
to produce a predictive model. The four variables examined
as predictors in a search for explanations of election out-

FIGURE 3.6

Major Domestic and International Events in Finland

Event	Date of Event	Date of Election Following the Event	Anticipated Impact on Incumbent Vote*	Anticipated Impact on Communist Vote
1. Trial of "war responsibles"	Nov. 1945-Feb. 1946			−
2. Allied Control Commission withdrawn	Sept. 1947		(the Communist party is the incumbent party)	+
3. Stalin's letter to President Paasikivi	Feb. 1948	July 1948		−
4. Communist seizure of power in Czechoslovakia	Feb. 1948			−
5. Treaty between Finland and the Soviet Union	Apr. 1948			Communist vote drops 3.5%
6. Strikes and Kemi riots	Summer 1949	July 1951	+ Incumbent vote drops 1.0%	Communist vote increases 1.6%
7. Final payment of war reparations to Soviet Union	Sept. 1952	Mar. 1954	+ Incumbent vote increases .9%	0 Communist vote unchanged

(continued)

99

FIGURE 3.6 (continued)

Event	Date of Event	Date of Election Following the Event	Anticipated Impact on Incumbent Vote*	Anticipated Impact on Communist Vote
8. Agreement on Soviet return of Porkkala to Finland	Sept. 1955		+	0
9. Membership in Nordic Council	Oct. 1955		+	0
10. Membership in United Nations	Dec. 1955		+	0
11. General strike	Mar. 1956	July 1958	0	–
12. Hungarian Revolution	Oct.-Nov. 1956		+	–
13. Open split within the Social Democratic Party	Apr. 1957		0	+
14. Devaluation of the Finnmark	Sept. 1957		– Incumbent vote drops 1.0%	+ Communist vote increases 1.6%
15. Recall of Soviet Ambassador in Helsinki	Sept. 1958		+	–
16. Tax increase on tobacco and liquor	May 1961	Feb. 1962	–	+
17. Membership in EFTA	May 1961		+	0

#	Event	Date	Incumbent vote	Communist vote
18.	Soviet note to Finnish government	Oct. 1961	+ Incumbent vote drops .1%	− Communist vote drops 1.2%
19.	New mark introduced	Jan. 1963	0	0
20.	Agreement on leasing Soviet section of Saimaa Canal	May 1963 Mar. 1966	+	0
21.	Sales tax reform	Jan. 1964	− Incumbent vote drops 1.8%	+ Communist vote drops .8%
22.	Devaluation of the Finnmark	Oct. 1967	−	+
23.	Warsaw Pact occupation of Czechoslovakia	Aug. 1968 Mar. 1970	+	−
24.	Open split within the Communist party	Apr. 1969	0	−
25.	Collapse of Nordek	Dec. 1969	− Incumbent vote drops 3.8%	0 Communist vote drops 4.6%
		Jan. 1972	+ Incumbent vote increases .7%	0 Communist vote drops .4%

*With the exception of events 6, 12, 13, and 15, the incumbent party on the eve of the election was also in power when the events occurred.

comes do not show strong and consistent correlations with voting. Although we think the kinds of quantitative analysis presented in the preceding section could possibly help the analyst to focus his thinking about elections in West European states, we see no formal transfer to multivariate and statistically based forecasting procedures.

However, the general purpose of this book is to suggest how INR analysts might attempt to improve their capacity to forecast. As we noted above, the forecasting components of INR studies on elections in these three states are small when compared with the descriptive and explanatory components. In addition, we have not discussed the need to forecast the consequences of elections. The preceding section deals with elections only as a dependent variable--something to be explained--when in fact one major concern of the analyst is to forecast the short-run and long-run political implications of an election in a particular country under study. To provide a method for forecasting not only elections results but also their consequences we conducted a modest experiment solely for the purpose of demonstration.

The intent of the experiment was to show the feasibility and utility of tapping expert viewpoints on future events and conditions. By way of example, we sent a brief questionnaire concerned with the March 1973 election in France to a group of scholars and State Department officials. We also requested responses from the editorial offices of six newspapers (New York _Times_, Boston _Globe_, Washington _Star_, Washington _Post_, Miami _Herald_, and _Christian Science Monitor_). Journalists were included in our sample for two reasons. First, an INR analysis of the 1972 election in Italy was in no small measure an effort to counter a journalistic parallel drawn between Italy and Chile--"spaghetti with chili sauce," as it was described in the New York _Times_. Second, there seems to be a feeling among INR analysts that policy makers are much influenced by the mass media, and that there is a certain amount of sensationalism as opposed to straightforward reporting even in the major newspapers. Of the six newspapers that received our questionnaire, four responded. The Miami _Herald_ did not return its questionnaire, and the _Christian Science Monitor_ felt unable to oblige because the questionnaire invited "speculative answers which we prefer to avoid." The New York _Times_, on the other hand, completed four questionnaires.

The questionnaire was completed by 23 scholars, 7 journalists and 10 members of the State Department. It

FIGURE 3.7

Questions for Quick Assessment of the March
1973 French Election

Please check your best estimated answer for each of the
following questions concerning the French National Assembly Election of 1973.

1. The leftist (Communist and socialist) percentage of
    the popular vote on the first round of balloting will
    be closest to which of the following figures:

    a. 10%_____ b. 20%_____ c. 30%_____ d. 40%_____

    e. 50% or more_____

2. Will the leftists win a majority of the seats in the
    National Assembly?

    Yes_____ No_____

3. What is the probability of the formation of a "Popular
    Front" government in the wake of the election?

    a. .8_____ b. .6_____ c. .5_____ d. .4_____

    e. .2_____

4. If a "Popular Front" government should materialize,
    what is the probability of a significant change in the
    French position on NATO?

    a. .8_____ b. .6_____ c. .5_____ d. .4_____

    e. .2_____

5. If a "Popular Front" government should materialize,
    what is the probability of a significant change in the
    French position toward the European Economic Community?

    a. .8_____ b. .6_____ c. .5_____ d. .4_____

    e. .2_____

contained five questions and was structured as indicated
in Figure 3.7. The results were tabulated and sent to the
department prior to the election, in the format appearing
in Figure 3.8. A number of interesting findings resulted
from this exercise.

FIGURE 3.8

Results of Expert-Survey of the French National Assembly
Election of 1973

▨ = Academic Respondents   ☐ = Journalistic Respondents   ■ = Others

1. The leftist (Communist and socialist) percentage of the popular
   vote on the first round of balloting will be closest to which
   of the following figures:

   40% Mean response of Academics

   40% Mean response of Journalists

   43% Mean response of Others

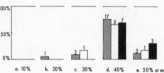

2. Will the leftists win a majority of the seats in the National
   Assembly?

3. What is the probability of the formation of a "Popular Front"
   government in the wake of the election?

   .33 Mean response of Academics

   .45 Mean response of Journalists

   .26 Mean response of Others

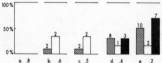

4. If a "Popular Front" government should materialize, what is the
   probability of a significant change in the French position on
   NATO?

   .44 Mean response of Academics

   .38 Mean response of Journalists

   .33 Mean response of Others

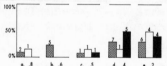

5. If a "Popular Front" government should materialize, what is the
   probability of a significant change in the French position toward
   the European Economic Community?

   .36 Mean response of Academics

   .31 Mean response of Journalists

   .34 Mean response of Others

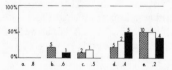

104

The first and perhaps most important finding for the long-range development of such a procedure is that there was substantially more consensus among State Department respondents than among either the scholars or the journalists. Table 3.5 shows the coefficient of variability for each of the three groups on the five questions. This statistic is based on the standard deviation, which measures the level of dispersion around the mean. In order to compare the standard deviations of various groups, we must divide by the mean of each group; it is the result of this division that is the coefficient of variability. The higher the coefficient, the less the agreement among the experts. In all cases, the State Department respondents had greater agreement than did either of the other two groups.*

TABLE 3.5

Coefficients of Variability for Each Group of Experts on Each of the Five Survey Questions

Respondent Group	Question Number				
	1	2	3	4	5
State Department	.11	0.0	.37	.35	.40
Scholars	.16	.11	.42	.47	.50
Journalists	.14	.28	.40	.64	.43

The implication of this particular finding is that those members of the department with an interest and competence in the 1973 French election were in relative agreement about the outcome and consequences of the election. Their estimates happened to be correct, as shown by the subsequent results of the election, and could have been communicated to INR users as an authoritative forecast to be compared with other information that was reaching American policy makers. The consensus also increases our confidence in the supposition that the questionnaire was understood in a similar way across experts.

---

*Whether such agreement is completely desirable is another question that is beyond the scope of this analysis. That is, it may be dangerous for officials concerned with a problem to be overly cohesive in their viewpoints.

The State Department officials were also different from the other two groups with respect to the question of radical electoral change and the probable impact of the election on French policies. On questions 2, 3, 4, and 5, the State Department officials clearly assigned the lowest probability to large-scale changes in French government structure and foreign policies growing out of the election when compared with the other two groups. Academics and journalists indicated that broader changes were somewhat more probable--although still highly unlikely.

The consistency across State Department experts in forecasting small probability of change contrasts sharply with the editorial statements appearing in newspapers before and after the French election. A perusal of editorials in the New York Times during the periods immediately preceding and following the French election (see Figure 3.9) reveals forecasts that are much more change-oriented than the responses of the journalists and State Department officials.

If we assume that users of INR reports are also readers of the New York Times, it is likely that these forecasts of possible revolution in French foreign policy were read with at least as much frequency and attention as the reports from the INR. Since, as reported earlier, a number of INR analysts spoke about the unnecessary concern that can be generated by flamboyant statements of newspaper writers, a brief forecasting questionnaire such as the one reproduced above could help to bring balance into a policy maker's view of upcoming events.

As far as the accuracy of the predictions goes, the results generated by questions 1 and 2 were confirmed as events unfolded. In the first round of balloting the leftist coalition received only 41.6 percent of the popular vote, and the second round of balloting made impossible the formation of a leftist coalition government. The success of the predictions generated by the questionnaire is by no means remarkable or significant evidence of the questionnaire's utility. Nevertheless, it does show how a valid and relatively authoritative analysis can be generated quickly and with relatively little cost.

This method contrasts to the existing procedures that are followed by an INR analyst when asked to forecast the results of an election. A well-argued but lengthy discussion of factors surrounding an election is sent to policy makers who express an interest in the outcome of a particular election. Although it cannot replace the type of presentation found in INR reports, a questionnaire could

FIGURE 3.9

New York _Times_ Editorials on the 1973 French Elections

Preelection Editorial

"A Left Union Government would pull France out of the Atlantic Alliance and adopt a neutral stance between East
and West--a step far beyond Charles de Gaulle's removal of
French forces from NATO commands. The Left is also committed to an economic program that would make Common Market
participation impossible."

Editorial After First-Round Voting

"The concern among France's partners in the Atlantic Alliance and the European Community over the possibility of
a Left government hostile to both organizations has not
been entirely eliminated by the first-round results; but
it has been eased considerably."

Postelection Editorial

"The election outcome brings great relief to France's partners in the Atlantic Alliance and the Common Market, who
had been concerned at the strong showing of the Communist-
Socialist tandem in the opinion polls. France is not an
easy partner, but the Left coalition was committed to programs that would have wrecked both Alliance and Community."

be used to supplement such a presentation. A questionnaire
is particularly effective if the user wants to get a "quick
assessment" in which he has a high degree of confidence
without worrying about the reasons behind a forecast.
    The use of experts to make forecasts is a well-devel-
oped procedure in technology assessment usually called
the "Delphi" technique.[4] The procedure involves having a
set of experts make long-range forecasts that are then examined as a total set. After this examination, the experts
are asked to adjust their initial forecasts. Although the
procedure has been used at great expense in a number of
fields, it is still controversial and has not been used
to predict political events and conditions. In any case,
it is substantially different from our quick assessment

forecasts, since our focus was on short-range forecasts, and the experts were not asked to reinterpret their results in the context of initial responses.

We have shown that it is feasible to get such forecasts in a relatively short period of time with a small amount of effort. We argue that such forecasts have utility for an INR user interested in a quick assessment that can be considered authoritative without studying the arguments presented. Ultimately, however, the success of this approach depends upon continuous usage over a substantial period of time and for a large set of different kinds of situations. If this were done, the complexity of conditions such as those behind an election could be reduced to a series of probability statements and a measure of agreement across those statements so that the time spent in writing and reading the report could be substantially reduced.

COSTS AND UTILITY OF QUANTITATIVE
TECHNIQUES IN ELECTION STUDIES

Our argument throughout this case study has been that quantitative techniques can be of only marginal utility to an INR analyst concerned with elections. Part of the reason for this modest utility lies in the unavailability of explanatory models that are relatively reliable across countries and time. The best that correlation techniques can do for the election analyst is to help him test the assumptions he makes about such factors as voter turnout, economic conditions, and major events. We think that some work in this area might increase the general precision and quality of the INR analyst, but not to such an extent that substantial financial or human resources outlays are warranted.

More specifically, we would like to suggest the following procedure for the INR analyst. In the second section of this case study, we discussed four factors that might affect elections in three countries. We will leave out voter turnout as a factor because its size cannot be determined prior to the election. We suggest that the INR analyst construct a checklist of factors and their general impact to use as a guide in systematically analyzing elections. To illustrate this procedure, Figure 3.10 contains information on the role of inflation, unemployment, and major events on communist votes in Finland. The arrows are based on the discovered correlations for Finland be-

FIGURE 3.10

Checklist of Multiple Factors To Be Used in Predicting the Communist Vote in Finland

	1948	1951	1954	1958	1962	1966	1970	1972
Inflation	→	→	←	←	←	→	→	←
Unemployment	←	←	←	←	→	←	→	→
Events	→	→	↑	←	→	→	↑	
Predictions	→	→	←	←	→	→	→	↑
Actual gain or loss (percent)	-3.5	+1.6	No change	+1.6	-1.2	-0.8	-4.6	+0.4

Note: The procedure used for generating the arrow for the impact of inflation and unemployment was to determine whether the mean value for the years previous to the election was greater than, the same as, or less than the mean for the total number of years. This information was related to whether the correlation for the total number of elections was positive or negative. If it was positive, then the arrow would indicate a positive impact if the mean value was less than the overall mean and an ambiguous impact if the mean value was the same for the years prior to the election than it was for the entire set of years. If the correlation was negative, a positive impact was indicated for values less than the overall mean and a negative impact for values greater than the overall mean. Since the correlation for Finland was negative for inflation as well as unemployment, the latter transformation was employed.

tween inflation and unemployment on the one hand and communist vote on the other. The arrows for the events are
taken from Figure 3.6.

As ongoing research discovers empirical relationships
between other variables and election outcomes, the INR
analyst could be given a more extensive checklist to use in
judging the likely results of different factors on election
results. In the particular case presented in Figure 3.10,
the predictions generated were correct in 1948, 1958, 1962,
1970, and (assuming that less than a 1 percent change is
no change at all) in 1972. Although the judgments of the
INR analysts are necessary to make useful interpretations
of a checklist similar to the one in Figure 3.10, we believe the checklist could help the analyst in producing
and presenting his conclusions.

As far as short-range election predictions go, the
INR analyst should continue to rely on the pollsters in
the various countries as well as on his own research in
the context of a particular election. There is no reason
for the analyst to collect or scrutinize data generated
by polls several months before an election. The pollster
has resources that surpass those of the INR analyst. Moreover, there is probably little demand for more than a
quick assessment of an upcoming election. If quick assessments are needed, we would suggest use of an inexpensive,
low-profile, questionnaire survey technique.

There is one area not covered in the substantive section of this case study, however, in which quantitative
techniques and more complex quick assessment polls could
be of value. This concerns the long-range (six months to
two years) impact of elections on the domestic and foreign
policies of a state. In our questionnaire we tried to
demonstrate how specific foreign policy questions can be
examined in terms of the impact of an election. However,
there is also a need to develop some type of profiling
system in which election results could be interpreted in
the context of specific policy decisions. Questions such
as the impact of the recent French election on French and
European trade policy or the attitude of the new Assembly
toward American business are probably of major concern to
INR users. Quantitative techniques could ultimately be
used to present these changes.

To develop quantitative indicators that measure policy
consequences such as these, however, would require extensive development work. Political scientists have rarely
focused on the role of election results in policy outputs,
particularly with respect to elections outside of the

United States. Without a substantial commitment to development work in the scholarly community, there is little that can be done beyond what has been demonstrated in this case study.

NOTES

1. For the countries covered in this study see, for example, the Finnish Gallup Poll, the Institut Francais D'Opinion Publique (IFOP), and CISER and DOXA for Italy.

2. For the countries covered in this study see, for example, Roy Pierce and Samuel H. Barnes, "Public Opinion and Political Preferences in France and Italy" (Paper presented at the annual convention of the American Political Science Association, Los Angeles, 1970); Pertti Pesonen, "Dimensions of Political Cleavage in Multi-Party Systems" (Paper presented at the annual convention of the American Political Science Association, Washington, D.C., 1972); and Pertti Pesonen, An Election in Finland: Party Activities and Voter Reactions (New Haven, Conn.: Yale University Press, 1968). Also see Gabriel A. Almond and Sidney Verba, The Civic Culture (Boston: Little, Brown and Co., 1965).

3. Data on voter turnout and the dependent variables of communist vote and incumbent vote are taken from the following sources: Jaakko Nousianinen, The Finnish Political System, translated by John H. Hodgson (Cambridge, Mass.: Harvard University Press, 1971); Philip M. Williams, French Politicians and Elections 1951-1969 (Cambridge, England: Cambridge University Press, 1970); Giaemilio Ipsevich and Enrico Zampetti, Elezioni 1972 Risultati e Confronti (Milan, Italy: Pan Editrice Milano, 1972). Unemployment and cost-of-living data are from the International Labor Organization's Yearbook of Labour Statistics, published annually. Data on major events was collected nonsystematically from the Bank of Finland Monthly Bulletin and from the Nousianinen book.

4. See O. Helmer, Social Technology (New York: Basic Books, 1966), and N. Dalkey, "Delphi," RAND Corporation, P-3704, 1967.

4

**EXPLAINING MILITARY
EXPENDITURES IN
LATIN AMERICA**

The purpose of this, our third case study, is to demonstrate how quantitative techniques might be used by foreign affairs analysts to explain and predict military expenditures in Latin America. It begins by identifying factors that INR analysts have mentioned in their reports as having some impact on general military expenditures as well as on specific arms acquisitions decisions. Statistical techniques are employed to determine whether some of these factors are associated with patterns in military expenditures. This discussion is followed by an attempt to develop a scheme to assess the overall relative importance of several leading indicators as they interact to help explain and anticipate a change in military expenditures. Finally, this study offers specific recommendations for the use of these techniques by analysts, with an eye to both their costs and benefits.

The chapter is organized into these three sections:

Measuring and Testing Factors that May Be Relevant to
  Patterns of Latin American Military Expenditures
A Multifactor National Profile Scoresheet As an Approach to Predictions
Costs and Benefits of the Techniques to the Foreign
  Affairs Analyst

MEASURING AND TESTING FACTORS THAT MAY BE RELEVANT
TO PATTERNS OF LATIN AMERICAN MILITARY EXPENDITURES

The purpose of this section is to demonstrate how quantitative techniques could be used to measure and test factors identified by INR analysts as relevant to patterns of military expenditures in Latin America. The procedure followed in this section was to study the work of INR analysts on military expenditures and arms expenditures in Latin America in order to identify a list of factors considered to have some impact. Once this was done, we explored ways of measuring these factors and determining the degree to which these measures were associated with patterns in military expenditures.

A number of relevant observations about the INR's work were made on the basis of our search through the INR literature on the subject. First, we found that INR analysts were primarily concerned with arms purchases rather than total military expenditures. Most of their forecasts had to do with whether a particular country or set of countries would purchase a particular type of military equipment rather than whether the total military budget would go up. We decided that we would use military expenditures as our dependent variable in all but one case, primarily because such data were more readily available to us on an unclassified basis. Although this decision restricts the direct application of the techniques explored in this case study to the concern for arms acquisitions, it should not affect the extent to which the case study demonstrates the feasibility and utility of the general techniques. We know from our discussion with INR analysts that the arms expenditure data are available to them on a basis that would allow the application of techniques similar to those applied in this case study.

The second aspect of the INR literature that we discovered was the highly sophisticated nature of the INR analyses. For a number of reasons, INR analysts tend to use quantitative data in their forecasts. They also tend to think in terms of factors. Our task was made easier in this respect. However, the analysts offered highly complex explanations of arms acquisitions policies, meaning that they saw the factors they identified as operating in a variety of ways. There were no simple statements of bivariate relationships between a given factor and military expenditures. Because of the complexity of the explanations and forecasts, we found that the only thing we could do in summarizing the INR work was to identify factors that could be relevant to Latin American military expenditures.

We searched the writings of INR analysts and developed the following list of factors that were considered important:

1. Economic conditions within the Latin American states.

2. The role of the military in the nonmilitary affairs of the government.

3. The need for internal defense.

4. Reactions to arms acquisition in other selected Latin American states.

5. Military allocations to particular service branches in other selected Latin American states.

6. Internal political support for the regime.

7. Age and condition of existing military equipment.

These factors were some of the ones identified as having some kind of impact on the acquisition of arms in Latin America and perhaps on overall military expenditures policies.* We decided to attempt to measure the first five factors and see whether there was some relationship between them and military expenditures. We omitted the remaining factors because the constraints of the project did not allow for data collection, although in principle it appears to be possible to acquire quantitative data relevant to these factors as well.

In attempting to test the factors mentioned above, we were faced with minor technical problems in gathering the data. Before one can gather data, one must operationalize the factors; that is, one must define each factor in such a way that reliable measurements can be taken. In the tests provided below, problems of operationalization will be discussed for each variable used.

Testing Factor 1: Economic Conditions Within the Latin American States

The problem of developing a precise definition so that quantitative data can be gathered is illustrated by our work on Factor 1. Before testing the influence that economic conditions within Latin American states exert on military expenditures, one must decide upon a definition for each of the concepts contained in the relationship

---

*There remains the problem that most of the relationships analyzed in INR reports were stated with arms rather than military expenditures as the dependent variable, whereas our analysis will focus on overall military expenditures.

that will facilitate reliable measurement and ensure an accurate test of the factor's influence.

We felt the gross domestic product (GDP) of each Latin American state to be an accurate measure of "economic conditions within Latin American states." The concept "military expenditures" is sufficiently self-explanatory. Changes in Latin American military expenditures as a function of GDP can be defined and measured in a number of ways. We will deal with two of the most common. One method is to present annual total military expenditures in raw figures; a second method is to measure the change in expenditures as a percentage of total GDP.[1]

In a scattergram, Figure 4.1, we have plotted the values for the two factors for 19 Latin American countries from 1967 to 1971. The horizontal axis relates countries according to their GDP (in millions of U.S. dollars). The vertical axis relates countries according to their total military expenditures (also expressed in millions of U.S. dollars). The graph seems to indicate that as GDP rises, so does the amount of money spent for military purposes. The diagonal line (regression line) through the graph traces the path on which all the points would fall if GDP were perfectly correlated with military spending. There is some dispersion on each side of the line; this tells us that the two are not perfectly correlated. However, most of the points are reasonably close to the line; this tells us that there is a strong positive correlation between GDP and military spending. In other words, if we know the level of a nation's GDP, we can make an accurate guess as to what the level of its military spending will be. If we guess that military spending is 3 percent of GDP, we will not be far wrong most of the time. There is a summary statistic to measure this degree of association between two variables. It is called the Pearson correlation, symbolized by the letter "r." This measure varies from -1.0 to +1.0. A minus number illustrates a negative linear relationship; a positive number indicates a positive linear relationship. The r for Figure 4.1 is +.88, indicating a very strong positive association between the level of GDP and the level of military spending. In this case we already knew, by inspecting the scatterplot, that the relationship was strong, and the Pearson's r did not tell us much more. However, when the relationship is not so obvious, it is useful to have such a statistic with which to measure the strength or weakness of the relationship.

FIGURE 4.1

Scatterplot of Military Expenditures by Gross Domestic Product, 1967-71

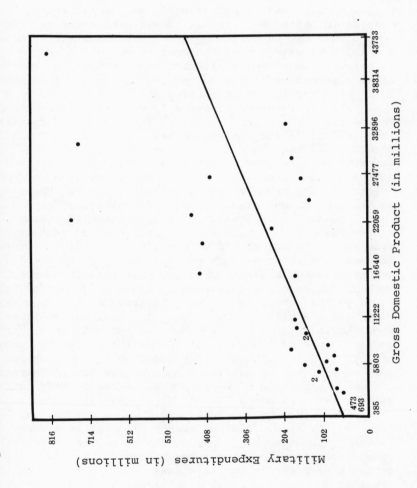

This analysis has told us only that as more money is available in Latin American economies, more is appropriated for military purposes. What if the increase in military expenditures is only U.S. $200 while the GDP jumps by 2 billion? Figure 4.1 and the Pearson correlation of .88 evaluate this increase as being equally significant if the increase in both GDP and military spending were $200 or if it were $2 million. In using raw military expenditure figures we are measuring increases, but we are not accounting for significant increases relative to the level of other factors in the nation. To account for these factors we will compute changes in military spending as a percentage of GDP. We can measure more accurately significant increases or decreases in spending over time and the degree to which this fluctuation is associated with changes in other variables, in this case, GDP. Figure 4.2 presents the scattergram for GDP again as the independent variable, with the change in military expenditures as a percentage of GDP as the dependent variable.

The results in graphic form and in terms of Pearson's r are quite different from our initial test of this factor. The wider dispersion of the points away from the regression line, and the r (which drops from +.88 to -.07), show that the strong association posited in Figure 4.1 does not hold up when we measure annual change as a share of GDP.

Translating these figures into verbal description, we can conclude that (1) both military expenditures and GDP increase over time and (2) there is not, however, a consistent relationship between level of GDP and the share of GDP used for military purposes. Since the percentage of GDP spent on the military varies independently of GDP, we will use this as a measure of military spending to see what factors, if any, predict changes in the share of military spending.

By changing our measure of military spending from an absolute figure to a percentage of GDP figure, we can conclude that increase in GDP leads only to larger expenditures in the sense of dollar volume. There appears to be no reason to assume that as the Latin American nations become wealthier, their actual policies regarding military expenditures change in a substantial and positive manner. In fact, the strong positive correlation between GDP and total military expenditures appears to be an artifact of the monetary consequences of a growing GDP and not evidence of increasing military armament.

117

FIGURE 4.2

Scatterplot of Military Expenditures as a Percentage of Gross Domestic Product, 1967-71

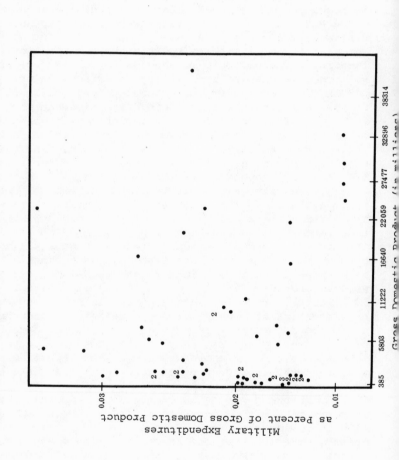

Testing Factor 2: The Role of the
Military in the Nonmilitary
Affairs of the Government

The problem of testing military expenditures as a
function of the role of the military in the nonmilitary affairs of government lies in finding a suitable definition
of the military's role in government. Fortunately, two
projects--one by the INR analysts and one by the Latin
American Military Behavior (LAMB) Project of Syracuse Uni-
versity--provide us with a relatively good definition that
is readily adaptable to testing procedures.

INR analysts classify the role played by the military
in the nonmilitary affairs of the government into three
distinct categories. Each category is assigned a number:
"1" corresponds to a situation where the military may be a
potentially significant political force but seldom mobilizes
for action because of the dominance of civilian groups;
"2" corresponds to a situation in which the military has a
limited but important part in the nonmilitary affairs of
government; and "3" corresponds to a situation in which an
ad hoc military group, or the armed forces as a whole, is
in fact the government.

This type of classification is called by social scientists a nominal scale. The categories 1 through 3 constitute an exhaustive and mutually exclusive set of categories
for classifying the role of the military in the nonmilitary affairs of government in all Latin American nations.
The numbers 1, 2, and 3 are used merely as symbols for the
categories and have no mathematical significance whatso-
ever.

Despite the care taken in its construction, this cate-
gorization is, like all nominal scales, a product of subjective judgment. In view of this, nominal scales can be
tested not for accuracy as such but rather for degree of
association with other nominal scales that attempt to measure the same phenomenon. Fortunately, such a scale, comparable to that of the INR, has recently been devised as
a part of a larger project studying military behavior in
Latin America.

In the LAMB Project of Syracuse University, domestic
acts in which the military was involved as either a target
or actor were coded into an event data set for 18 Latin
American nations for the period 1960-70. One of the categories coded was the "role of the military in government,"
consisting of a threefold nominal scale corresponding almost exactly to the INR scale. To test the degree of as-

119

sociation between the two, we did a simple correlation analysis on 18 nations that showed a moderate association between the rating of the military role by both scales.*
When the classifications of only those nations on the continent of South America were correlated, the association between the two scales was even stronger. It should be noted that in view of the fact that these scales were independently generated, with very different resources and by different analysts with different purposes in mind, the correlations reported here lend credibility to both scales.

A nominal classification scheme allows for a relatively simple but extremely useful quantitative technique often referred to as a cross-tabulation of variables. To construct such a table, the dependent variable, change in military spending, must be transformed into a similar type of nominal scale. This is done by grouping all decreases in spending as a percentage of GDP into category 1, all zero changes into 2, and all increases into category 3. The result is a three-by-three matrix, as presented in Table 4.1.

Data for the two scales was collected and aggregated for the six leading Latin American arms spenders--Argentina, Brazil, Chile, Colombia, Peru, and Venezuela (hereafter referred to as the "Big Six")--for the time period 1960-70. The independent variable, the role of the military, is shown in the columns of the table, and the dependent variable, the change in arms spending, is shown in the rows. The numbers in each cell, called cell frequencies, refer to the number of times that the particular condition of the column and the particular condition of the row are simultaneously satisfied. This cross-tabulation procedure is useful because it permits the findings to be expressed a number of ways: raw frequencies, percentages, or a summary statistic of association similar to the correlations that have been previously discussed.

If the assumption about the role of the military leading to high spending is valid, we would expect the matrix to show two basic trends: (1) when there is little or no involvement of the military in the nonmilitary affairs of government, there will be decreases in military spending; (2) when the military is somewhat involved in the nonmilitary affairs of the government, there will frequently be no changes in spending; (3) when the military is very in-

---

*We used Yule's Q, a statistic that computes correlation between two variables measured on nominal scales.

TABLE 4.1

Cross-Tabulation of the Change in Military Spending as a
Percentage of GDP, by the INR View of the Role of the
Military in the Nonmilitary Affairs of Government,
the Big Six, 1960-70

Change in Military Spending as a Percentage of GDP	Role of the Military			
	Little or No Involvement	Limited Involvement	Very Involved	Row Totals
Decrease	11	12	8	31 (51.7%)
Zero change	5	2	0	7 (11.7%)
Increase	8	11	3	22 (36.7%)
Column totals	24 (40.0%)	25 (41.7%)	11 (18.3%)	60 (100%)

volved in the nonmilitary affairs of the government, there
will be frequent increases in military spending.

In scrutinizing the matrix we can see that it does
not conform to the pattern predicted by the factor. The
inconsistent patterns in the decrease and increase rows
show that expenditures do not consistently vary with different roles of the military. Moreover, the spread and
patterns between entries are not great enough to posit any
relations. If the cells in the "Increase" row (reading
from left to right) read something like 1, 4, and 17, respectively, this would indicate that the more involved the
military, the greater the likelihood of an increase in
military spending. As the table shows, this is far from
being the case. The statistic of association for cross
tabulations further bears out these disparities. The measure, scaled in the same way as a Pearson's correlation
(-1.0 to +1.0) and called Kendall's Tau b, was computed
to be .01, so close to zero as to suggest complete randomness between the two variables. These results are consistent with INR analyses, which find little relationship between the role of the military and military expenditures.

However, the cumulative percentages of the rows and the columns do offer some interesting information pertinent to this factor. In 1960-70, for the largest-spending Latin American countries, changes in expenditures as a percentage of GDP decreased from those of the previous year 51.7 percent of the time, remained unchanged from one year to the next 11.7 percent of the time, and increased 36.7 percent of the time. (These are the row percentages of Table 4.1.) Among other things this shows the relevance of studying spending increases and decreases. It is also noteworthy that despite the prominent role of the military in both Argentina and Brazil during this time period, the military dominate governments of the Big Six only 18.3 percent of the time, while the remaining 80 percent is split about equally by the other two categories in the INR's scheme.

Testing Factor 3: The Need for Internal Defense

The concept "need for internal defense" also presents problems in operationalization, since a variety of measurements might be developed. Our response to this ambiguity was to employ two different types of data in measuring the concept.

The first type of data was generated as part of the LAMB Project described above. Those data were used to produce an index of the security police role of the military in Latin American societies. Events such as arrests and armed conflicts in each nation were coded and tabulated. The total of such events was then divided by the total number of domestic events reported for that nation for each year.

A second measure of "need for internal defense" was developed by using an index of violence reported in the second edition of the World Handbook of Political and Social Indicators (New Haven, Conn.: Yale University Press, 1972). This index includes the numbers of riots, deaths from domestic violence, and political protests.

Having developed two separate measures of "need for internal defense," we are ready to perform a number of statistical analyses. The first determines the degree to which the two measures were intercorrelated. If we assume that the two measures were tapping the same phenomenon, we would expect a high correlation between the two. However, knowing that the "need for internal defense" is a complex factor containing a variety of dimensions, we would have been surprised if the two were highly correlated. This was particularly true since the procedures for collecting the data were different and concerned somewhat different categories. The Pearson's correlation of the two measures for the Big Six states, from 1960 to 1967, is .47, which suggests that they are measuring the same general phenomenon but picking up different dimensions of that phenomenon.

In any case, the lack of a very close fit between the two variables suggests that we correlate each separately with military expenditures. In both cases, however, there is no correlation. The first measure, from the LAMB data (military acting as a security force), generated a .02 correlation, whereas the index of domestic violence from the Handbook yielded a -.04 correlation. Our failure to uncover a relationship between military expenditure and two different measures of "need for internal defense" suggests strongly that there is no systematic relationship between that factor and growth of military expenditures for the Big Six Latin American countries from 1960 to 1967.

Testing Factor 4: Reactions to Arms Acquisitions in Other Selected Latin American States

Tests of the three preceding factors have relied upon measures of statistical association that describe the strength of a relationship between variables. However, other types of quantitative analyses are possible, particularly when dealing with events occurring at one point in time that are assumed to have an impact on events and conditions at another point in time. Factor 4 is readily suited to this kind of analysis. We will be applying a technique for this and the following factor referred to as Markov chain processes based on probability analysis. The technique assumes that through establishing initial probabilities and conditional probabilities, one can predict a future occurrence. It provides a method for predicting what Nation X will do at a future time if we know what Nation Y did in the past; or, stated more specifically for the above factor, it is a method for testing if an increase in arms expenditures by one nation leads to a reaction by another nation to increase its acquisitions.

The calculations involved in the Markov chain analysis are rather complex, involving as they do matrix algebra. However, the entire scheme is based on relatively straight-

forward notions of conditional probability. Consider this
simple example. Suppose that over a time span of 10 years,
Nation X acquired one or more high-performance weapons
(HPWs) in four of those years. On the basis of this observation alone, we could say that for this period there
is a probability of .40 that Nation X acquires HPWs within
a given year. Suppose that we also observe that Nation Y,
a neighbor and presumed rival of X, has acquired HPWs in
six of the 10 years, and that half of these acquisitions
(three of the six) were in the years preceding the years in
which Nation X acquired its HPWs. On the basis of these
observations, we can establish the following probabilities:
(1) the probability that Nation Y will acquire HPWs is
6/10, or .6; (2) the probability that Nation X will acquire
HPWs in the year following Y's acquisition of HPWs is 3/6,
or .5.

This leads to a simple conditional probability calculation: The long-run probability that Nation X will acquire HPWs is the probability that Y will acquire a weapon
(.6) times the probability that Nation X will acquire a
weapon in the year following Y's acquisition (.5), or
.6 × .5 = .30.

What we have done in this simple example is to take
a model based on the assumption that X is responding to Y's
HPW acquisitions and to operationalize it with a conditional probability. This gives us a predicted long-run
probability that X will acquire HPWs in three out of ten
years, which is quite close to the observed result of Nation X's HPW acquisition rate of four out of ten years.
In the absence of a more powerful explanation, we would
conclude that this model had validity in explaining Nation
X's HPW acquisition policy. In the actual analyses that
follow, we have performed the same type of calculations,
although they are somewhat more complex. The primary reason is that we assume not merely that one nation is reacting to the other but that both are reacting to one another
in their weapons acquisition policies.

The actual cases we examine are Chile-Peru and Brazil-
Argentina. These two pairs of countries are frequently
cited as potential arms rivals, although they are not the
only rivals in Latin America. We have chosen them because
they show the different sorts of findings that can be generated with probability techniques, and because they are
relatively simple two-way rivalry patterns, rather than
patterns involving three or more nations, which involve
complexities exceeding the data available to us.

It is important to note here that what we are testing
is a reactive pattern between two nations and not reaction
as an independent variable to explain military spending.
This latter factor could be tested in much the same manner
as factors 1-3, but for the purpose of demonstrating
whether or not the reactive notion operates at all between
nations, our probability test seems of greater significance.
Figure 4.3 presents: A, the matrix of initial probabilities with the corresponding conditional probabilities by
which the cells are to be multiplied to produce B, the
chain process of transitional probabilities, and finally C,
a diagram of the rivalry patterns that emerge. The data
contained in the cells was produced from an analysis of
Chilean and Peruvian acquisitions of high-performance air-
craft and combat sea vessels.

For the factor concerning reactive behavior among nations to be a valid explanation, a basic pattern would have
to hold in the Markov process. Over time, the difference
between the transitional probabilities of each nation would
decrease. In other words, if two nations really see one
another as referents and act accordingly, the probabilities
in Figure 4.3B should move toward identity and at the very
least remain fairly stable over time. Looking at Figure
4.3B, we see that this is precisely the case with Peru and
Chile; graph 4.3C more clearly illustrates the pattern that
emerges. In 1967 the probability that Chile would acquire
a weapon was .2, while that of Peru acquiring a similar
weapon was .3. Acquisitions by both nations at some time
prior to time t, 1967, sparked a referencing maneuver
whereby the two rivals not only reacted and moved toward
one another but also reacted in such a way that the propensity of each to acquire a weapon in 1968 was exactly
that of its rival in 1967. The situation in the years
that follow shows that the movement toward the position of
the rival establishes a stable equilibrium.

Another finding of interest emerges from the Markov
scheme. The initial matrix 4.3A shows that at no time in
the five-year span measured in this data did Chile acquire
a weapon at time t+1 when it had acquired a weapon at time
t. The same relationship holds for Peru. Further, the
matrix 4.3B of transitional probabilities shows that 50
percent of the time neither nation will acquire any weapon
at all. Given this fact (that neither nation will acquire
a weapon at time t), the matrix suggests that the drive
by each nation to then acquire an arms advantage over the
other is only .4 for Chile and .2 for Peru. This notion
seriously challenges a theory of arms races, for our analy-

FIGURE 4.3

Markov Chain Analysis of Rivalry Between Chile and
Peru in High-Performance Weapons

A. INITIAL PROBABILITY MATRIX

Transitional
Probabilities

		Time (t+1)			Conditional Probability
		Neither	Chile	Peru	
Time (t)	Neither	0.4	0.4	0.2	0.5
	Chile	0.5	0	0.5	0.2
	Peru	0.67	0.33	0	0.3

Initial
Probabilities

B. TRANSITIONAL PROBABILITIES CHAIN

Time

T	T+1	T+2	T+3	T+4
0.5	0.5	0.48	0.50	0.49
0.2	0.3	0.27	0.27	0.27
0.3	0.2	0.25	0.23	0.24

C. GRAPH OF HPW REACTIVE PATTERNS BETWEEN CHILE AND PERU

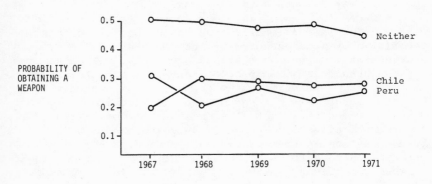

126

sis shows that a dampening reaction is the key explanatory phenomenon of weapons acquisition and produces shifts, if not outright changes, in a nation's military appropriations.

Testing Factor 5: Military Allocations to Particular Service Branches in Other Selected Latin American States

This factor can be construed in two ways: first, as one pertaining to intranational service competition for national military appropriations, and second, as one pertaining to transnational branch rivalries. In dealing with the first we operationalized the concept of interservice competition by measuring the share of military spending for each service branch. If allocations to the branches were related, a stable equilibrium or share for each could be identified and then deviations from that norm could be calculated. However, glancing at our data for the Big Six for 1940 to 1970, a pattern emerges that renders the factor from the internal perspective untestable by the Markov process.

Table 4.2 contains the percentage distribution for each of the Big Six nations at five-year intervals. It seems that since the air force as a service branch had a later beginning in these six than in other nations, increases over time tend to reflect not competition among rivals but rather the desire of governments to modernize their total armed forces. In view of this we chose to concentrate our analysis of this factor on the idea of transnational service rivalries.

A different and simpler use of the Markov technique will be implemented in this test. Figure 4.4 contains the data that will be used to test the rivalries between selected Latin American nations for the years 1960 to 1970. We will use only the matrix of initial probabilities and will include the raw frequencies that generated these probabilities. Matrixes A and B test Brazil's and Argentina's reactions to each other, while Matrix C tests the reactions of Peru to Chile.

For the factor to have explanatory power, we would expect that the highest initial probabilities would occur in those diagonal cells where one nation at time t and another nation at time t+1 both increase or both decrease relative to each other. In both the case of Brazil's reaction to Argentina and Argentina's reaction to Brazil,

TABLE 4.2

Share of Total Appropriations, the Big Six, for Five-Year
Intervals, 1940-70

	Argentina			Brazil		
Year	Army	Navy	Air Force	Army	Navy	Air Force
1940	61.8	38.2	0	70.9	29.1	0
1945	69.9	26.0	9.1	56.6	21.7	21.7
1950	47.6	31.5	20.9	47.4	25.8	26.8
1955	46.5	33.4	20.1	46.7	28.3	25.0
1960	50.7	29.9	19.4	49.6	24.9	25.5
1965	51.1	31.1	17.8	50.0	24.3	25.7
1970	43.3	30.2	26.5	48.1	24.2	27.7

	Chile			Colombia		
	Army	Navy	Air Force	Army	Navy	Air Force
1940	45.9	44.3	9.8	64.1	18.6	17.3
1945	60.5	30.4	9.1	na	na	na
1950	45.7	39.9	14.4	na	na	na
1955*	61.2	27.7	11.1	60.5	24.0	15.5
1960	33.7	44.3	22.0	60.1	21.8	18.1
1965	32.5	45.5	22.0	66.3	17.9	15.8
1970	37.5	42.0	20.5	55.0	19.0	26.0

	Peru			Venezuela		
	Army	Navy	Air Force	Army	Navy	Air Force
1940	62.9	37.9	0	85.0	15.0	0
1945	58.4	17.9	23.7	89.0	11.0	0
1950	61.4	18.6	20.0	na	na	na
1955	59.0	15.8	25.2	na	na	na
1960	60.6	18.7	20.7	37.6	35.2	27.2
1965	49.3	26.3	24.4	42.5	33.3	24.2
1970	46.2	27.4	26.4	41.7	33.3	25.0

*Data for Colombia, 1957 figures.

FIGURE 4.4

Interservice Rivalries, 1960-70

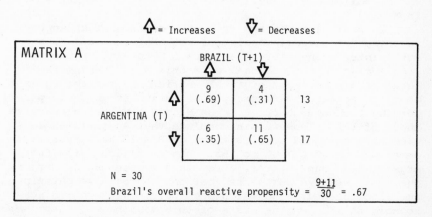

⇧ = Increases   ⇩ = Decreases

MATRIX A

BRAZIL (T+1)
⇧   ⇩

ARGENTINA (T)

⇧
| 9 (.69) | 4 (.31) | 13 |
⇩
| 6 (.35) | 11 (.65) | 17 |

N = 30

Brazil's overall reactive propensity = $\frac{9+11}{30}$ = .67

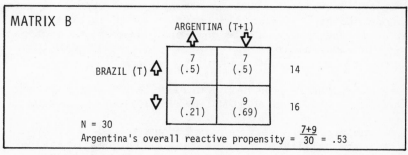

MATRIX B

ARGENTINA (T+1)
⇧   ⇩

BRAZIL (T) ⇧
| 7 (.5) | 7 (.5) | 14 |
⇩
| 7 (.21) | 9 (.69) | 16 |

N = 30

Argentina's overall reactive propensity = $\frac{7+9}{30}$ = .53

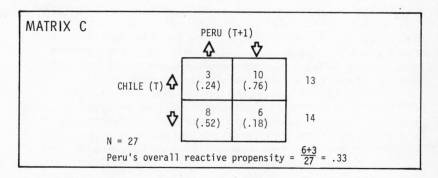

MATRIX C

PERU (T+1)
⇧   ⇩

CHILE (T) ⇧
| 3 (.24) | 10 (.76) | 13 |
⇩
| 8 (.52) | 6 (.18) | 14 |

N = 27

Peru's overall reactive propensity = $\frac{6+3}{27}$ = .33

this pattern emerges (Matrixes A and B). However, the reverse relationship is the case with respect to Peruvian armed forces in reference to those of Chile, as shown in Matrix C, where the diagonal probabilities are lower than those in the other cells. Chile's responses to Peru (not shown) follow a nonreactive pattern similar to that shown in Matrix C.

In examining the raw frequency patterns that appear in these reactive diagonals for both Matrix A and B, another interesting pattern appears. By adding up the raw frequencies in the diagonal of Matrix A and taking the total as a percentage of total entries, we see that Brazil's reactive index with respect to Argentina is .67. In performing the same computation on Matrix B we get a reactive index of .53. Thus we can conclude that Argentinian service branches tend to view those of Brazil as referents to a stronger degree (.67 to .53) than Brazilians view their Argentinian counterparts. From this simple use of Markov analysis, we have postulated not only a reactive pattern but also the degree to which each participant nation seems to hold to it. On the basis of this finding we accept that the service branches in Argentina and Brazil do refer to one another and that this pattern is an identifiable one. In the case of Chile and Peru, however, no such pattern is discernible.

A MULTIFACTOR NATIONAL PROFILE SCORESHEET AS AN APPROACH TO PREDICTIONS

The preceding section may be summarized in two points. First, the utility of quantitative techniques in making sound explanations is directly related to the clarity of definition and precision of measurement of the variable that will be scrutinized. Second, the way one chooses to define concepts contained in a factor frequently determines the types of quantitative technique appropriate for its testing. Thus, factors postulating relationships between certain factors and a change in arms spending are best tested with correlation analysis: factors measured in nominal or interval scales are easily analyzed through cross-tabulation procedures. Relationships that claim that variables interact in conditionally dependent patterns lend themselves to some form of probability analysis.

In light of the preceding tests, how well do the factors identified by INR analysts fare when subjected to quantitative analysis? We feel the tests support the following conclusions:

1.   There is no strong relationship between changes in national economic growth, as expressed in GDP, and changes in military spending.
2.   Although we can identify reasonably well the role of the military in the nonmilitary affairs of the government, this variable does not provide reliable explanations and predictions of fluctuation in military spending.
3.   Although the role of the military as a security force may be important for other reasons, it does not predict changes in military spending over time.
4.   The level of domestic violence in a nation is moderately related to the role of the military as a security force, but it too does not account for changes in military spending.
5.   Rivalry patterns with respect to high-performance weapons do operate in Latin American nations, some more than others, and this causes a shift in arms acquisitions behavior of a nation.
6.   Service branches of rival nations tend, in some cases, to view one another as reference points for establishing their share of arms spending.

At first glance, these may appear to be quite limited findings. But it must be remembered that the factors abstracted for this case study from the INR reports were arbitrarily organized in this book as a series of single-factor explanations of military spending. That is, our five factors identified five separate independent variables. We should not let this form of presentation lead us to believe, as the INR analysts well know is not the case, that any one variable can adequately explain fluctuations in military expenditures.

What we need is a mode of analysis in which Latin American military spending can be predicted through a technique that simultaneously takes into account all the relevant explanatory factors. Our ability to predict changes in the dependent variable should increase if we can systematically relate several of the factors to the changes in military spending.

We must make one more change in our approach. In the foregoing analysis we assumed that patterns were uniform from one country to another. That is, we took data from either the Big Six or the set of 19 Latin American countries and treated them as one sample. This type of analysis is frequently called "cross-sectional" analysis because it looks at a cross section of cases for one time period. With cross-sectional analysis, a failure to find high correlations is sometimes caused by this lumping together of all countries. One relationship between factors could exist in one country while a different pattern might prevail in another country; in such a case, the cross-sectional approach could have resulted in the canceling out of the two patterns and a failure to find any correlation.

An example of how cross-sectional analysis failed to uncover a pattern that in fact did exist can be seen in the relationship between the role of the military as a security force and changes in military spending. Cross-sectional analysis of the Big Six countries from 1960 to 1967 produced a correlation of .02. But for Argentina alone, during the same time period, the correlation is a much-higher .43, and for Colombia alone it is .56. Hence, analysis of individual countries leads to higher correlations than does the cross-sectional analysis of all countries taken together.

Pointing out the advantages of single-country analysis over time does not mean rejecting the comparative approach and cross-sectional analysis. There are advantages to that form of analysis since it provides a larger set of cases upon which to conduct quantitative analysis. In fact, the first case study, "Predicting Political Instability in Tropical Africa," made use of a cross-sectional design to generate correlations that applied with high consistency for all black African nations.

However, in this case a multiple-factor analysis of each country over time seems more appropriate. The standard quantitative response to this problem is the use of multiple regression techniques. Multiple regression is a method for estimating the relationship between one dependent variable and a set of several independent variables. It is useful to social scientists because it shows the importance of each independent variable, relative to the importance of all other independent variables, in explaining variation in the dependent variable. However, when the policy analyst wishes to forecast, he is only concerned with how well a set of independent variables, taken together, will predict changes in another variable. Therefore, we are proposing a procedure roughly comparable to multiple regression, but much simplified--and, we might add, much simpler to use and understand. It is called a National Profile Scoresheet (NPS). Its purpose is to use current patterns of information on each country in such a way that the foreign affairs analyst can develop a checklist of factors leading to increases or decreases in military expenditures. It lists the major factors along with the probabilities that those factors would contribute to either increase or decrease in military expenditures.

There are four basic ideas underlying the use of NPS:

1. Given that different factors predict a change in military spending in Latin America in different nations, each country must be studied individually.

2. The set of factors on the NPS are the same for each nation. National profiles are comparable in terms of how different nations react to one another or to change in domestic conditions; of course, the relative importance of each factor is likely to be different from one country to another.

3. A knowledge of the previous relationships between factors will help us predict what that relationship will be in the future.

4. Quantitative techniques are useful in this analysis because the correlations or probabilities for a particular prior period constitute the relevant "historical" information for making projections into the future.

In Tables 4.3 through 4.8, we have provided the tests of the NPS on the Big Six nations. The goal is to predict changes in military spending as a percentage of GDP in each nation for two years, 1967 and 1968. Section A of each table lists the correlations between each separate independent variable and the change in spending. These serve as historical tendencies identifying the most salient factors that cause changes in each particular nation. The measure r^2 is the amount of variance each factor explains in changes in military spending.

Section B of each table describes in symbolic form the state of the factors at the time specified. In the column headed 1966, the arrows pointing upward ($\blacktriangle$) indicate increases over that of the previous year; the arrows pointing downward ($\blacktriangledown$) signify decreases; and horizontal arrows ($\rightarrow$) mean no change. On the basis of these trends we assign positive or negative values to a "conditional r^2," sum the results of the present situation, and divide by the original or highest possible r^2 score from column A to arrive at a probability of change. The higher the probability, the greater the probability of a large increase. The lower the probability, the more likely a decrease in spending between 1966 and 1967. In Sections A' and B' of each table, the same operations are performed to assess the change that will occur in 1968.

TABLE 4.3

NPS Tests Predicting Changes in Military Spending as a Percentage of GDP in Argentina, 1967-68

A Variable Relationships (1960-65)	r²	B Present Situation 1966	Conditional r² (cr²)	A' Variable Relationships (1960-66)	r²	B' Present Situation 1967	Conditional r² (cr²)
1 Change in GDP with change in arms expenditures (r = .06)	.00	1 GDP ←	0	1 Change in GDP with change in arms expenditures (r = -.39)	.15	1 GDP ↑	+.15
2 Role of the military in government as a predictor (r = .14)	.02	2 Role of the military in government →	0	2 Role of the military in government as a predictor (r = .17)	.03	2 Role of the military in government →	0
3 Role of the military as a security force as a predictor (r = .43)	.19	3 Security role of military ↓	-.19	3 Role of the military as a security force as a predictor (r = .41)	.17	3 Security role of military ↓	-.17
4 Correlation of domestic violence with arms spending (r = .21)	.04	4 Level of domestic violence ↓	-.04	4 Correlation of domestic violence with arms spending (r = .22)	.05	4 Level of domestic violence ↓	-.05
5 Reactive rating to rival acquiring HPW = .50	.03	5 HPW acquisitions by rival ↓	-.03	5 Reactive rating to rival acquiring HPW = .5	.03	5 HPW acquisitions by rival ↑	+.03
6 Transnational service rivalry rating = .61	.37	6 Interservice rival ↑	+.37	6 Transnational service rivalry rating = .62	.38	6 Interservice rival ↓	-.38
Total = .65		Total = +.11		Total = .81		Total = -.42	

Conditional $\dfrac{r^2}{r^2} = \dfrac{+.11}{.65} = .16$

Conditional $\dfrac{r^2}{r^2} = \dfrac{-.42}{.81} = -.52$

Prediction: small probability of increase in spending (for 1967)

Prediction: moderate probability of decline in spending (for 1968)

Reality: decrease of .2 percent GDP

Reality: decrease of .2 percent of GDP

TABLE 4.4

NPS Tests Predicting Changes in Military Spending as a Percentage of GDP in Brazil, 1967-68

A Variable Relationships (1960-65)	r²	B Present Situation 1966	Condi- tional r² (cr²)	A' Variable Relationships (1960-66)	r²	B' Present Situation 1967	Condi- tional r² (cr²)
1 Change in GDP with change in arms expenditures (r = .37)	.14	1 GDP ←	+.14	1 Change in GDP with change in arms expenditures (r = .38)	.15	1 GDP ←	+.15
2 Role of the military in government as a pre-dictor (r = .14)	.20	2 Role of the military in government →	0	2 Role of the military in government as a pre-dictor (r = .08)	.01	2 Role of the military in government →	0
3 Role of the military as a security force as a predictor (r = .05)	.01	3 Security role of military ←	+.01	3 Role of the military as a security force as a predictor (r = .06)	.00	3 Security role of military →	0
4 Correlation of domestic violence with arms spending (r = .62)	.38	4 Level of domes-tic violence ←	+.38	4 Correlation of domestic violence with arms spending (r = .63)	.40	4 Level of domes-tic violence →	-.40
5 Reactive rating to rival acquiring HPW = .42	.18	5 HPW acquisi-tions by rival ←	+.18	5 Reactive rating to rival acquiring HPW = .42	.18	5 HPW acquisi-tions by rival →	-.18
6 Transnational service rivalry rating = .49	.24	6 Interservice rival →	+.24	6 Transnational service rivalry rating = .49	.29	6 Interservice rival →	-.29

Total = 1.15   Total = +.95   Total = 1.03   Total = -.62

$$\frac{\text{Conditional } r^2}{r^2} = \frac{.95}{1.15} = .83 \qquad\qquad \frac{\text{Conditional } r^2}{r^2} = \frac{-.62}{1.03} = -.61$$

Prediction: substantial probability of increase in (for 1967) arms spending

Reality: increase .8 percent of GDP

Prediction: moderate probability of decline in (for 1968) spending

Reality: decrease .3 percent of GDP

TABLE 4.5

NPS Tests Predicting Changes in Military Spending as a Percentage of GDP in Chile, 1967-68

A Variable Relationships (1960-65)	r^2	B Present Situation 1966	Condi- tional r^2 (cr^2)	A' Variable Relationships (1960-66)	r^2	B' Present Situation 1967	Condi- tional r^2 (cr^2)
1 Change in GDP with change in arms expenditures (r = .24)	.06	1 GDP	+.06	1 Change in GDP with change in arms expenditures (r = .17)	.03	1 GDP	+.03
2 Role of the military in government as a predictor (r = 0)	0	2 Role of the military in government	0	2 Role of the military in government as a predictor (r = 0)	0	2 Role of the military in government	0
3 Role of the military as a security force as a predictor (r = -.15)	.02	3 Security role of military	0	3 Role of the military as a security force as a predictor (r = -.14)	.02	3 Security role of military	0
4 Correlation of domestic violence with arms spending (r = .27)	.07	4 Level of domestic violence	-.07	4 Correlation of domestic violence with arms spending (r = .27)	.07	4 Level of domestic violence	+.07
5 Reactive rating to rival acquiring HPW = .25	.06	5 HPW acquisitions by rival	+.06	5 Reactive rating to rival acquiring HPW = .25	.06	5 HPW acquisitions rival	-.06
6 Transnational service rivalry rating = .72	.52	6 Interservice rival	+.52	6 Transnational service rivalry rating = .71	.50	6 Interservice rival	-.50

Total = .73   Total +.59   Total = .68   Total = -.46

Conditional r^2 = $\frac{.59}{.73}$ = .77

Conditional r^2 = $\frac{-.46}{.68}$ = -.67

Prediction: moderate to large probability of increase in spending (for 1967)

Reality: no change

Prediction: moderate to large probability of decrease in spending (for 1968)

Reality: decrease of .4 percent of GNP

TABLE 4.6

NPS Tests Predicting Changes in Military Spending as a Percentage of GDP in Colombia, 1967-68

A Variable Relationships 1960-65	r²	B Present Situation 1966	Conditional r² (cr²)	A' Variable Relationships 1960-66	r²	B' Present Situation 1967	Conditional r² (cr²)
1 Change in GDP with change in arms expenditures (r = -.49)	.24	1 GDP	+.24	1 Change in GDP with change in arms expenditures (r = -.67)	.45	1 GDP	+.45
2 Role of the military in government as a predictor (r = 0)	0	2 Role of the military in government	0	2 Role of the military in government as a predictor (r = 0)	0	2 Role of the military in government	0
3 Role of the military as a security force as a predictor (r = -.42)	.18	3 Security role of military	-.18	3 Role of the military as a security force as a predictor (r = -.38)	.14	3 Security role of military	+.14
4 Correlation of domestic violence with arms spending (r = .25)	.06	4 Level of domestic violence	-.06	4 Correlation of domestic violence with arms spending (r = .35)	.12	4 Level of domestic violence	-.12
5 Reactive rating to rival acquiring HPW' = .14	.02	5 HPW acquisitions by rival	-.02	5 Reactive rating to rival acquiring HPW = .14	.02	5 HPW acquisitions by rivals	+.02
6 Transnational service rivalry rating = .56	.31	6 Interservice rival	+.31	6 Transnational service rivalry rating = .62	.38	6 Interservice rival	-.38

Total = .81   Total = +.29

$$\text{Conditional } r^2 = \frac{.29}{.81} = .36$$

Prediction: a small probability of increase in spending (for 1967)

Reality: decrease of .1 percent GDP

Total = 1.11   Total = .11

$$\text{Conditional } r^2 = \frac{.11}{1.11} = \frac{.11}{1.11} = .10$$

Prediction: slight probability of increase in spending (for 1968)

Reality: increase of .3 percent GDP

TABLE 4.7

NPS Tests Predicting Changes in Military Spending as a Percentage of GDP in Peru, 1967-68

A Variable Relationships 1960-65	r²	B Present Situation 1966	Conditional r² (cr²)	A' Variable Relationships 1960-65	r²	B' Present Situation 1967	Conditional r² (cr²)
1 Change in GDP with change in arms expenditures (r = -.55)	.30	1 GDP	+.30	1 Change in GDP with change in arms expenditures	.08	1 GDP	+.06
2 Role of the military in government as a predictor (r = .28)	.08	2 Role of the military in government	0	2 Role of the military in government as a predictor (r = .44)	.19	2 Role of the military in government	0
3 Role of the military as a security force as a predictor (r = -.41)	.17	3 Security role of military	+.17	3 Role of the military as a security force as a predictor (r = -.31)	.10	3 Security role of military	-.10
4 Correlation of domestic violence with arms spending (r = -.65)	.42	4 Level of domestic violence	-.42	4 Correlation of domestic violence with arms spending (r = -.65)	.42	4 Level of domestic violence	-.42
5 Reactive rating to rival acquiring HPW = .33	.11	5 HPW acquisitions by rival	+.11	5 Reactive rating to rival acquiring HPW = .43	.18	5 HPW acquisitions by rival	-.18
6 Transnational service rivalry rating = .39	.15	6 Interservice rival	-.15	6 Transnational service rivalry rating = .33	.11	6 Interservice rival	+.11
Total = 1.26		Total = .1		Total = 1.08		Total = -.53	

$$\text{Conditional } r^2 \big/ r^2 = \frac{.1}{1.26} = .08$$

$$\text{Conditional } r^2 \big/ r^2 = \frac{-.53}{1.08} = -.49$$

Prediction: no change in spending (for 1967)

Reality: increase of .8 percent of GDP

Prediction: moderate probability of decrease in spending (for 1968)

Reality: decrease of .2 percent GDP

TABLE 4.8

NPS Tests Predicting Changes in Military Spending as a Percentage of GDP in Venezuela, 1967-68

A Variable Relationships 1960-65	r^2	B Present Situation 1966	Conditional r^2 (cr^2)	A' Variable Relationships 1960-65	r^2	B' Present Situation 1967	Conditional r^2 (cr^2)
1 Change in GDP with change in arms expenditures (r = .39)	.15	1 GDP	+.15	1 Change in GDP with change in arms expenditures (r = .22)	.05	1 GDP	+.05
2 Role of the military in government as a predictor (r = 0)	0	2 Role of the military in government	0	2 Role of the military in government as a predictor (r = 0)	0	2 Role of the military in government	0
3 Role of the military as a security force as a predictor (r = -.14)	.02	3 Security role of military	+.02	3 Role of the military as a security force as a predictor (r = -.27)	.04	3 Security role of military	-.04
4 Correlation of domestic violence with arms spending (r = .44)	.19	4 Level of domestic violence	-.19	4 Correlation of domestic violence with arms spending (r = .33)	.11	4 Level of domestic violence	-.11
5 Reactive rating to rival acquiring HPW = .27	.07	5 HPW acquisitions by rival	+.07	5 Reactive rating to rival acquiring HPW = .27	.07	5 HPW acquisitions by rival	-.07
6 Transnational service rivalry rating = .56	.31	6 Interservice rival	+.31	6 Transnational service rivalry rating = .57	.32	6 Interservice rival	0
	Total = .74		Total = .36		Total = .59		Total = -.17

$$\frac{\text{Conditional } r^2}{r^2} = \frac{.36}{.74} = .48$$

Prediction: moderate probability of increase in spending (for 1967)

Reality: increase of .1 percent GDP

$$\frac{\text{Conditional } r^2}{r^2} = \frac{-.17}{.59} = -.27$$

Prediction: slight probability of decrease in spending (for 1968)

Reality: decrease of .2 percent of GDP

Note that the calculations for A' and B' utilized what is contained in A in addition to the patterns found for the year being predicted in B. In this way, the procedure implies a continuous system for updating the correlation coefficients. If foreign affairs analysts were to use this procedure over a period of time, the National Profile Scoresheet would incorporate past events in the form of changed correlation coefficients. A yearly update of the basic coefficients would allow the NPS to change as patterns and conditions within each of the countries changed.

The success rate for two predictions on each of the Big Six countries was eight correct in 12 attempts. These tests suggest that the NPS is a reasonable approach. Of course more experiments must be done and more explicit decision rules formed for predicting change in military spending. But in light of the evidence of the 12 tests, we see this approach as one viable way of incorporating clearly defined variables, quantitative techniques of analysis, and the important discriminating character of the Latin American nation, all of which appear to be essential to making accurate explanations and predictions about changes in Latin American military spending.

THE COSTS AND BENEFITS OF THE TECHNIQUES
TO THE FOREIGN AFFAIRS ANALYST

The preceding pages have suggested a broad range of quantitative techniques that could be used by the analyst in dealing with dependent variables such as military spending in Latin America. Basically, we see two very different uses for foreign affairs analysts. The first is to use the techniques to check assumptions about the world. We showed how quantitative techniques ranging from two-by-two table analysis to regression and probability analysis can test the assumptions made by analysts about relationships among variables. The second use is to construct some type of checklist of the several factors that have in the past been correlated with military spending patterns in Latin America so that the analyst can take into account all of the factors when making forecasts.

In terms of costs to the analysts, we see little in the way of expenditures of any sort. The data we used, except for the LAMB data, were acquired from INR analysts already working on the problem of military expenditures in Latin America. The LAMB data set was put together at a very small cost, and in many ways it could be easily duplicated by INR analysts without substantial additional costs. The procedures required to conduct most of the analyses carried out here are already programmed on the Department of State computer. This is true for all but the Markov chain analysis. The only programming one might want to develop that does not now exist is a procedure for generating the NPS from raw data that might be supplied on a periodic basis. However, this procedure could be initially carried out by hand.

The training of INR analysts that would be required to conduct the kinds of analyses presented in this chapter is not formidable. Part of the reason for this is that most of the INR analysts who have worked on military spending already think in terms of variables and quantitative indicators. What they lack is the knowledge of a small number of simple analytical techniques that would allow them to move from descriptive concepts, such as correlation, to probability. The kinds of training would be no more complicated than those described in Chapter 2, "Predicting Political Instability in Black Africa" and in the general package described in the final chapter.

While the costs would be minimal, the benefits would be substantial. As analystical procedures are established, the INR analyst could continually update NPSs for each country and across all Latin American countries. We saw in the preceding section that time-series analysis works better than cross-sectional analysis, since patterns seem to be specific to countries. INR analysts could benefit by continually testing propositions both over time for each country and across all countries. Continuous updates could provide profile sheets that would alert analysts and users to major changes in trends. It would also help to formalize the solid analytical work that has already been done in the area of Latin American military expenditures so that this work is not lost to future INR analysts working on this and related problems. The construction of a series of NPSs relevant to dependent variables such as the climate for foreign investment, political instability, or willingness to pursue population control policies could be undertaken. In addition to improving the quality of the analysts' work, all of these activities would help to establish a communication structure with the policy maker, since he could become accustomed to the format and meaning of a NPS.

NOTE

1. All data pertaining to military expenditures, unless otherwise indicated, were taken from Gertrude E. Heare, Trends in Latin American Military Expenditures, 1940-1970: Argentina, Brazil, Chile, Colombia, Peru and Venezuela (Department of State Publication 8618, December 1971). Also available to us was an updated memo from the same author for expenditures for 22 nations for 1967-72. Figures are adjusted for currency revaluations and inflation.

The purpose of this case study is to explore the utility and feasibility of acquiring policy-relevant information by systematically surveying specialists. It points to the possibility of developing full-scale monitoring systems to provide on a regular basis information relevant to a variety of topics important to American foreign policy. For illustration as much as anything, this study deals with monitoring the bargaining between governments of North and South Korea over the outcome of an agenda of legal, political, social, and economic issues.

This exploratory study is designed to allow the reader to estimate the utility and feasibility of a foreign policy monitoring system utilizing information estimates supplied by experts. We are interested in showing how the monitoring system might be employed and some of the costs involved in its implementation. For this case study we surveyed academic and government specialists on Korean affairs. In the collection of the data we were assisted by Young W. Kihl of Juniata College and by State Department officials concerned with Korean affairs.

This chapter is organized into five parts:

The Rationale for a Foreign Policy Monitoring System
A Description of the Data
The Utility of the Data
Some Methodological Issues
Costs in Developing and Maintaining a Foreign Policy
  Monitoring System

THE RATIONALE FOR A FOREIGN
POLICY MONITORING SYSTEM

The rationale for this study stems from the conviction that knowledge about the dynamics of international relations has been hampered by the lack of systematic and organized data about behavior in the international system. The policy-making community suffers from a seriously inadequate data base for the efficient management of foreign policy. Indeed, the compelling need for such data is frequently voiced.[1]

The problem is not that information is unavailable. Indeed, there is too much information, a problem stemming from the growing complexity of transnational conditions. This complexity is caused in part by the increased number of parties that American policy makers must take into consideration. This includes not only the larger number of nation states, which is important in itself, but also the larger number of actors other than nation states that have the capacity to affect the outcome of issues important to the United States. Moreover, there has been an equally formidable increase in the number of policy issues and outcomes that have significance for the United States. Added to the traditional categories of national security and promotion of American economic interests (which themselves have become more complex) are issues growing out of the increasing social interdependence of the world. Taken together, all these factors have such a powerful multiplier effect on complexity that efficient use of existing information by policy makers is becoming extremely difficult.

The problem is that all this information is not translated into systematically organized data that can be used efficiently. Instead of organizing data--whether verbal or nonverbal--the analyst gathers and analyzes information through what might be termed "immersion" procedures. These procedures are especially apparent with respect to the activities of officials in the Department of State. Typical examples involve the study of all possible relevant "intelligence" on the subject in question, accompanied by more or less organized verbal interchanges among relevant experts to try to make sense out of the ever-expanding incoming information. This technique, which has, if nothing else, the force of tradition behind it, can still no doubt support rational policy making concerning some relatively simple issues. However, for complex matters, it requires the kinds of resources at both the input (information gathering) and output (analysis and presentation) stages that are simply not presently available for a large (and growing) part of the transnational environment of the United States.

American foreign policy makers have attempted to deal with the growing complexity of transnational conditions through the use of social science techniques and computer technology. The Department of State, for example, through several in-house and externally funded projects, has undertaken activities involving systematic information retrieval systems, the use of quantitative data in policy analysis, and the application of various forms of operations research procedures. These projects include the Traffic Analysis by Geography and Subject (TAGS) system of categorizing the content of incoming cables;[2] the procedures of the Program Analysis and Resource Allocation (PARA), focused on improving internal operations within the State Department;[3] and the Computer-Aided System for Handling Information on Local Conflicts (CASCON), a bank of retrievable data on internal conflicts in which the United States or some other outside power has become involved.[4] The State Department has been relatively conservative as far as the use of social science techniques are concerned. But its needs have become so great that it has begun exploring new forms of information processing and analysis.

However, it is by no means certain that major changes in information handling for policy making will take place as a result of these efforts. There is a strong possibility that the dominant existing approaches cannot render more tractable the kinds of complexity with which the policy maker must deal. Two different patterns characterize the bulk of these attempts to deal more efficiently with relevant information, both of which do not auger well for the policy maker. The first is the use of cataloging systems that assume that the analyst will be able to use available information more efficiently. In the case of the State Department's CASCON project, for example, it is assumed that by being able to access information about similar conflicts, the policy maker, or his advisers, will be able to make better judgments. However, for the policy maker and the analyst who are already overburdened with information about the specific event with which they are attempting to deal, the prospect of having an expanded memory bank at their disposal simply adds more information and is not very helpful.

The other pattern of employing systematic approaches to information grows out of the planning-programming-budgeting system movement and is exemplified in the PARA activities. This approach involves an attempt to develop a

comprehensive procedure for ranking objectives vis-à-vis
selected divisions of the department, and for collecting
and interpreting information in terms of those objectives.
This approach may well be valuable for budgeting and resource allocation tasks. However, it is little help in
formulating strategies for achieving specific policy outcomes. It may help in determining, for example, how many
consular officials should be sent to Turkey, but it does
little to help the policy maker deal with the problems of
getting that country to control its drug production.

The first pattern of information handling is to increase the amount of information available to the policy
maker, whereas the second pattern is to severely constrain
it. Most of the individuals involved in the policy-making
process in the State Department are predisposed to accept
the former pattern as potentially more useful because of
their familiarity with the "immersion" technique. However,
from the outside observer's point of view, the former
creates information-overload, while the latter fails to
deal with the problem of measuring some of the most significant aspects of what is going on in a complex environment.
To state the same point in somewhat different terms, the
former does not introduce enough structure into the infor-
mation-handling process, while the latter introduces too
much.

The solution to the problem, therefore, depends on
providing information that is sufficiently structured so
that it can be used efficiently, but not so structured as
to prevent its being used flexibly. The solution offered
in this study is based on a model of information acquisition, transmission, and analysis that recognizes the tremendous complexity produced by the proliferation of issues
and actors in contemporary policy making. The system that
we present is based on the analyst's preference for using
experts as one of his major sources of information, whether
those experts are "functional" specialists with knowledge
in policy areas or "area" specialists with knowledge of
countries and regions. The purpose of the system is to
organize parsimonious quantities of information acquired
from the experts so that the analyst can efficiently man-
age the data. At the same time it attempts to increase
the reliability of these experts' viewpoints, the speed of
communicating their viewpoints to higher-level officials,
and the ability to integrate the viewpoints of the various
experts so that the policy maker can be most efficiently
informed.

The traditional model is based on the assumption that the expert should determine the amount of information the user needs to make his decision. Accordingly, the specialist usually presents that information in a layered structure. That is, the policy maker can first read or listen to a short abstract, with the option of delving more deeply into the detailed reasoning of the specialist. The application of information retrieval techniques has had as its intention allowing the policy maker to acquire his own source of information to check against the advice he receives from experts. However, for the policy maker to deal effectively with the added information available to him, he must invest almost as much time as the specialist, if not more. In short, the whole premise of the system is that the policy maker can gain confidence in the expert and his information by checking his argumentation. In fact, however, the policy maker's only option is to go to more detailed information if he is unsure of the expert's conclusion.

The model we are dealing with is quite different. It treats the specialist as a data generator. Under it, the policy maker will be assisted by receiving not only the consensus, but also the range, of experts' opinions. The information coming to him is organized and parsimonious. The user can check for reliability not by evaluating the logic of the expert, and/or by trying to duplicate his research, but by examining a range of expert viewpoints. When that range is broad--that is, there is little consensus--he may then embark upon the more traditional procedures of assessment. However, when a consensus emerges from the viewpoints expressed, the user can more confidently accept that viewpoint. At the same time, of course, the user will check the validity of the experts' consensus against other evidence (for example, subsequent events and different empirical indicators).

The policy maker as information user is the critical figure in the operation of the system. He must formulate the questions and indicate the criteria upon which the experts will be selected. Unless he is involved in this process, it is possible that the data provided him will not be relevant. Because the kinds of policy problems are relatively similar, however, we would expect that a standard list of questions will be formulated over a period of time by the policy maker so that as he uses the system the amount of time required from him will decrease.

To illustrate the model we have in mind, let us consider the U.S. policy concerning continued access to Mid-

147

dle Eastern oil. (This example will be of necessity highly simplified, but it should serve to illustrate the kind of system we hope to develop.)

Assume that officials in the State Department as well as those in interested agencies outside the foreign policy establishment (for example, the Office of Emergency Preparedness) wish to assure agreement between oil-producing governments and the major petroleum corporations. The policy area has both a geographical dimension--the Middle East --and a technical dimension--petroleum needs and supplies. Both dimensions must be dealt with. Accordingly, a set of specialists with differing expertise must be selected. Those responsible for the policy must formulate the problem in sufficient detail to allow them to identify specific policy outcomes that they would like to see occur. Such outcomes might include agreed rate structures and increased participation by the governments of the producing countries. The users of the information would then select a set of experts inside or outside the U.S. government who are knowledgeable about either the countries involved or the issues of petroleum production, distribution, and consumption.

Each expert would be asked to complete a questionnaire similar to the one reproduced in Appendix B. This questionnaire asks for estimates on how significant political actors ranging from national governmental leaders to local community leaders now feel about the issues, and the amount of influence they might have in determining the outcome of the issues. In addition, the expert can attach information indicating how confident he feels about the values he assigns. Once the expert has been trained to use the form, he can complete it in a relatively short period of time at regular time intervals.

There have been some attempts to tap experts on a systematic basis. Perhaps the best-known effort has been undertaken by Olaf Helmer who, along with others, developed the Delphi technique at RAND.[5] The system we are proposing shares one feature with the Delphi technique in that it uses information supplied by experts. However, our proposed system departs radically from the Delphi method because it asks for estimates on what now exists rather than, as is typically done in Delphi, projections of what might exist in the near or distant future. Instead of placing the severe demands on the expert to estimate the future, this system asks him to formalize his perceptions of the

148

present.* For that reason alone, we expect the reliability and technical problems to be much more tractible for our project than has been the case for most of the Delphi efforts.

The use of specialists to generate quantitative estimates is not new to the State Department. A number of experimental and training projects have been undertaken with State Department personnel, including members of the INR, to make probability estimates (using Bayesian statistics) of future events. In addition, the Net Assessment Project, used to analyze U.S. policy toward Western Europe, has tried to get officials to provide estimates on the positions of states on U.S. policy goals. For both the probability estimates and the Net Assessment, however, the usual procedure has been to have a group of experts meet to develop a consensus on a series of quantitative indicators. In no case has there been an attempt to deal with the feeling, expressed by many participants and observers of the process, that the numbers assigned are arbitrary. This feeling represents a major roadblock in the development of expert-generated quantitative estimates, since it precludes the serious use of those estimates by INR analysts and their users.** For this reason alone, we feel that a case study that begins to deal with these considerations and with more flexible modes of using experts is desirable. Although the kind of methodological work required to make an operational system has yet to be completed, a pilot case study could serve to demonstrate both the utility and the difficulties of one such system.

---

*We will make projections about the future, but they will be generated from the data on present conditions provided by the experts.

**That is, the users of expert-generated data want to validate the perceptions of experts. When there is no "objective" criteria by which perceptions can be validated, social psychologists argue that people look for a group consensus for validation. Essentially, our procedure systematically taps the extent of consensus in order to validate quantitative estimates. (See Leon Festinger, "Informal Social Communication," Psychological Review 57 (1950): 271-82.

A DESCRIPTION OF THE DATA

The choice of bargaining between North and South Korea over the future political, social, economic, and legal relationships between the two states as the subject for this case study was based on several considerations. First, during the winter of 1973, relations between the two states were in flux. Therefore, we could expect some movement of the two states on a variety of issues. Second, the question of present and future issue positions of these two states permeates the documents produced by INR analysts. Third, the information required to make judgments on North-South Korean bargaining is like information about most foreign policy questions in that it is difficult to acquire and always "soft." That is, it is not data based on readily available measures such as votes or balance of payments or aid flows. Finally, this particular topic was the subject of intensive study through traditional measures by INR and other foreign affairs analysts. Therefore, it could serve as a test of whether knowledge gained by the expert through the conventional "immersion" in the subject could be formalized in quantitative terms and effectively communicated to the user.

Our data collection began with a systematic study of INR reports on bargaining between North and South Korea between January 1971 and January 1973. We abstracted from those reports a list of issues--that is, future events and conditions over which there was some contention between the two states--that might be suitable subjects for our study. After consultation with members of the department knowledgeable in Korean affairs, we identified the 10 issues appearing in Figure 5.1.

Note that each issue is stated in the form of an event or condition (that is, set of events) that could occur in the future. The format of these statements is critical because the generation of the quantitative estimates is based on the wording of the issues. This will become more evident when we describe the variables on which data was collected.

Once the list of issues between North and South Korea was chosen, our next task was to identify actors that would be important in the determination of the outcome pictured in the issues. After considerable discussion with scholars in the field and with members of the State Department, we decided that we would take only two actors--North Korea and South Korea. The informal consensus was that we would be unable to identify enough experts who would be suffi-

FIGURE 5.1

Issues in North-South Korean Bargaining

A. Set up a relatively permanent operating secretariat to
deal with problems of divided families. (FAMILY)

B. To hold a Park-Kim summit meeting by the end of 1973.
(SUMMIT)

C. The elimination of anticommunist laws in South Korea.
(LAWS)

D. North Korea allows South Korea to fish in northern
waters, given comparable economic concession by the
South. (FISH)

E. Establishment of mail service between the two states.
(MAIL)

F. Establishment of limited cultural exchanges between
the two states. (CULTURE)

G. Establishment of a supreme assembly where representatives from North and South Korea would discuss points
of mutual interest but no domestic affairs of either
side. (ASSEMBLY)

H. Both sides would support joint admission to the United
Nations. (UN)

I. Mutual reduction of armed forces and/or armaments.
(ARMS)

J. Establishment of bilateral "nongovernmental" negotiations between political parties, North and South.
(PARTIES)

ciently informed on the important subnational actors in
the two Koreas. Undoubtedly, gathering information on
subnational actors would greatly enhance the credibility
and usefulness of the data. However, for our present illustrative purposes, we considered the focus at the nation-
state level to be adequate.

The following procedures were followed in gathering
the information. Each of the 10 issues was then given two
questionnaires, one for each Korea. The questionnaire requested the respondent to supply estimates on five variables concerning the issues vis-à-vis North and South Korea.
A brief description of each of them is provided below.

1. Importance--the degree to which the actor considers the issue to be important, ranging from zero (no importance) to ten (extremely high importance).
2. Power to Support--the degree to which the actor
can unilaterally bring about the event or condition pictured in the issue ranging from zero (no power) to ten
(complete capability to create the condition).
3. Power to Oppose--the degree to which the actor
can unilaterally prevent the event or condition pictured
in the issue, ranging from zero (no power) to ten (complete
capacity to block the condition).
4. Issue Position--whether the actor supports, opposes,
or is neutral regarding his preference for the conditions
pictured in the issue. This is a nominal variable consisting of three categories--Support, Neutrality, and Opposition.
5. Firmness--the degree to which the actor's issue
position is likely to change, ranging from zero (highly
probable it will change) to ten (highly improbable it will
change).

The data was collected during the last two weeks of
February 1973. The experts were asked to assign values
for the time period for which they were completing the
form. A total of 25 experts were surveyed--16 academic
scholars and 9 from the department. In order to make it
possible to keep this report unclassified, we will call
the two categories of experts "Group I" and "Group II"
without identifying which were the academic and which were
the government officials.

THE UTILITY OF THE DATA

How could an INR analyst employ the data we have described in the preceding section? The best way to answer
this question is to replicate some of the analyses found
in INR reports from January 1971 to January 1973. These
reports are primarily devoted to describing current conditions between the two states.

Generally speaking, the INR analysts attempted to describe the nature of the issues and the likely positions of the two states on those issues. Some general predictions were made concerning the likelihood of possible agreement between the two states. However, such predictions were always couched in highly qualified terms. We will attempt to show in this section how data collected by the survey of experts could be used to describe the positions of the two states and to project likely situations regarding the relations between North and South. The format for doing this will be the hypothetical INR report which follows.

INTELLIGENCE NOTE: Evolving Issues in North and
                     South Korea Negotiations

Date: February 26, 1973

Over the past 20 months, there has been substantial decline in rigidity on the part of North and South Korea concerning the issues that divide them. As a result, we have conducted a survey of observers inside and outside the government to obtain estimates of the positions of North and South Korea on 10 issues that are actual or potential topics of negotiations between the two. Twenty-five experts were surveyed during the week of February 19-23. Statistical tests were run that showed no consistent differences between the estimates provided by the two groups--government officials and scholars.

To gain some idea of the extent of consensus among the judges, we looked at the scores they assigned for the issue positions of the two countries on the 10 issues. Figure 5.2 shows the results of this analysis. The more even the distribution of judges across the three categories--that is, the more similar the height of the bars for the categories--the more disagreement among judges, as for Issue G. Conversely, where one bar is much taller than the others, there is a high level of agreement, as for Issue C. For the issues on which there is high agreement among the judges, we can be fairly sure that the issue positions of the nations are accurately represented. For the issues on which there is much disagreement, we must acquire more information by some other kind of process before we can be confident of the estimates of issue position.

FIGURE 5.2

Distribution of Issue Positions Assigned by the Experts

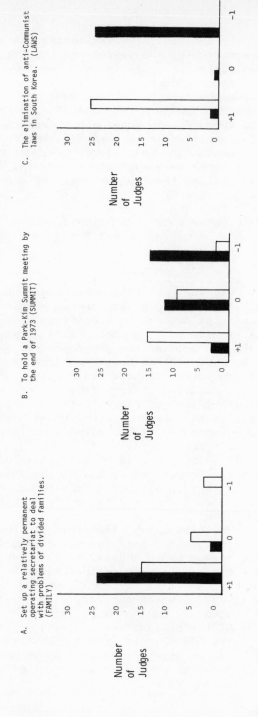

A. Set up a relatively permanent operating secretariat to deal with problems of divided families. (FAMILY)

B. To hold a Park-Kim Summit meeting by the end of 1973 (SUMMIT)

C. The elimination of anti-Communist laws in South Korea. (LAWS)

FIGURE 5.2 (continued)

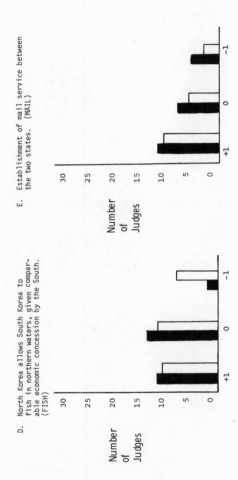

D. North Korea allows South Korea to fish in northern waters, given comparable economic concession by the South. (FISH)

E. Establishment of mail service between the two states. (MAIL)

South Korea   North Korea

FIGURE 5.3

Index of Short-Term Likelihood of Resolution of Issues

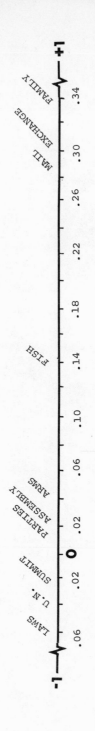

We have generated two indexes of the likelihood of resolving the 10 issues. The first is a short-term estimate of the probable disposition of each issue during the next month. The second is a long-range estimate of the probable disposition of each issue over the next 12 months.

Figure 5.3 displays the issues according to the short-term likelihood of resolution. The closer an issue is placed to +1.0, the greater the likelihood it will be resolved. The closer it is to -1.0, the more likely it is to become a dead issue, no longer the topic of negotiation. The closer it is to 0.0, the more likely it is to continue as a topic of negotiation.

In general, most of the issues surveyed appear, in the short run at least, to be likely to continue as a subject of negotiation between the two parties. None of the issues is close to being either resolved or dropped as a subject of controversy. Those which do have some slight outlook for acceptance are the social issues of family reuniting, cultural exchanges, and mail services. The question of fishing and comparable economic benefits is the most likely "substantive" issue to be resolved, although its short-run chances are quite slim. The domestic political and foreign policy questions are all grouped close to the midpoint, indicating virtually no chance of early resolution.

The preceding hypothetical intelligence note succinctly presents a fairly rich array of information about the current and future state of relations between the two Koreas. It may be worth noting that the details of several calculations were not explained in the document—only the descriptive results of those calculations. In fact, the typical reader of this report probably had no more knowledge of the techniques involved than the typical policy maker would have. Despite this, it was, we feel, possible to communicate a rather wide spectrum of information.

We will now discuss some of the calculations that were used to present the information in the report. The first conclusion of the report was that in the survey undertaken there were no systematic differences between the two groups of respondents, government officials and scholars. The basis for this conclusion was a statistical test that calculates a probability measure of the likelihood that the differences between the two groups occurred by

157

chance fluctuations of responses, as opposed to the differences occurring because of systematic differences between the two groups. For example, one group might systematically assign more positive issue positions to North Korea, more power to South Korea, or any number of other consistent differences. To determine the likelihood of such systematic differences, we performed a "t-test," which is not a typographical error but is the somewhat arcane label used by statisticians for this procedure.[6] Since each respondent made five estimates on each of 10 issues for both North and South Korea, there are 100 comparisons that can be made between the two groups. In the overwhelming proportion of these (88 out of 100), the t-test indicated that the slight difference in average scores between the two groups was almost certainly due to chance. Since the 12 instances of significantly high difference were scattered throughout the data without apparent pattern, we concluded that the two sets of experts were responding to essentially the same cues in the real world. (If more significant differences had turned up, the normal procedure would have been to systematically compare the differences between the two groups, and to evaluate whether one group was better informed than the other, or whether each group was responding to valid, but nonoverlapping, information sources. This latter conclusion, of course, must be made on the basis of qualitative judgment rather than on the basis of any statistical technique.)

Below we will continue the discussion of the meaning of differences or similarities between variously defined groups of respondents. Let us now turn to some of the other calculations in the hypothetical INR report.

Figure 5.2 is pretty straightforward. We simply arrayed each of the judges in the bar graph according to whether he assigned for each, North Korea and South Korea, an issue position of favor, oppose, or neutral. The purpose was simply to show the agreement among judges. We could also look at the percentages of judges who assigned each of the three categories. This same procedure could have been performed for the other four variables generated by the questionnaire.

We have also developed an index of the likelihood of resolving issues for the short run (within a month) and the long run (over the next 12 months), of which the former is reported in Figure B of the report. The short-range probability estimates were made by multiplying the sign of the issue positions (+, 0, or -) times the firm-

ness of the issue position times power (to support or oppose) times the importance of the issue to the actor.

The reasoning behind these calculations is as follows:
An issue will be more likely to be resolved positively,
that is, to occur as stated, to the extent that the actors
involved have positive and firm issue positions, have high
power on that issue, and attach high importance to the issue. To the extent that the actors involved have negative
issue positions and high scores on the other factors, the
issue is likely to be negatively resolved, that is, eliminated from the agenda of active topics. The overall estimate of an issue's probable disposition is calculated by
determining the net score contributed by each actor. In
principle, as many actors as necessary for any set of issues could be used for the probability estimates. In this
case study only two actors have been analyzed: the numbers
are generated by the net scores of North and South Korea
on each issue. The scores are normalized into the index
range of -1.0 to +1.0 by dividing the score for each issue
by the maximum possible score. Since issue position firmness, power, and importance can each have a maximum score
of 10, each actor (two in this case) could potentially contribute a score of $\pm 1,000$. Therefore, in this study the
scores were normalized by dividing by 2,000. The sign of
the number indicates whether the overall predictors were
contributed primarily by actors with positive or negative
issue positions. The estimates presented in Figure 5.3
are produced through a computer simulation model for political research, observation, and evaluation (PROBE).[7]

In order to assess the hypothetical report, we looked
at three INR Intelligence Notes and two "Para Memos" that
were written between December 1971 and February 1972. Of
the 16 pages written in those five reports, over 14 were
concerned with description (nine and one-half) and explanation (four and one-quarter). Although this lack of forecasting analysis is typical of all the INR documents we
surveyed for fiscal year 1972, as discussed in Chapter 1,
this proportion of forecast to description and explanation
was as small as any we have found in comparable sets of
INR reports. Notwithstanding the very important caveat
that our sample consists of only a portion of the INR's
output--Research Studies, Intelligence Notes, and Miscellaneous Memoranda--we feel that analyses attempting to estimate future issue positions of states or groups are particularly difficult to make, especially when compared with
budgetary, economic, or social trend projections. It is,
therefore, an important feature of the hypothetical report

presented above that a number of specific forecasts are made about future political positions of states.

The predictions we did find in the reports surveyed, which were not as precise as the ones presented in the hypothetical report, were (1) that talks could easily be broken off between North and South Korea, (2) that carefully controlled exchanges were possible within the next three to five years, and (3) that South Korea might reduce its opposition to a joint application for membership to the United Nations. Exact comparisons between these predictions and the ones in the hypothetical report are not possible because the issues were phrased somewhat differently in the two sources and because they were written in different time periods. However, there is no question that the level of specificity and explicitness of the forecast are much higher in the hypothetical report than in the INR reports.

The preceding hypothetical report, we feel, provides the user with a great deal of information in more quickly digestible form than do traditional report formats. The user is provided, in addition to general background information, with an assessment of the probable outcome of issues important to American foreign policy officials. The user also knows that these estimates are derived from a wide spectrum of experts, rather than just one or two. And he can quickly see on which of the issues the experts have high consensus and on which they are reporting uncertainty or conflicting information.

Many questions of proper method and procedure must be answered before the system outlined above can be used. Nevertheless, we believe that the benefits of such a system could be substantial. In addition to forming the basis for reports such as the one provided above, the system would produce data that could be used in several other ways. First, since data on a particular set of issues could be collected periodically, INR analysts and their users could monitor trends over time in the evolving relationships between two or more states. Second, the users, as they became familiar with the techniques, could look at more detailed displays of the data. They could inspect scatterplots and other frequency distributions to determine the extent of agreement among experts on the estimates of changes in issue positions among the states. Third, as country desk officers as well as those in the field became familiar with the questionnaire, data could be gathered on subnational groups whose collective activities influence the positions of the states being monitored.

Over the long run, the development of a system to yield this kind of data could increase the INR's capacity to monitor, describe, and ultimately project the positions of a wide variety of actors--subnational groups, governmental ministries, and both governmental and nongovernmental transnational actors. Information involving technical and functional expertise as well as knowledge of the politics of a particular state or institution could be integrated and displayed on a continuing basis, in accordance with the priorities of policy makers. In addition, with the accumulation of data over time, statistical analyses could test and adjust models such as PROBE to make projections of the future state of the relations between states and the resolution or elimination of various issues. The development of such a reliable method of political projection would, of course, have immense value as a policy-making tool. It would not only provide projections based on the actual current state of affairs, but it would also permit the simulation of alternative policies and their estimated future consequences.

The data available from such a monitoring system would also provide a basis for policy evaluation. Such evaluation is not frequently part of the routine procedure of INR operations. Nevertheless, this system would permit the INR, or other divisions of the State Department, to supply policy makers with quantitative indicators that could be used in judging the relative success of American foreign policy. The system could provide data for input into procedures like Net Assessment and PARA. These procedures could then be used with greater confidence, since the numbers assigned would less likely be viewed as arbitrary and/or the product of face-to-face group pressures. Furthermore, the time series data on selected issues could allow policy makers to see whether a particular policy had the desired results in relation to established goals.

In conclusion, we expect that a foreign policy monitoring system utilizing expert-generated information could have a major impact on improving the work of the INR. It would allow the bureau to do more than the usual background reporting, post hoc explanations, and the tentative estimating now undertaken. It would aid the INR in establishing a common conceptual framework with the policy maker so that analyses could be more rapidly communicated. Finally, it would enable the INR to help the policy maker evaluate the costs and benefits of both past and projected foreign policy actions.

SOME METHODOLOGICAL ISSUES

This section deals with some problems of method and procedure involved in the establishment of an on-going system of surveying experts. Unfortunately, there has been relatively little systematic study of the methodological issues involved in using expert-generated data. The major work has been in the field of psychometric scaling and variations of the Delphi technique. However, neither of these approaches adequately confronts the principal problems that must be solved to institute the kind of system we have described.

Two major questions are raised by the use of any quantitative data: the problem of "reliability" and the problem of "validity." Reliability refers to the stability of the data obtained, that is, consistency of the values generated for the same variable at the same point in time. Validity refers to whether or not the data generated accurately describes the conditions in the real world it is supposed to be describing. It is generally the case, of course, that as reliability and validity increase, there is an increase in the usefulness of the data for INR and other users. In the following discussion we will briefly examine the special implications of reliability and validity for the kind of system we have been discussing.

Social scientists usually require their data to be highly reliable. Data generation techniques such as content analysis, for example, require high agreement among different coders before they can be used. If sufficiently clear rules can be developed to instruct people in assigning numbers and/or categories to qualitative material, so that two different people assign the same value, the results are considered to be reliable. Researchers normally consider data generated through content analysis that has agreement less than 80 percent to be unreliable and therefore of little use.

A question arises as to whether the same standards of reliability should be applied to the generation of data by experts. In content analysis procedures, each coder is assumed to be operating according to explicit rules and to be dealing with the same qualitative information (for example, a sentence describing a foreign policy act). Therefore, a lack of agreement between two coders can only be a result of inadequacies in the rules and procedures of the coding or the incompetence of the coders. In contrast, we know that experts draw on different sources of information in their understanding of complex questions. Therefore, a lack of agreement may be a result of differences in information rather than errors in responding to a questionnaire.

It must still be admitted that low agreement among respondents in expert-generated data procedures could result from one or both of two reasons: weaknesses in the procedures or differences in information available to various experts. To determine the cause of any particular disagreements would require detailed analysis beyond the scope of this case study. However, we will examine below the degree to which reliability was achieved in this case study.

In our particular case, there are two sorts of questions to be asked about agreement between and among respondents. One, which we have already mentioned in our discussion of the "t-test," is the pattern of differences between the two groups of respondents, government officials and scholars. The second, to which we now turn, is the possible extreme deviation of any particular judge or judges from the pattern of the rest. For the most part, this is a problem that must be dealt with over time in a series of responses. Any judge who was consistently beyond the norm over a series of surveys would lead to one of two responses: either make inquiries into what special information the deviant respondent possessed or eliminate him from future surveys.

In any event, there is no unequivocal procedure for deciding at what point a respondent indeed becomes a "deviant" and should be subjected to special treatment of one sort or another. As an illustration of one possible method, we have performed a factor analysis on the totality of all responses in our case study. Simply stated, we have used factor analysis as a procedure for estimating the extent to which the responses of the various experts are correlated with one another. Respondents with high amounts of such intercorrelation are grouped together in what are called "factors." Our factor analysis of the respondents grouped the experts into five factors for South Korea and four factors for the North Korean data. After factor analysis is performed, it is still necessary to choose between an "easy in" and an "easy out" selection policy. The "easy in" approach leads one to include in the remaining sample all respondents except those who are extremely deviant from the group. In our case, this would lead to excluding only one respondent, who scored on the final factor in both the North Korean and South Korean estimates. The "easy out" approach leads us to exclude all except those who are extraordinarily similar in their responses. In our case this would lead to including only 13 respondents who were grouped together in Factor I on the South Korean estimates, and the 10 on Factor I for North Korea. In maintaining an ongoing monitoring system, the "easy in" or "easy out" choice would be made according to a number of considerations, such as the characteristics of the respondents, known biases or the previous record of the experts, and similar criteria.

In our examination of the reliability of our expert-generated data, we reanalyzed the data twice, once with the lone deviant judge excluded and once excluding all but the judges who were grouped together on Factor I. Our analysis focused on the measure of issue position. When the one deviant judge was excluded, there were no substantial shifts in the data. When all those but the "Factor I" judges were excluded, there was only one major shift in the data: the estimate of North Korea's issue position on joint application to the United Nations (issue H) went from support to opposition. One explanation for the similarity of the reanalyzed data to the original data is that the deviant scores were not biased in one direction but were spread evenly to either side of the norm for all respondents.

One conclusion of this analysis is that just about the same information is being obtained from the smaller group of Factor I respondents as from the entire sample of 25. If these results held up over time, it would be advisable to use a smaller sample in the monitoring system, with confidence that basically the same information was being obtained as from a larger, and therefore costlier, sample.

A word of caution must be entered here. We are not advocating "getting rid" of deviant judges in some kind of purge so that complete homogeneity of viewpoints is produced. Indeed, we argued earlier for the value of competing viewpoints. The value of this approach is that those individuals with different perceptions can be identified so that the analyst can then determine what kind of information they are responding to and what leads them to perceive the value of a particular variable as different from the values assigned by other respondents. In a sense, therefore, the procedure systematizes the examination of differing viewpoints by alerting the analyst to those differences and giving him the opportunity to decide how to handle the differences.

The conclusion that we have reached from this analysis and our general experience with the questionnaire is that substantially more work must be done to improve the reliability of the procedure. We would not expect to achieve the level of agreement among experts now found among coders in content analysis procedures. Given our assumption about varying information sources, such a level would not even be desirable as a general goal. However, we do expect to improve substantially the reliability among experts who have the same information base. Experimental procedures can be developed to refine a questionnaire that will accomplish this purpose.

We must also deal with the question of validity. In this case, work in social science provides even less help than it did in the case of reliability. Among social scientists the meaning of validity, let alone the procedures for establishing it, always generates controversy. For the purposes of developing a foreign policy monitoring system, we might suggest three different types of validity tests. The first is what might be called "face validity." Do knowledgeable individuals agree that reasonable values are generated by a particular technique? This question generally asks for a qualitative assessment, although it might imply having a second set of experts systematically "validate" the data generated by an initial set of respondents. One can also ask face validity questions by looking at the extreme values of the data produced. In the case of the Korean data, for example, it appears reasonable that South Korea and North Korea are most widely divergent on the issue of eliminating anticommunist laws in the South. It would be highly suspect if our data showed a high probability of this particular condition changing. If that were the case, we would seriously question the entire data set on the grounds of face validity.

A second way to check for validity is to determine whether experts from different organizational roles achieve a consensus. Significance tests on the differences between Group I and Group II were carried out to estimate whether these differences were unsystematic and random, or whether they were so consistent as to suggest that the two groups had a different picture of reality in responding to the questionnaire. For North Korea, there was only 1 instance out of 50 in which a significant, systematic difference occurred. For South Korea a significant difference occurred in 11 out of 50 instances. Taking agreement between the two groups as a measure of validity, it would appear that the experts generated more valid data on North Korea than on South Korea.

In developing a full-fledged monitoring system, it would probably be desirable to pay attention to detailed categories of experts. It might be useful to compare four groups--INR analysts, country desk officers, officers in

the field, and nongovernmental experts. If a panel of respondents was created from representatives of these categories, it would be possible to conduct a more thorough
analysis of consensus and divergence within and between the
various groups. It would then be possible to set the minimal levels of between-groups agreements at which estimates
could be considered valid.

Finally, what is called the construct validity of the
data could be checked through follow-up studies of the situations being monitored. Using more conventional data generation techniques such as content analysis, the picture
of the world emerging from the questionnaire responses
could be compared with public statements and other behavior.
These follow-up studies would help determine the extent to
which the expert-generated estimates were confirmed by other
information that was subsequently made available. These
studies would only be applied in selected cases, since it
can be assumed that once a monitoring system had proved
valid in some situations it would continue to provide valid
information.

It should be pointed out that reliability and validity
are not all-or-nothing questions. What is needed is a
basic acceptance of the possibility of a reliable and valid
method. Once members of an organization accept this, the
goal is then to work for incremental improvements of the
reliability and validity of the specific estimates provided
by the system. In other words, the credibility of the expert-generated estimation procedure has to be created much
as that of conventional INR analyses has been--that is,
through the trust that comes from continuous and extensive
usage. The long-run payoff for the effort could be forecasts that are more precise and more succinct, and that
can be more flexibly used for analysis and evaluation of
policy.

COSTS IN DEVELOPING AND MAINTAINING
A FOREIGN POLICY MONITORING SYSTEM

The costs of developing and maintaining a capability
to collect expert judgments on a set of political issues
for the Department of State can be discussed from a number
of perspectives. The discussion below assumes that the
methodological problems discussed in the preceding section
have been resolved in one way or another. It would probably take about one year of work to develop a survey instrument that is relatively reliable and yields substantial

validity. During the same period the training manuals and computer software necessary to generate, test, and analyze the data would also be developed. After these essentially technical problems were overcome, a series of further steps involving organizational costs and commitments would have to be taken. Some of these costs would be essentially financial, as in the maintenance of computer programs and the means for in-putting the raw data into those programs. The programs necessary to receive, organize, and analyze the kinds of information that we collected in this case study would be relatively simple to develop and maintain. Such programs would involve displays of frequency distributions, the calculations of composite indexes, and perhaps some simple projective devices similar to those described in Appendix C. The data itself would come from experts in the field and in Washington as well as outside the government, whose participation would involve a relatively small amount of time. Government respondents would participate as part of their normal duties. Outside experts, should they be used, might have to be induced with a small consulting fee. An additional inducement would be the offer to regularly share with them the unclassified portions of the information collected. After initial training, respondents could provide the data in a relatively short period of time. Since the data would already be in quantitative form, it could be easily processed by the computer programs, and distributed to users.

Relatively speaking, the monetary costs for computer program maintenance and the acquisition and use of the data are minimal. However, the organizational costs are formidable. Those costs involve training not only the INR analyst but also potential experts throughout the government and potential users at all levels of government. Previous experience with a variety of information systems suggests that getting cooperation from potential generators of the expert data will be extremely difficult. Equally, if not more, difficult will be getting the users to appreciate this kind of information.

The latter obstacle is extremely important because the INR analyst can use a system such as the one proposed in this case study only if it can be applied to issues in which the users are interested. This means that the users of INR output must identify the kinds of questions they have about the political world with which they deal. For many reasons it may be extremely difficult to apply this system to the issues most salient to users. However, without the understanding on the part of users as well as their

demand for this type of analysis, there is little the INR
analyst can do.

Even if the INR analyst succeeds in discovering a set
of political issues that his user would like to be examined,
the analyst would have considerable difficulty in getting
other Washington experts as well as field representatives
to supply the data. From our experience with this case
study, we know that the supply of experts on a particular
subject is quite limited if one is confined to the Washington community. Identifying appropriate respondents in the
field would be no less difficult unless an understanding
of the questionnaire procedure and a commitment to the procedure were acquired from the officer before he entered
the field.

In indicating these organizational costs, we are not
attempting to argue that the development of a capability
within selected geographical areas and for selected functional questions might not be feasible. On the contrary,
there are issues like the laws of the seas, the control of
the flow of narcotics, and the pursuit of energy policy in
the interest of the United States where the functional complexity combined with the geographical specificity of the
information needed creates conditions in which the users
of INR research no doubt feel overwhelmed by the data.
Some of the more conventional areas of American foreign
policy interests such as alliance policies and disarmament
issues are also sufficiently technical and geographically
specific that a crisper formatting of available information
would be welcomed by policy makers. In short, the need
by INR clients for clearer information and better forecasts
in subject areas where there is a great deal of political
complexity might be sufficient to overcome the organizational costs involved.

From the INR analyst's point of view, the benefits
would clearly be worth the costs. The survey of INR documents reported in Chapter 1 indicates clearly that the INR
makes very few forecasts. Only 22 percent of the documents
surveyed made forecasts that identified an explicit time
frame. In addition, a concern that the output of the INR
is receiving too little attention by potential users might
increase a willingness to develop a system that helps the
analyst communicate more efficiently with the user. With
such a system, the INR analyst would perform the role of
synthesizing opinions across a wide range of experts, and
of serving as the intermediary between the user and experts
(in the intelligence community and in the field). It would
seem that the INR would considerably benefit in terms of

organizational capability from performing such a role. Furthermore, it is a role that few other agencies in the present constellation of the foreign policy-making process could play.

The benefits to the experts who provide the responses might also be sufficiently high to pay for the costs incurred. First, the experts would receive feedback as to the relationship of their viewpoints to the viewpoints of others in the governmental and the scholarly community. The opportunity for an expert to check his views (normally through informal means) is usually welcomed. Therefore we would expect that the opportunity for a check through a somewhat more formal system would also be welcomed. Second, the system would allow the experts another avenue through which their opinions could be heard. A common feeling among specialists is that policy makers do not adequately listen to their viewpoints. Although the system we proposed would force the expert to constrain his viewpoint within a relatively formalized structure, it would nevertheless be an additional conduit to those whom he thinks should be reached. Finally, the system would create a built-in feedback process to reduce the anomie that is generated by a large bureaucratic structure that appears to be impervious to the hard work and honest effort of the rank and file foreign service officer. He would no longer suffer the deprivation of thinking that he understands the problem while others neither understand it nor solicit his views.

In other words, it can be argued that the system might produce some general organizational benefits quite aside from the actual utility of the data produced. This is a subsidiary argument, however. Our main purpose was to show that data similar to that which was generated for the Korean negotiations could substantially improve the clarity and usefulness of forecasts about evolving political conditions. The capacity to see the distribution of experts on various estimates of existing political positions and capabilities will, we feel, help the policy maker better comprehend the complexity of existing conditions. It will also enable the INR analyst to write reports that are relevant and concise, and to make forecasts and evaluations that are helpful to the policy maker.

In short, we are describing a system that would be relatively inexpensive to establish and maintain in financial terms and that has the potential for substantial direct and indirect benefits to the INR and the foreign policy community at large. While the organizational costs, less measurable in dollar terms, are large, it appears they are not insurmountable and that they may indeed be worth surmounting.

NOTES

1. For a recent statement of the problem by a U.S. government official, see Arthur Vogel, "Toward a Foreign Policy Reporting System," World Affairs 133, 2 (September 1970): 106-14. Also see Frank L. Klingberg, "Studies in Measurement of the Relations Among Sovereign States," Psychometrika 6 (1941): 335-52.

2. Department of State, "Traffic Analysis by Geography and Subject" (Washington, D.C.: U.S. Government Printing Office, March 1973).

3. The PARA system is discussed in PARA: Process, Problems and Potential (Ann Arbor, Mich.: Bendix Aerospace Systems Division, 1972).

4. The CASCON system is described in Lincoln P. Bloomfield and Robert Beattie, "Computers and Policy-Making: The CASCON Experiment," Journal of Conflict Resolution 15 (March 1971).

5. Olaf Helmer, Social Technology (New York: Basic Books, 1966).

6. See Herbert M. Blalock, Social Statistics (New York: McGraw Hill, 1960), pp. 144-49.

7. The model is described in Michael K. O'Leary, William D. Coplin, and Gary Brey, "PROBE User's Manual" (Syracuse, N.Y.: Syracuse University International Relations Program, 1974).

6

PROJECTING VIOLENCE IN
THE MIDDLE EAST

The purpose of this case study is to demonstrate how existing quantitative techniques might be used by INR analysts to project the occurrence of violence in the Middle East. The study focuses on the interactions among four states--Israel, Egypt, Syria, and Jordan--for the time period January 1965 through January 1970. Our major concern is to determine the degree to which events data can be used in projecting the outbreak of violence among the four states during that time period.

We have been fortunate in being able to draw upon the work of Edward Azar, Department of Political Science, University of North Carolina.[1] Azar is a substantive specialist on Middle East conditions who has collected substantial data banks in quantitative form. A description of the data will be provided below.

The time period covered in this case study includes both periods of low conflict and also periods of extreme violence. Our problem is how to employ quantitative techniques to aid the INR analyst whose job it is to project conditions that might lead to violence. Our first step was to examine closely the documents written by INR analysts for the period 1965 through 1969. We extracted from those documents projections relevant to the domain of the data. These projections were then compared with the patterns found in the data in terms of the following questions:

1. Do the conditions (independent variables) and consequences (dependent variables) found in the INR analyses correspond with the data?

2. Were the projections made by the INR analysts consistent or inconsistent with events reported in the data?

3. Would the use of data have strengthened the INR projections?

4. How useful would the INR analyst find different levels of aggregation and different forms of data manipulation (for example, raw frequency counts, weighted frequency counts, or pictorial display of verbal descriptions of events)?

5. How could data be provided that is similar to the Azar data and that is up to date and relatively inexpensive?

6. Would the benefits be worth the costs?

To answer these questions, we first must describe our procedures for abstracting the projections. This will be followed by a discussion of selected projections in terms of the data in answer to questions 1 and 2. A further selection of projections will be made in order to explore questions 3 and 4. A final section of the case study will focus on questions 5 and 6.

The organization of the case study is as follows:

INR Projections
Fitting the Data on the Projections
Using Quantitative Techniques for Projections
Using Quantitative Methods to Test Assumptions
Utility of Data and Techniques to INR Analysts

INR PROJECTIONS

Our aim was to abstract as many statements as possible that made projections concerning the likelihood of violence among the four states from January 1965 to December 1969. We read all of the relevant INR documents (for the time period) that were classified no higher than "secret." For those documents with higher classifications, members of the INR's Office of Near East and South Asia abstracted and paraphrased projections.

Nineteen projective statements were identified. The earliest was November 1966 and the latest was September 1969. The projections are listed in Figure 6.1 along with the dates of the reports from which they are abstracted.

The dominant theme in most of the projections is that previous violent or other conflictive events will lead to either more or less violent or other conflictive events in the future. Although some other kinds of independent variables were employed (for example, internal conditions

FIGURE 6.1

INR Projections for Middle East Violence, 1965-69

Projection Number	Date	Projective Statement
1	November 1966	Should Syrian attacks continue, Israel is likely to resort to force in reply.
2	November 1966	Israeli reply will probably take the form of air attacks but not the seizure and holding of Syrian territory.
3	November 1966	Reprisals by Israel are likely against Jordan.
4	November 1966	Syria will not reply to Israeli reprisal by the use of force but will rather protest diplomatically.
5	January 1967	Continued daily firings and incidents across the cease-fire line could lead to a more serious clash.
6	January 1967	The breakout of major Arab-Israeli hostilities is not expected at this time.
7	January 1967	Progressive deterioration of the situation over time could lead to major hostilities.
8	July 1967	Despite the increase in incidents/clashes along the Suez Canal, the UAR is not likely to resume major hostilities with Israel.
9	October 1967	Neither side (UAR/Israel) is expected to initiate major hostilities in the Suez Canal area.
10	February 1968	If Arab terrorists mount a major attack across the cease-fire line, Israel is expected to respond quickly with a punitive raid.
11	March 1968	Jordan is now likely to become even more dependent on UAR politically and provide military support as a result of the Israeli attack.
12	September 1968	There is no evidence that the UAR is planning any significant military action in the near future--offensive action "not likely."
13	November 1968	Despite its increased ability to harass Israel along the Suez Canal, the UAR is not expected to resume general hostilities.
14	March 1969	To the extent Israel seems to be firming its occupation along the Suez Canal, the UAR will continue to initiate violent incidents.
15	April 1969	Splits within the Syrian regime mean that another direct confrontation, perhaps involving the use of armed force, could happen during the next several months.
16	May 1969	Nasser may decide that some sort of military action, regardless of consequences, is the least risky course left to him.
17	June 1969	There is a small likelihood that the Arabs will mount a dramatic initiative against Israel in the next few months.
18	September 1969	Egyptian suspicion/hostility toward Israel is unlikely to diminish under Nasser or his successors.
19	September 1969	The prospects for Israeli-Egyptian accommodation are dim.

173

within states or actions by states outside the area), there
is clear evidence from this list that the INR analysts are
most often projecting from past patterns of violence to
likely future patterns. This style of projection corresponds to the quantitative techniques employing trend analysis similar to those used in the analysis of stock prices.
In order to replicate quantitatively the qualitative projections of the analyst, many of the independent and dependent variables implicit in the INR projections must be employed in the Azar data.

FITTING THE DATA ON THE PROJECTIONS

In this section, we are interested in answering two
relatively distinct questions: (1) To what degree can the
available data sets be used to measure the events discussed in the projections, and (2) to what degree can the
data be used to check the accuracy of the analyst's projections. Our interest here is not so much to evaluate the
analyst as to see whether the data itself has some face
validity. We found substantial evidence that the data did
fit the projections and that the projections were on the
whole consistent with events subsequently reported in the
data. Since we were not interested in conclusive evidence,
we did not test all of the projections reported above.
Rather, we selected those that could best illustrate the
variety of projections and the complexity and problems
that could arise in applying the data.

Applicability of the Data Set

To deal with the question of whether the Azar data
could be fitted to the kinds of projective statements found
in the documents, it is necessary to provide some explanation of the procedure employed by Azar to create his data.
We will report the procedure in summary fashion, referring
the reader to Azar's work for a more detailed description
(see note 1).

Azar's data-generation procedure can be divided into
two steps: the identification of events and the scaling
of events. The first step involved the survey (that is,
foreign policy acts) of 32 sources such as newspapers and
periodicals that report events in the Middle East. The
procedure for identifying events requires the coder to

specify actor, target, activity, and issue area in a systematic format. The scaling procedure is one initially
developed at Stanford University and used extensively by
Azar and others. A high degree of intercoder reliability
was developed for a 13-point scale that ranges from high
degrees of cooperation at the lower end of the scale to
intense conflict at the upper end of the scale.

Both the raw sentences abstracted by Azar and the
scaling procedure applied to those sentences produce data
that is conceptually similar to the dependent variable (occurrence of violence) in the State Department projective
statements. The sample raw sentences reproduced in Figure
6.2 include general acts of reprisal and violence as well
as specific actions such as air attacks. The projections
reported in Figure 6.1 referred to similar events. In general, the INR projections show a concern for the frequency
and intensity of violence or conflict and, to a lesser degree, cooperation. The scale used by Azar represents a
similar conceptual framework.

Merely to point out the conceptual similarities between the projective statements of the State Department
and the data generated by Azar does not, of course, provide
conclusive evidence of the compatibility between the two
sources of information. To acquire more evidence beyond
this face validity, we correlated the existence of a particular projection by an INR analyst with the frequency of
violent acts. Assuming that the INR reports would be written before or during the perceived escalation of violence,
we can see the degree to which the Azar data conformed to
the picture of the world presented in the INR reports.
Figure 6.3 shows the average frequency of conflict acts
per month between Israel and three Arab states over time.
The graph also indicates the points at which INR projections were made. The evidence is clear that in general
the periods of high conflict as measured by the Azar data
were also the periods when most INR reports were written.
Assuming that high conflict is most likely to attract the
attention of the analysts, the co-occurrence found in Figure 6.3 provides substantial validity to the Azar data.

Using the Data to Check
INR Projections

To see whether the analyst's projections were confirmed by the data, we performed the analysis reported in
Figure 6.4. In some cases, the INR analysis projected in-

FIGURE 6.2

Some Selected Foreign Policy Events in the Azar Data

Israel charges Egypt with Arab sabotage activities

Israel warns Egypt of retaliatory measures against recent acts

Israel denounces Egypt's blockade

Israel expresses to Egypt concern for the Jordanian-Egyptian defense pact

Israel exchanges fire across the Suez Canal with Egypt

Israel warns Egypt to expect heavier strikes

Israel warns Syria against continuation of sabotage operation

Israel reports that Syrian terrorists shelled Israel from Lebanon

Egypt refuses direct negotiations with Israel

Egypt states to Israel that another battle with her is inevitable

Egypt states to Israel that a political settlement of the conflict is impossible

Egypt raids Israel's positions in Suez

Israel exchanges prisoners with Syria

Israel complains to Syria of advocating military action

Israel accuses Syria of truce violations

Israel clashes with Jordan in Judean Mountains

Israel protests to Jordan about sabotage incidents

Israel imprisons Jordanian citizens for terrorism

Israel captures Egyptian fishing boat

Israeli clash with Syria in Jordan valley

Israel kills Syrian infiltrators

Israel arrests Egyptian spies

FIGURE 6.3

Production of INR Reports Compared with Average Frequency of Conflict Acts: Israel ⇌ UAR, Syria, and Jordan, 1965-70

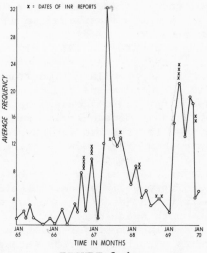

FIGURE 6.4

Comparison of INR Projections with the Azar Data

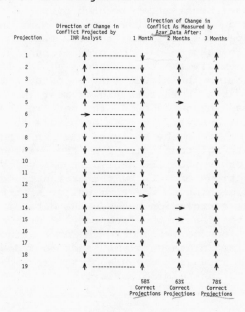

Projection	Direction of Change in Conflict Projected by INR Analyst	Direction of Change in Conflict As Measured by Azar Data After:		
		1 Month	2 Months	3 Months
1	↑	↓	↑	↑
2	↑	↓	↑	↑
3	↑	↓	↓	↓
4	↑	↓	↑	↓
5	↑	↑	→	↑
6	→	↑	↑	↑
7	↑	↑	↑	↑
8	↓	↓	↓	↓
9	↓	↓	↓	↓
10	↑	↓	↓	↓
11	↓	↓	↓	↓
12	↓	↑	↓	↓
13	↓	→	↓	↓
14	↑	↑	→	↑
15	↑	↑	→	↑
16	↑	↑	↑	↑
17	↓	↓	↑	↓
18	↓	↑	↑	↑
19	↑	↑	↑	↑
		58% Correct Projections	63% Correct Projections	78% Correct Projections

177

creased violence while in other cases, the analyst suggested
that the conflict would either remain at about the same
level or decrease. The basic trend projected in each statement is illustrated in Figure 6.4 by the direction of three
arrows: " " violence is expected to increase, " " violence
is expected to stay the same, and " " violence is expected
to decrease. An arrow was assigned to each of the 19 projective statements.

In order to evaluate the INR analysts' projections
with the data, it is necessary to make a number of assumptions regarding the appropriate time frame. Frequently,
the reports did not give a specific time frame for projections. We assume that in all cases the time frame was
three months or less. Consequently, Figure 6.4 reports the
success percentage for the projections for violence one
month, two months, and three months after the projection
was made in an INR document.

Figure 6.4 provides strong evidence either that the
INR analysts did very well (assuming the data is valid) or
that the data is valid (assuming the INR analyst is correct).
Within a three-month span, only three projections, Numbers
3, 6, and 10, were incorrect for all three months. Figure
6.4 also suggests that the analysts themselves may have had
a three-month span in mind, since their percentage of correct predictions was highest for that time period.

Even though the "batting average" of the analyst appears to have been extremely high over the four-year period,
Figure 6.4 and this analysis suggest that the question of
time is especially critical for the analyst. The INR analyst tends to make open-ended projections that do not explicitly identify the time frame. (This characteristic is
not peculiar to the Middle East reports, but, as noted in
Chapter 1, is a characteristic of most INR estimates.)
Nevertheless, by juxtaposing the data to the verbal statements of the analyst, we have been able to get some feel
for the time frame the analysts have in mind.

Our general conclusion from the evidence presented in
this section is that the Azar data has validity. The verbal descriptions of acts by the Azar data correspond closely
in content meaning to the terminology of the INR analyst.
The general correlation between the date of the INR projection and the rise in the frequency of events suggests that
INR perceptions correspond to the Azar data. Finally, the
"success rate" of the analyst tends to support the validity
of the Azar data as a measure of the reality of violent
interactions in the Middle East.

USING QUANTITATIVE TECHNIQUES
FOR PROJECTIONS

This section examines some of the uses that might be made of a data set similar to the set we have used in this case study. We are especially interested in illustrating how quantitative projection techniques and visual displays of quantitative data can be used to aid the analyst in examining his subject and communicating his conclusions about the future. To use quantitative techniques effectively, two basic decisions must be made: what level of aggregation to use and what particular visual displays and statistical analyses to employ.

Choosing the Level of Aggregation

In the data analysis that we have presented so far, we have made two important aggregation decisions. First, we have looked only at the simple frequency of conflictive acts sent by one state to another. Second, we have examined these frequencies within one-month time units. These aggregation decisions were appropriate for the questions we asked in the preceding section. However, they may not be appropriate for making projections of interest to the user of INR analyses. For that reason, we must consider the aggregation problem in more detail.

In a sense, the decision to use quantitative data to represent reality already requires a level of aggregation decision, since it requires the transformation of the verbal description of an act to some kind of quantitative symbol. The reason we make such a transformation is to enable us to use analytical techniques that can be applied only to quantitative data. With quantitative techniques we can efficiently handle large amounts of information. However, there is no question that we lose information in making the transformation.

In fact, the entire aggregation problem is similar to the dilemma posed by transforming verbal descriptions into quantitative form, because we are making a trade-off of detail in order to acquire analytical power. The benefits of trade-off are always open to debate and can be only tentatively resolved in terms of the actual use made of the analysis. Therefore, it is not possible to provide a complete set of rules from which to make aggregation decisions. Hopefully, the discussion that follows will illustrate the importance of aggregation decisions and provide some gen-

eral guidelines for them. Let us turn to our decision to
examine the simple frequency of violent acts and to aggregate for month-long periods.

The first aggregation decision we made was to take only
raw frequency as a measure of the level of violence. In
doing this, we elected not to make use of the procedures
for scaling acts from 1 to 13 (cooperation to conflict).
We could have weighted the frequencies in a variety of
ways to take into account the scale values. Azar has suggested a measure that he calls the "dv"--dimension of vio-
lence--which is generated by multiplying the median scale
value for the time period by the frequency of acts for
that period (in this case a month). Another method would
be to multiply each event by the scale value and then divide by the total number of events. This would provide a
weighted average frequency for each time period.

No matter what the formula, however, the question of
weighting the frequency to take into account the scale
value focuses on decisions relating to aggregation. Such
a decision would make the measure more complicated to interpret and understand but also richer in meaning. The
question that must be asked is whether important information is lost by the simplifying procedure.

To answer this question, we decided to determine the
correlation coefficient between frequency of acts and dv.
If the two are highly correlated, then we can use the simpler measure (frequency) without affecting the sophistication of the analysis. Figure 6.5 presents the correlation
coefficients and their significance levels for actions
from Israel to the UAR, Syria, and Jordan as well as ac-

FIGURE 6.5

Correlation of Average Frequency of Acts per Month to "DV"
per Month, 1965-70

	Correlation	Significance
Israel → Egypt	0.85624	0.00001
Israel → Syria	0.68151	0.00001
Israel → Jordan	0.70366	0.00001
Egypt → Israel	0.81508	0.00001
Syria → Israel	0.85729	0.00001
Jordan → Israel	0.50342	0.00002
Israel → Egypt, Syria, Jordan	0.79989	0.00001
Egypt, Syria, Jordan → Israel	0.77736	0.00001

tions from these three states to Israel. The figure shows
a strong relationship between the two measures for the
various dyads. The higher the average frequency of violent
acts per month, the higher the dv score. Thus, not much
is gained in an analysis by adding the conflict weights to
the measure of the average frequency of acts.

Average frequency of acts is not, of course, the lowest level of aggregation for the data we are using here.
The most disaggregate form is the individual event, such
as those listed in Figure 6.2. A somewhat less disaggregate form of the data would be the scale value assigned to
each event-statement. Both the statements themselves and
their scale values are highly disaggregate forms of information that might be used in visual displays by the analyst
to "get a feel" for the sequence and trend of events. However, we cannot apply statistical methods for projection
to data in this extremely disaggregated form.

If we assume that the frequency of conflictual foreign
policy acts is a useful measure of the level of violence
between two states, we still have not settled all the questions posed by aggregation. The question of the most appropriate time unit also must be dealt with. The analyst
can determine frequencies for a unit of time as small as a
day or as large as the entire five-year period studied.
Choice of unit of time depends upon statistical constraints
as well as policy-making interpretations. Generally speaking, the more data points, the more reliable the statistical analysis. A unit of time that would allow 1 value, 5
values, or even 60 values creates substantial constraints
on the user of statistics. At the same time, however,
choosing a unit of time in which there are many empty cells
(that is, cases where there are no observations) creates
substantial impediments to statistical analysis. For example, if we choose days as the unit of analysis for the
Azar data, the large number of days in which nothing happens would create havoc with most statistical procedures.
From a statistical point of view, one must choose the unit
of time that will yield the largest number of data points
but not create conditions in which a large number of those
points are zero.

From the forecasting perspective of this case study,
we need as small a unit of time as possible. Violence can
rapidly escalate and deescalate. A quick visual inspection of Figure 6.3 will illustrate that pattern in this
data set. This means that a unit of time that is too
large would contain such wide variations within each time
frame that important conditions might be overlooked. More

important, predictions might be too general to be of use.
The time frame of a month, for example, might be too large
to uncover the statistical relationships that must be found
if forecasts are to be made. Daily units would probably
be best, if it would be possible to surmount the statistical problems of empty cells indicated above.

Our response to the kinds of aggregation problems we
have just discussed is to use as the basis for our projections the simple frequency of conflictive acts between the
states, measured by weeks and by months. The weekly figures represent the smallest time unit that we can employ
without creating a statistical problem of too many zero
observation points. The major point of this discussion,
however, is that no single aggregation formula can be provided. Instead, the analyst must choose levels of specificity and time units that are at once statistically adequate and make sense in terms of his forecasting tasks.

Forms of Analysis for Projective
Purposes

This section will present a variety of methods for
making projections using the Azar data. To illustrate the
range of methods, we will consider the problem of projecting the increase or decrease of violent acts between Israel
and the UAR. Our presentation will start with the most
specific technique and progress to the more general aggregate use of the data. We will also move from trend projections of one type of event over time to projections using
one type of event to predict other events.

The most concrete use of the data would be an examination of a print-out of the events reported in the Azar
data. The analyst might be given a series of events similar to the one appearing in Figure 6.6 in which the raw
descriptive sentences are printed in chronological sequence.
This list would constitute a simple description of the sequence of events; it would maximize detail but minimize
the editorial and rhetorical writing found in the normal
report. This form for reporting events would allow the
INR analyst or, in some cases, the user of the INR product,
to save time in "getting the facts."

Figure 6.6 presents the set of events contained in the
Azar data set between Israel and the UAR from May 21 to
May 26, 1967. The analyst using this data could apply the
information he has acquired through other channels in an
attempt to discover patterns of interactions between the

two states. He could attempt to piece together the reported sequence of events in order to project likely trends in the violence that might follow during the month of June, or in subsequent time periods. At the same time, he might find the format of the information useful in presenting a briefing or writing a report to communicate to policy makers the likely sequence of events.

While there would be a maximum of descriptive richness in this running list of events, such a format would make analysis almost as difficult as it now is. The task of forming generalizations about patterns of interactions and trends would be almost as difficult because the information would still be in verbal form and too bulky for concise and explicit analysis.

The next step toward greater aggregation would be to score each of Azar's sentences on a violence scale. As noted earlier, Azar has provided one possible such scale over a range of cooperation and conflict. One feature of the scaling procedure is that each event is assigned a violence weight independent of each other event. Hence, an air space violation is always given the same scale value irrespective of its occurrence along with other events. However, this type of judgment can be made by the analyst; that is, he can supply the links between the scale values in his analysis.

Figure 6.7 presents the intensity scores on the violence scale of each event between May 21 and May 26 listed in Figure 6.6. Figure 6.7a merely lists the scale values of the events while Figure 6.7b plots those scale values in a time-series graph.

For purposes of analysis as well as presentation, the analyst will probably want to graph the flow of events in a form similar to that in Figure 6.7b. The question then becomes what to graph--the frequency of acts (from Figure 6.6), or the scale value of acts (from Figure 6.7). The answer depends largely on the analyst's intentions and the data available to him. In this analysis we have a measure generated by Azar that includes both frequency and scale value of acts. This is the dimension of violence (dv) discussed above. However, since we found that dv and frequency are highly correlated, we can substitute one for the other with no loss of information. Thus we can show the flow of violence by graphing the frequency of acts over time.

Figure 6.8 plots the frequency of events by day for the two-month period May 1 to June 30, 1967. (This of course includes the week described in Figure 6.6 and Fig-

FIGURE 6.6

Events Between Israel and Egypt, May 21 to May 26, 1967

Date	Conflict Act, Israel to Egypt	Conflict Act, Egypt to Israel
May 21	Take political measures to assure full Israeli rights Complete partial mobilization of reserves	Occupy Sharm El-Shaykh Move UAR cruiser and six other vessels south Mobilize reservists
May 22	Call for mutual withdrawal of troops	Close Gulf of Aqaba to Israeli ships Close Gulf of Aqaba to ships carrying Israeli material
May 23	Condemn UAR closing of Straits of Tiran Declare closing Straits of Tiran constitutes aggression	Close Straits of Tiran to all Israeli shipping
May 24	Deny clash along Gaza strip	Call up all reserve forces Announce Gulf of Aqaba mined Mine Gulf of Aqaba
May 25	--	Report clash in Gaza strip Warn entry of Israeli ship into Gulf of Aqaba is aggression
May 26	State they have right to break blockade if United Nations did not Condemn closing of Gulf of Aqaba	Announce completed buildup in Sinai State closing of Gulf of Aqaba might mean war State objective of war with Israel is to destroy Israel

FIGURE 6.7

Scale Values of Individual Acts Between Israel and Egypt,
May 21 to May 26, 1967

Figure 6.7A: List of Scale Values by Day

	Israel to Egypt	Egypt to Israel
May 21	08 09	08 08 09
May 22	06	11 08
May 23	08 08	11 08
May 24	08	09 09 11
May 25		11 08
May 26	08 08	09 08 08

Figure 6.7B: Flowchart of Scale Values by Act

Israel to Egypt _____
Egypt to Israel - - - -

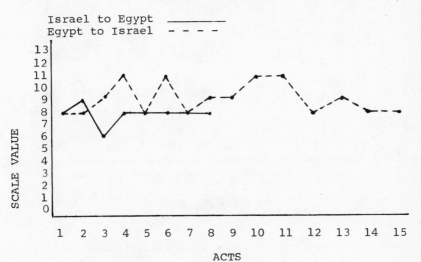

ACTS

185

FIGURE 6.8

Frequency of Acts Between Israel and Egypt by Days

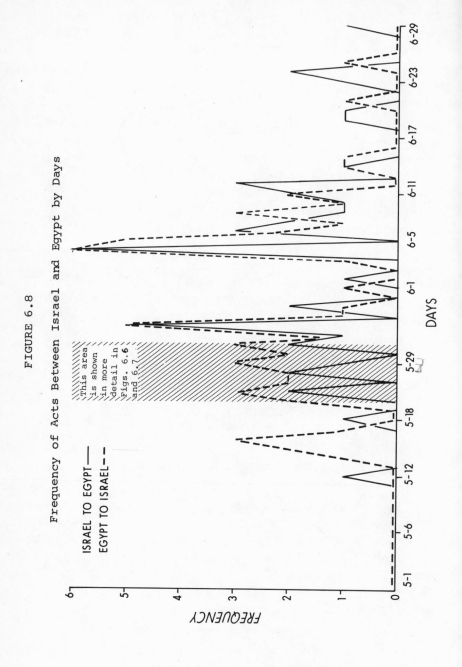

ure 6.7.) Note the trade-off involved in presenting a graph like this: we lose the detail of description given in Figure 6.6 but we gain a better (and a quicker) appreciation for the flow of interactions between the two nations over time.

The analyst can make a projection on the basis of visual inspection of the graph. In doing so, he should mix his own judgments with the indications of the graph. This is necessary in order to overcome the limitations of trend analysis based on graphs. For example, population growth was expected to be enormous, based on a trend analysis of demographic data. When other factors were included in an analysis, however, the expected rate was considered to be substantially lower. The point is that such graphs of trends should be considered no more and no less than one piece of evidence in an analysis. INR analysts should use graphs as analytical tools in forming their conclusions and as presentational devices for communicating more efficiently and effectively with users of their oral and written reports.

One point is clear from a visual inspection of Figure 6.8 and graphs for other time periods. There is no clear linear trend in the flow of violence between Israel and Egypt. Increases and decreases are quite substantial from the monthly, weekly, and daily viewpoints. Because there is such substantial variation, simple linear trend projections are unlikely to be of any use. To say this is to argue that one cannot simply take the data points for April and May and accurately estimate a linear trend for June. There is neither inductive nor logical basis for such a conclusion, since there is no necessary cumulative effect of the growth in frequency of violence.

A more complicated statistical analysis of the data is required if any type of projection is to be made. Unfortunately, as we have mentioned above, the "empty cell" problem makes the use of daily events unfeasible. For that reason, we will describe the use of statistics for projective purposes on monthly and weekly data. To use statistical measures, the analyst has to translate predictive propositions into statistical formulas; that is, he must apply generalizations about the outbreak of violence to the calculations of measures. If he can do this, he can use statistics to analyze his data. To put it another way, he can apply his generalizations consistently across a variety of data points.

To illustrate, let us examine what might be considered a trite projective proposition: "violence begets

violence." A systematic observation of the behavior of individuals, groups, and nations suggests that this proposition is not without foundation, although there are obviously
qualifying circumstances.* This proposition suggests calculating a running average that takes the frequency of
violent acts averaged over some specified past period to
represent a trend that is likely to feed upon itself. By
using a running average in which new conditions at each
data point add incrementally to previous levels, the analyst controls for isolated patterns and identifies the cumulative trend implicit in the proposition.

Another proposition that might be considered useful
in making projections is the generalization that consistency within trends increases the probability that the
trend will continue in the projected direction. Statisticians are quite adept at measuring consistency, so we could
choose from a variety of index constructions. For our particular purposes, we have chosen the standard deviation
for the set of data points used to construct a running average. The standard deviation can be interpreted as a measure of the dispersion of data points above and below the
mean. The lower the standard deviation the closer the data
points to the mean. Assuming a normal distribution of
events around the mean, 67 percent of the data points used
to construct a given mean will be contained within the
range of one standard deviation.

Figures 6.9 and 6.10 present cumulative standard deviations (and cumulative averages) for monthly and weekly
data points. If our consistency assumption is correct,
we would expect the band representing one standard deviation to be rising and to become more narrow with the escalation of violence. As the cumulative effect of rising
violence takes its toll and there are fewer extreme ebbs
and flows in the pattern, it makes sense that the escalation of violence is imminent. The reasoning that led to
our use of the running average and standard deviation is
confirmed by the patterns plotted in Figures 6.9 and 6.10.
Knowing this to be the case, the analyst might have projected that there was likelihood for a substantial increase
in violence prior to the actual outbreak of the Six-Day
War in 1967. This quantitative projection could have been
a valuable tool in strengthening the analyst's argument.

---

*One qualification is that nonviolent actions may be
preparatory moves that later lead to violence; these should
be considered in a full explanation.

FIGURE 6.9

Frequency of Acts Between Israel and Egypt by Weeks, with Standard Deviation

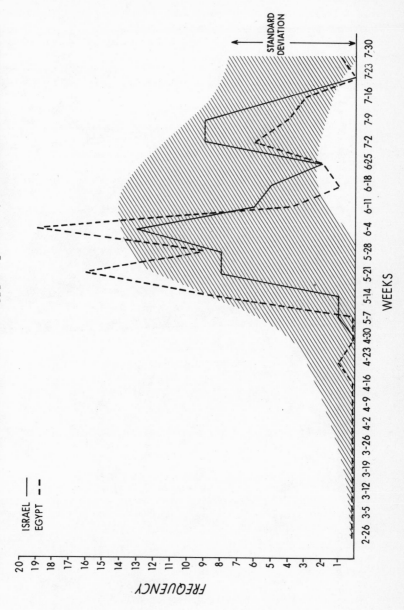

FIGURE 6.10

Frequency of Acts Between Israel and Egypt by Months, with Standard Deviation

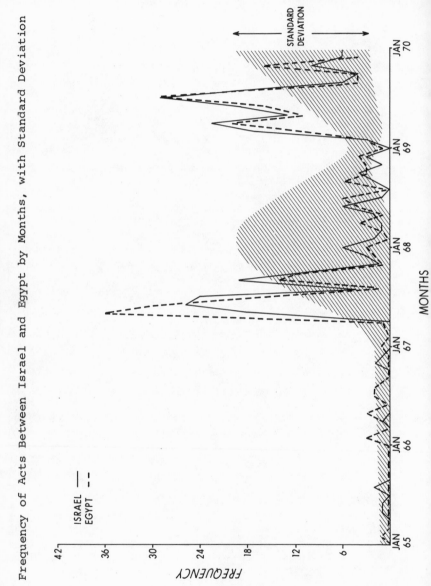

There is a fundamental problem in the argument so far. What of the possibility that consistent violence begetting greater violence (a combination of the two propositions) does not apply across all of the time periods that the analyst might want to consider? An inspection of the running averages and standard deviations throughout the 1965-69 period suggests that there are several exceptions to this proposition in the Middle East conflict. One advantage of doing systematic quantitative analysis over time is that the exceptions can be identified and then examined for the unique factors that make them exceptions.

There is insufficient evidence at this point to support a universal "law" of conflict escalation. First of all, we have noted exceptions in the case under study. Second, we have not performed the necessary next step of comparison across a variety of conflict situations (for example, India and Pakistan). However, this does not mean that the analyst cannot use statistical measures such as the running average and standard deviation as a tool in his analysis as long as he recognizes the limitations. The analyst can use this and any other measure that he deems reasonable, just as he now uses historical precedents and logical deductions. The formalism required by the statistics does not mean that the analyst has to have any more confidence in his projective assumptions than he now has, although it does require that he state those assumptions in more precise terms.

So far we have discussed projections that are made on trends in one type of event over time. More complex projections can also be made. The first case study, Predicting Political Instability in Tropical Africa, demonstrates the use of some of these more complex techniques for making predictions by identifying internal social, political, and economic conditions that are "determinants" of elite and communal instability in black Africa. Similar variables could also be used to develop and test complex models for predicting the likelihood of increased violent acts between the Middle Eastern states. Given the vital importance of domestic political conditions for events in the Middle East, such analysis would not be unreasonable. We have not performed it here because the methods would be similar in structure and format to the present case study.

We will instead look at patterns of interaction between Israel on the one hand and Syria, Jordan, and the UAR on the other. We can statistically test whether the pattern of interaction between the two sides is systematically associated with the increase in violence. Our proposition here is that as violence increases, the two sides will act more symmetrically. Our measure of violence is the one we have been using throughout this case study--the frequency of violent acts per month. Our measure of symmetry is the correlation between the number of acts sent from Israel to the three Arab states and the number of acts sent from the three Arab states to Israel. That is, as the number of acts from one side increases, the number of acts from the other side also increases--a symmetrical pattern of interaction. Table 6.1 shows the relationship between the two variables. Assuming that cut-off points of r = .50 and 5 = .70 (Pearson's correlation coefficients) are meaningful, we constructed a table in which complete support for our proposition would be indicated by zeros in all cells but the diagonal ones. The data in Table 6.1 strongly supports our proposition, although there are some anomalies.

On the basis of this analysis, we can conclude that symmetry is a characteristic of interactions between states that are increasing their violence toward each other. Given the empirical evidence as well as the logic of that position, we can add some method of calculating symmetry to our projective technique. This calculation might be the correlation coefficient already used, or it might be a simple formula in which a ratio of the frequency of acts sent by one state to the frequency of acts sent by the other is calculated. As that ratio approaches one to one and as the frequency of violence is rising, the probability of an increase of violence can be projected.

TABLE 6.1

Relationship of Magnitude of Conflict to Bilateral
Symmetry by Month (January 1967 to December 1968)
for Israel ⇌ UAR, Syria, Jordan

Magnitude of Conflict	Symmetry		
	$0 < R < .5$	$.5 < R < .7$	$.7 < R < 1.0$
Less than 10 conflict acts per month	8	3	0
11 to 20 conflict acts per month	2	4	2
More than 20 conflict acts per month	0	0	3

Using statistical procedures, the analyst could make three relatively independent tests of the patterns found in graphs of weekly frequencies of hostile acts. He could look at the running average to see if the level of violence is rising; he could examine the running standard deviation to see if the dispersion around the mean is decreasing; or he could look at the patterns of bilateral interactions to see if the two parties are responding symmetrically to one another. Any one of these indicators might not be significant. But a finding that all three indicators were pointing in the same direction would be substantial evidence that could be used in generating projections.

Using this reasoning, a computer program could be designed to project violence. One possible procedure that could be programmed is summarized in the flowchart in Figure 6.11. We followed these procedures to analyze the INR projections reported in Figure 6.4. Figure 6.12 compares the projections that used our procedures with the projections of the INR analysts. If we consider there is agreement when our projection is high or moderate and the INR projection is an increase, and when our projection is low and the INR projection is a decrease, then the table indicates agreement between the two in 15 out of the 19 cases. (Numbers 5, 6, 7, and 17 are incorrect.) Figure 6.13 presents projections made on the basis of the flowchart for each week of 1967. Although we did not have weekly INR projections with which to compare this data, we did find it interesting that the procedure yielded consistent escalatory projections for the weeks prior to the Six-Day War in June. If this procedure had been used in the INR, clear warning signals would have emerged by the middle of May predicting hostility in early June.

Once again, we would emphasize that the convergence between our projections and those of the INR in Figure 6.12 and the post hoc validity of our projections in Figure 6.13 are more an indication of the face validity of our data and procedures than anything else. Nevertheless, even with data based exclusively on public sources and our highly simplified analytical procedures, we feel that the similarity between the two sets of projections raises the prospect that quantitative techniques applied to a fuller range of data could be a useful tool to the INR analyst.

USING QUANTITATIVE METHODS
TO TEST ASSUMPTIONS

In addition to the forecasting procedures we have so far described, the data could also be used to test the ex-

FIGURE 6.11

Illustrative, Simplified Flowchart of a Computer Program
for Producing Estimates of Future Escalation Based on Each
Week's Pattern of Conflict

S·T E P   1:   Is this week's frequency of violence greater
               than the mean for the previous 12 weeks?

| If Yes, go to Step 2 | | If No, Report:
"Low Probability of
Escalation" |

S T E P   2:   Is the cumulative standard deviation for this
               week smaller than the cumulative standard de-
               viation for last week?

| If Yes, go to Step 3 | | If No, Report:
"Moderate Probability
of Escalation" |

S T E P   3:   Is there increasing symmetry in the frequency
               of conflict between opposing sides?

| If Yes, Report:
"High Probability
of Escalation" | | If No, Report:
"Moderate Probability
of Escalation" |

planatory assumptions of INR analysts. The analyst could
use the data to study the patterns of behavior of the
states. Such a study could then be used to test strategic
assumptions made by foreign policy makers and to suggest
alternative strategies. To illustrate, let us consider
the general Israeli position that substantial but limited
escalation can be used to deter the continuation of Arab
violence. The implicit assumption is that by meeting limited violent acts by Arab states and/or terrorists from
those states with an unequivocal and substantial set of

194

FIGURE 6.12

Comparison of Projections of the Case Study Flowchart and of the INR for Increase of Violence

Projection	QUEST Projection of Probability of Escalation	INR Projection
1	High	↑
2	High	↑
3	Moderate	↑
4	High	↑
5	Low	↑
6	Low	→
7	Low	↑
8	Low	↓
9	Low	↓
10	Moderate	↑
11	Low	↓
12	Low	↓
13	Low	↓
14	High	↑
15	Moderate	↑
16	Moderate	↑
17	High	↓
18	Moderate	↑
19	Moderate	↑

↑ Will increase
↓ Will decrease
→ Will remain the same

195

FIGURE 6.13

Weekly Projections of Violence for 1967--Israel ←→ Egypt

WEEK	PROJECTION		WEEK	PROJECTION
1	↓		27	↓
2	↓		28	↓
3	↓		29	→
4	↓		30	↓
5	↓		31	→
6	↓		32	↑
7	↓		33	→
8	↓		34	→
9	↓		35	↑
10	→		36	→
11	↓		37	↓
12	↓		38	↓
13	→		39	↓
14	→ APRIL		40	↓
15	→		41	↓
16	→		42	↓
17	↑		43	→
18	↑ MAY		44	↓
19	↑		45	↓
20	↑		46	→
21	↑ JUNE WAR		47	→
22	↑		48	↑
23	↓		49	→
24	↓		50	→
25	↓		51	↓
26	↓		52	→

violent actions that are clearly escalatory, the Arabs will refrain from future violence. Although we will not perform an empirical analysis of this assumption here, let us briefly point out how the data might be used to test the assumption.

The proposition implies that we must take into account the frequency and the intensity of violence and, most important, the time lag between Arab acts and Israeli reprisals. One method of testing the proposition would be to visually inspect the graph of the flow of violent acts over some time period, as has been done for a six-month period in Figure 6.9. The impressionistic evidence from Figure 6.9 is mixed in terms of this hypothesis; at some points Israeli violence appears to follow Arab violence as predicted, but at other points the opposite relationship appears. We would have to look at a longer time period and graphs for Israeli interactions with states other than the UAR, for most reprisals have been directed at Syria, Lebanon, or Jordan.

Any impressionistic reading of a graph can be no more than suggestive of a pattern of interactions. A more careful study of the extent to which Israel does in fact follow a "behavior-modification" policy and, more significantly, the extent to which it appears to work, would require more complex study consisting of:

1. The analysis of daily and weekly interactions over a substantial time period.
2. A consideration of Israel vis-à-vis each of the neighboring Arab states.
3. The analysis of a fuller range of data beyond the public sources used in this case study.
4. More complex analytical procedures, such as time-lag regression analysis and computer simulation which programmed the hypothesized decision-rules followed by the two sides.

This further study is especially necessary to understand the pattern involved, since, while the visual inspection of the graphs appears to lend some support to the proposition under discussion, the correlation analysis of monthly data sets does not. The analysis performed in the preceding section shows increasing symmetry between Israel and the Arabs with increasing violence. This suggests that the increase in conflict by one side leads to more, rather than less, violence by the other side. The conflicting interpretations between a visual inspection of the graphs and the correlations suggest that visual inspections may sometimes be misleading. Hopefully, further studies would help reconcile these two interpretations.

This brief analysis does demonstrate that policy-relevant propositions can be tested with data of this sort. The findings are often mixed and therefore not decisive in confirming the validity of a particular assumption that may underlie a specific doctrine. However, they are no more mixed than the citation of historical incidents and logical statements that now serve as the basis for making evaluations of strategic assumptions. Hence, this kind of quantitative data might well become part of the analytical tools of the INR analyst when he is exploring policy assumptions.

UTILITY OF DATA AND TECHNIQUES
TO INR ANALYSTS

The purpose of this section is to discuss the costs and benefits that might accrue if some type of data similar to the Azar data was available to the INR analyst. Some of the more general costs of data acquisition and management as well as training in quantitative techniques are discussed in Appendix C. Here we will comment on the utility of the kinds of analytical tasks discussed in this case study.

The preceding sections illustrate that the data such as Azar's might be a useful supplement to the INR analyst in monitoring levels of violence not only in the Middle East but in other areas of the world where interstate conflict is frequent and intense. As events in Africa, Asia, and Latin America have unfolded over the last two decades, there is evidence for the development of patterns of escalation in violence similar to those in the Middle East. Given the large number of areas of possible violence and the constrained resources of INR, a system of monitoring interactions and making projections would have some use. Although it would still require the careful analysis by knowledgeable specialists with full understanding of particular contexts, a computer-based conflict-monitoring system built on data similar to Azar's could provide more extensive coverage than is now provided by the INR, particularly in areas where one analyst is responsible for a large number of countries. Programs could be developed that used some of the projective calculations discussed in the preceding pages that automatically flagged patterns that might lead to escalation in violence. The INR analyst could then be alerted and do a more detailed study.

In addition to the use of the data for projective reasons, the data could also be used for the exploration of policy strategies. The effects of U.S. actions on the relationships between a pair of violence-prone states could be examined. Likewise, the effects of other factors such as internal conditions within the countries or intervention by other states from outside the region could be included. Although this capability would not be as far-reaching as the monitoring capability, it certainly could be used to write reports on general background conditions and to inform policy makers in their selection of actions.

Given these potential uses, what are the costs? The answer to this question in specific terms cannot be supplied. However, some general comments can be made.

The costs of using Azar's procedures would be prohibitive. Assuming that public documents were not the only ones surveyed but also that incoming information from various governmental sources were included, the volume of events to be identified and scaled would require perhaps a full-time clerk for every state whose behavior was being monitored. We say perhaps because it might require more than a clerk, since problems of contradictory information would have to be checked and rechecked just as Azar has done. Vernard Lanphier's project on Venezuela attempted to do just what we are suggesting and yielded 1,200 acts over a three-month period (compared to Azar's average of 25 for a three-month period in Israeli foreign policy).[2] Of course, sampling techniques could cut down on the volume somewhat, but it is clear that the costs would be substantial.

In addition to the cost, there is also the problem of immediate accessibility. The procedures followed by Azar create a time lag of at least six months before information is in usable form. This situation could be remedied by having an on-line system for coding events as they come in. However, the creation and maintenance costs for such a system would be substantial.

Content analysis procedures similar to those in the Conflict and Peace Data Bank project do not appear to be feasible, given the financial and time constraints. However, such data could be generated from the resources that already exist in the State Department. Instead of collecting volumes of information on violent events among states and then coding that information so that quantitative techniques can be applied, it might be possible to use a system of daily or weekly questionnaires from the field to collect similar data. Since personnel at diplomatic mis-

sions write extensive descriptive reports that are read by
the INR analyst (if there appears to be a reason for it),
a short questionnaire that could be on machine readable
forms could be attached to the report procedure and could
be automatically fed into a data bank. The bank would be
up-dated automatically and the computer could generate
weekly violence patterns. When those patterns are considered to be significant (according to a priori criteria set
by the INR analyst) he would be alerted and then could read
the relevant reports.

In fact, the indexing procedure for cable traffic in-
stituted as of March 1, 1973, for all overseas diplomatic
missions could be used to supply data on a daily basis.
The system for Traffic Analysis by Geography and Subject
(TAGS) provides for both geographic and subject matter
classification of incoming cables by the author of the
cable. A decision could be made in high conflict areas,
such as the Middle East, to monitor the frequency of cables
dealing with specified subject matter categories in TAGS,
such as PBOR (Boundary, Territory, and Water Claims) and
MOPS (Military Operations). If procedures were established
that gave promise for adding to the accuracy of information
based on the cumulative mean, standard deviation, symmetry,
or other patterns, then a program could be written to select all appropriately coded messages as they were received,
test the frequencies for critical patterns, and report out
estimates of the likelihood of conflict escalation. This
procedure would be the least costly, since it would involve
only aggregating and analyzing data that is presumably already being collected on each cable. However, it would
also be relying on quite general information about the content of each cable. Depending upon the utility of the
quantitative analysis procedures developed, a decision
could be made to provide additional coding for the content
of the cables--to code them as to violent or nonviolent
events, or to code them for the level of violence. Nevertheless, the analysis of the frequencies of events based
solely on the TAGS-coded cables might well prove to be the
optimal cost-benefit decision.

This idea for generating quantitative data is not new.
Substantial organizational costs would be involved in constructing such a monitoring system, but the data processing costs would be much less than those involved in content
analysis and scaling. In effect, the field reporter would
be formalizing his perceptions instead of there being a
formalizing procedure carried on through content analysis
and scaling.

Periodically, an outside contractor could be called in to compare the patterns in his data with those found in the data generated by the mission reports. This comparison would serve an an evaluative instrument to check the validity of the monitoring system and could be done for a small amount of money.

We believe that the procedure described above could be cost-effective for American missions in areas of high violence. It would extend the coverage of the INR analyst so that the occurrence of violence between states would be better anticipated. It would allow him to concentrate on the areas of particular concern at the moment without totally ignoring other areas. It would also serve as a basis for more precise reporting to users and more systematic evaluations of foreign policy strategies. The costs would be relatively small once organizational and start-up training and programming procedures are overcome, since it would build on the existing coverage already supplied by the department.

NOTES

1. Data used in this study was obtained from Edward Azar's Conflict and Peace Data Bank (COPDAB). For a description of the data, see Edward E. Azar, "Conflict and Peace Data Bank: A Codebook," in Studies of Conflict and Peace (Chapel Hill: University of North Carolina, 1971), mimeo.

2. Vernard A. Lanphier, "Foreign Relations Indicator Project" (Paper presented at the annual convention of the International Studies Association, Dallas, 1972).

7

**MEASURING AND MODELING
COALITIONS IN GLOBAL
OIL POLITICS**

The purpose of this case study is to explore the utility of quantitative techniques in forecasting the strength of the evolving coalitions among petroleum-exporting countries (PECs) and petroleum-importing countries (PICs). As a result of technological developments and economic conditions, patterns of bargaining over oil issues have developed in recent years in which the two groups of states have confronted one another as blocs. The PECs have established more formal patterns of cooperation through the creation of the Organization of Petroleum Exporting Countries (OPEC). But the PICs have cooperated informally and may in the future establish their own formal institutional structure. This case study will attempt to evaluate the extent to which quantitative techniques can be used to aid the foreign affairs analyst in projecting conditions and events relevant to American global oil interests, with a particular focus on the strength of the two coalitions. It will begin with a discussion of how INR analysts have treated the subject and discuss two very different uses of quantitative methods. The first will be the use of quantitative techniques to measure a series of factors associated with different dimensions of the strength of the two coalitions. The second method will be the application of nonverbal symbols to the exploration of theoretical relationships that might be used in making forecasts. A final section will briefly assess the costs and benefits of using the tools identified in the case study.
This chapter consists of four parts:

INR Views of Global Oil Politics
Quantitative Methods of Measuring Coalition Strength

INR VIEWS OF GLOBAL OIL POLITICS

To determine the concerns of the INR analyst in the field of global oil politics, we surveyed in detail nine Intelligence Notes classified no higher than "Secret" between February 1971 and November 1972. We attempted to determine what kinds of conditions and events the analysts tried to forecast and the factors the analysts used in their predictions. We also looked at the methods employed in making the forecasts.

All of the documents analyzed in our sample attempted to describe, explain, and sometimes forecast actions taken by the major oil-producing states. Most of the reports were concerned with recent past or forthcoming events in which particular oil-producing states or OPEC as a group took actions vis-à-vis the oil industry. The types or actions analyzed appear in Figure 7.1. They can be classified roughly into those issues in which there is general agreement among all of the oil-exporting states and those issues in which the exporting countries themselves might be expected to have substantial disagreement (as noted by the asterisked actions in Figure 7.1).

From this brief list, we can discern a number of things. First, the major concern of the INR analyst is with actions taken by the PECs that affect the oil companies and the PICs. The companies are viewed in the INR analyses primarily as agents of the oil-consuming states although they are accorded an important role in the overall bargaining process. The critical question that is usually explored is the degree to which the two sides--producers and consumers--are able to achieve their bargaining goals vis-à-vis each other. Second, the kinds of actual and anticipated actions discussed represent typical issues in coalition formation processes. Most of the actions pit PEC interests squarely against PIC interests; however, a substantial number of issues also produce differential gains and losses for the PECs themselves. Third, the variety of issues demonstrates the substantial complexity across all of the questions involving the two coalitions. This complexity introduces opportunities for innumerable different bargaining outcomes and makes it extremely difficult to offer precise predictions (such as predicting a specific rise in price rather than a change in taxes).

FIGURE 7.1

Actions by Oil-Producing States Analyzed in INR Reports

Establishing oil tax rates
Raising posted prices
Increasing revenue payments from oil industry
Demanding more participation in ownership and/or manage-
  ment of oil companies
Altering production rates
Nationalization of oil companies
Ownership of natural gas companies
Increasing oil price to offset devaluation policies of
  importing states
Increasing or decreasing the amount of oil extracted*
Abrogation of oil concession agreements*
Taxing auxillary activities (port duties, for example)*
Admission of new members to OPEC*
Supporting or not supporting actions by an individual mem-
  ber of OPEC*
Regional negotiations rather than OPEC-wide negotiation*
Establishing premium charges for oil close to primary
  markets*

_____

    *Issues in which disagreement among producing states
is likely.

        In spite of this complexity, the situation presented
here seems to conform to one of the major principles of
collective bargaining in modern society. This principle
is that the success of either bloc in the bargaining process is a direct function of the relative internal cohesion enjoyed by each bloc. Therefore we can expect that
patterns of bargaining outcomes will be largely determined
by the relative PEC and PIC capacities to present a common
front in facing their antagonists. Although the INR analysts are concerned with specific bargaining outcomes and
the resultant actions by the oil-exporting states, the
general problem with which they are faced is forecasting
the relative cohesive strengths of the two blocs.
        When we speak of a bloc's "cohesion" in this case
study we have in mind a definition that is quite narrow,
but one that is useful for a study of the politics of this

issue area. For purposes of this study "cohesion" is defined as the probability that, in the event of a confron-
tation over oil issues, the members of a given bloc will
support whatever collective action is decided upon by other
members of the bloc. This notion, we feel, is at the heart
of much of the projection over the future of world oil politics. At the same time, it is an extremely difficult notion to measure. For in this formulation, cohesion does
not necessarily mean identical policies at a given time on,
for example, the extent of PEC participation in refining,
the setting of royalties, or any other specific issue.
Agreement on these or other issues may be a partial indicator of the extent of the future-oriented concept of cohesion as we have defined it, but it is not a direct indicator. Indeed, with such a definition we are necessarily
forced to rely upon indirect measures. Nevertheless, we
feel that what we lose in precision we gain in relevance.

Our examination of Intelligence Notes indicates that
the conclusion of the INR analysts on this particular question is that there is more PEC cohesion than PIC cohesion.
Although the producers are not infrequently out of step
with each other on many specific questions, they have been
able to produce a generally united front in the early 1970s.
Recent PIC moves suggest that this solidarity is clearly
recognized and that there is a felt need to create greater
PIC solidarity.

In examining the documents, it is also clear that although the INR analysts appreciate the use of quantitative
data in constructing their analyses, they do not attempt
to employ quantitative techniques of analysis. Figure 7.2
lists the types of quantitative data appearing in the nine
reports studied. Almost all of the quantitative data presented appeared in textual form. There was no use of
graphs and no use of statistics for either descriptive or
inferential purposes, and there was only one tabular presentation of data. While the INR analysts were using quantitative data to illustrate specific points or to suggest
specific trends, they did not employ techniques of analysis that would have given explanatory and predictive power
to their analyses.

Given the analytical concerns of the INR analyst and
his willingness to use some quantitative data, although
to a limited extent, we decided to suggest how the kinds
of data found in the reports, supplemented by other data
where necessary, could be used to measure PIC and PEC cohesion. We felt that such an exercise would constitute a
logical extension of present INR analysis. Whether it

FIGURE 7.2

Quantitative Data Appearing in INR Reports on Global Oil
Politics

1. Estimated increased OPEC revenue, 1971-75
2. Estimated Arab oil producers' monetary reserves by 1975
3. OPEC's share of all oil traded internationally
4. OPEC members' magnitude of imports from the United
   States
5. Annual revenue loss to OPEC members for each one-per-
   cent devaluation of the dollar
6. Shares of participation demanded by various OPEC members
7. Rises in a particular country's export oil prices
8. Average demand for oil per day
9. Levels of export quotas
10. Production level of an oil field since 1961
11. Amount of one oil company's investment in a particular
    field
12. Annual payment of one oil company to a PEC
13. Predicted price rise resulting from OPEC negotiations
14. 0.1 revenue increase to a Persian Gulf country result-
    ing from agreement with oil companies
15. Dependence of oil customers on Gulf countries
16. Proposed oil tax rate
17. Extent of revenue increase
18. Concession shares owned by various oil companies
19. Annual production of oil
20. Annual receipts from oil production
21. One country's revenues derived from petroleum taxes
    and royalties
22. Annual revenue from pipelines
23. Annual production growth rate increase
24. 0.1 production allowance decreases
25. Estimated loss to one country from allowing the pound
    sterling to float freely

could be a sufficiently valuable extension to warrant the cost is an open question that will be discussed in the final section of this chapter.

In addition to using quantitative techniques in order to generate information more relevant to the question of the cohesion of the two blocs, we will also show how some formal modeling techniques might be used to clarify and ultimately improve forecasts. A study of the propositions made by INR analysts shows a number of theoretical relationships posited between various conditions and events. While we could scarcely begin to test all of these relationships in this case study, we feel that it would be valuable to show how various visual techniques now used in mathematical and computer modeling could be employed to articulate the assumptions of INR analysts about global oil politics. These techniques will be demonstrated in the second and third sections of this case study.

QUANTITATIVE METHODS OF MEASURING COALITION STRENGTH

The purpose of this section is to develop some quantitative indicators to measure the past, present, and potential cohesion within each bloc and hence the relative strength the blocs will have in dealing with each other.

For purposes of analysis, we will make two distinctions in identifying those factors associated with the cohesion of PEC and PIC blocs. The first distinction is between oil-related conditions and nonoil conditions. Some factors of bloc cohesion are directly related to oil production, such as amount of proven reserves (for PEC) or amount of domestic production (for PIC). At the same time, other conditions not directly related to oil, such as trade, investment, and general political relationships, must be considered in assessing the overall cohesion within each bloc. The second distinction we wish to make is between economic and social transactions among states, on the one hand, and official international political positions that states take, on the other. The flows of goods, services, and people across the boundaries of states have been shown in a number of instances to correlate with the degree to which states engage in conflict or cooperation. At the same time questions of general political relationships among states that become international issues (for example, policy toward Israel) also are barometers of cooperation and conflict among states.

207

FIGURE 7.3

Examples of Factors Associated with Cohesion Within
Petroleum-Exporting and Petroleum-Importing States

	Oil	Nonoil
Transactions	Oil imports Oil exports (a)	Trade flows (b)
Political issues	Unilateral acts by PEC states toward oil companies (c)	Votes in the United Nations (d)

The two distinctions we have just discussed generate
the two-by-two matrix appearing in Figure 7.3. This matrix
presents the distinctions and provides examples of the factors that correspond to each of the four cells.

There are a number of ways we can associate the ele-
ments listed in the four cells. One way would be to consider all four categories of variables as indicators of
cohesion and to research for some way of assigning relative weights to each factor in order to calculate one or
more indexes of bloc cohesion. Another approach would be
to distinguish between independent and dependent variables.
If we were to do this it would be reasonable to consider
the factors in cells a, b, and d as the independent variables that "explain" or "predict" the dependent variable in
cell c.

Since the primary purpose of this section of the case
study is to identify quantitative techniques for measuring
aspects of bloc cohesion, it is not necessary to make a
decision on this question at this point. Instead, we will
be concerned with ways of generating quantitative indicators that might be used in analyzing the cohesion of either
bloc and the bargaining between the two blocs. We will assume that if INR analysts had such quantitative indicators
they would be able to use them for a variety of explanatory
and predictive purposes.

The data we have chosen to use for this case study is drawn from readily available public sources. If the procedure presented in this case study were actually to be used by INR analysts, other data and data sources might be employed. However, we feel that public information is adequate for our present purpose, which is to demonstrate the utility of quantitative approaches in measuring dimensions of cohesion within the two blocs.

Figure 7.4 lists the data and sources employed in gathering information on the four types of factor we have identified above. The transaction measures are relatively straightforward and require no comment. The data measuring the political issues is less readily available than the transaction data. For oil issues, the data we employed consisted of publicly reported actions by the larger PEC states involving the relationships of the oil companies operating within their territory. These events were classified according to a number of criteria and generally cover the spectrum of political issues over which the two blocs have bargained. For nonoil political issues, we have used voting agreements in the UN General Assembly. We are aware of the viewpoint, shared by scholars and government analysts, that these votes are not always representative of a state's true position on issues. Nevertheless, we feel that by analyzing a large number of votes, we can get a reasonably accurate estimate of the relative positions of states on a variety of nonoil issues.

FIGURE 7.4

Raw Data on Factors Associated with Cohesion

	Oil	Nonoil
Transactions	Oil production Oil consumption	Direction of trade statistics (IMF)
Political issues	Events reported in public sources affecting relationships between PEC states and oil companies	United Nations roll call votes

Before we discuss the kinds of analysis performed on the data described in Figure 7.4, we should identify our sample. We will be studying the 34 states listed in Figure 7.5. The list includes all of the major oil-producing and consuming states except the Soviet Union. One state, Canada, is listed in both the consuming and producing columns. For this analysis, however, we have classified Canada as a consuming state. We will be studying these 34 states for a seven-year period (1964-70).*

Our basic design will be to generate and analyze data for each year to see whether we can develop some measure of factors that might be associated with bloc cohesion. Various transformations will be employed to dimensionalize cohesion generated by oil transfers, by general trading relationships, by issue agreement or disagreement on nonoil issues, and by oil-related acts of PEC states. An attempt will be made to interpret the patterns found in these measures over the period 1964 to 1970.

Cohesion Associated with Patterns
of Oil Exchanges

In looking at the patterns of oil trade among states in the two blocs, we found it necessary to formalize a set of assumptions into mathematic rules for the transformation of the available data on oil patterns. To begin with, we have assumed that patterns of dependence between the two blocs will directly affect the cohesion of each bloc. More specifically, our primary assumption is that the more the dependence of a state on oil flows is concentrated on one or a few states in the other bloc, the less cohesive one member will be within its own bloc. The logic behind this reasoning is that if a consuming state were highly dependent on one or two oil-producing states, it would be more likely to strike a separate deal and ignore the wishes of the other consuming states, because of its vulnerable position.

To translate this reasoning into an index measuring bloc cohesion associated with oil-trading patterns, we first had to develop a formula to measure the dependence of one state on oil imports from, or exports to, another state. The following formulas were employed:

---

*In some cases, not all states will be analyzed, because of missing information.

a. For oil-producing states:

$$Dependence_{ij} = \frac{Oil\ Exports_{ij}}{Total\ Oil\ Production\ of\ i}$$

where "i" is an oil-producing state and "j" is an oil-consuming state

FIGURE 7.5

Major Oil-Consuming and Oil-Producing States

Oil-Consuming Countries on Both the Demand and Import Lists (with the constraint that they account for at least 75 percent of both demand and imports)	Oil-Producing Countries on Both the Production and Export Lists (with the constraint that they account for at least 75 percent of both)
United States	(Canada)
Canada	Venezuela
Brazil	Nigeria
United Kingdom	Algeria
Netherlands	Libya
Belgium and Luxembourg	Iran
France	Iraq
Spain	Egypt
West Germany	Saudi Arabia
Italy	Kuwait
Finland	Trucial States
Sweden	Oman
Denmark	Qatar
South Africa	Indonesia
South Korea	
Australia	
Japan	Account for 75 percent
India	of production and 85
Singapore	percent of exports
Philippines	

Account for 74 percent
of demand and 85 percent of imports

211

b. <u>For oil-consuming states</u>:

$$\text{Dependence}_{ji} = \frac{\text{Oil Imports}_{ji}}{\text{Total Oil Consumption of } j}$$

where "i" is an oil-producing state and "j" is an oil-consuming state

These two formulas are relatively simple ways of conceiving of dependence for producing and consuming states. The dependence score is really a percentage of oil exports or imports for one state of its total oil production or consumption. There are many ways in which this measure could have been formulated, but the one we have used is sufficient to demonstrate the general use that could be made of generating a measure of dependence on oil.

We apply these formulas to determine the dependence of each PEC on each PIC and also of each PIC on each PEC for every year between 1964 and 1970. However, our concern is not with this rather simple measure of dependence but with the degree to which any producer or consumer was dependent upon a few, rather than many, other states. This formulation is based on our assumption, stated above, that the more concentrated a state's dependence on other states, the more likely it will be vulnerable to separate deals with the other bloc. As stated above, we are assuming that if an oil-producing state has most of its exports going to a few consuming states, it will be less committed to a cohesive bloc of all producers. Similarly, the more concentrated a consuming state's source of oil, the less willing it would be to form a strong consuming bloc.

To measure the degree to which each state's oil dependence is concentrated, we calculate what is called a "Gini index." This index is frequently used by social scientists to measure concentration or equality in the distribution of some quantity. The Gini index is calculated in such a way that if one state (say, a PEC country) shipped equal amounts of oil to all PIC countries it would have a Gini index of zero. If a state shipped oil exclusively to only one other state, it would have a Gini score of 1.0. The Gini index is expressed as a decimal fraction; the closer the number is to 1.0, the more concentrated the state's oil dependence on other states.

Table 7.1 presents the scores for each of the 34 countries for the period 1964-70. It shows that in general the PEC bloc has more heavily concentrated trade in oil

TABLE 7.1

Gini Index as a Measure of Concentration of Dependence of PEC States on PIC States for Sales and of PIC States on PEC States for Imports

	1964	1965	1966	1967	1968	1969	1970
Producers (PEC)							
Venezuela	0.86	0.79	0.77	0.76	0.74	0.72	0.76
Iran	0.74	0.81	0.71	0.75	0.74	0.73	0.78
Iraq	0.82	0.71	0.68	0.75	0.75	0.79	0.89
Kuwait	0.77	0.74	0.77	0.71	0.67	0.68	0.69
Qatar	0.83	0.76	0.84	0.73	0.76	0.80	0.79
Saudi Arabia	0.75	0.68	0.65	0.65	0.64	0.68	0.70
Trucial States	0.82	0.82	0.80	0.76	0.72	0.75	0.70
United Arab Republic	0.86	0.90	0.94	0.89	0.83	0.82	0.70
Indonesia	0.95	0.92	0.90	0.92	0.89	0.92	0.94
Algeria	0.88	0.90	0.89	0.90	0.82	0.89	0.88
Libya	0.84	0.84	0.79	0.76	0.77	0.76	0.77
Nigeria	0.91	0.88	0.84	0.75	0.73	0.66	0.70
Average Gini scores	0.84	0.81	0.80	0.78	0.75	0.77	0.77
Consumers (PIC)							
United States	0.65	0.70	0.72	0.75	0.69	0.66	0.67
United Kingdom	0.53	0.57	0.54	0.59	0.61	0.61	0.61
Belgium	0.74	0.75	0.72	0.80	0.53	0.58	0.55
Denmark	0.76	0.71	0.65	0.62	0.60	0.70	0.63
France	0.63	0.59	0.58	0.61	0.55	0.58	0.58
West Germany	0.54	0.74	0.65	0.55	0.65	0.64	0.64
Italy	0.67	0.68	0.66	0.62	0.60	0.60	0.61
Netherlands	0.61	0.59	0.61	0.59	0.64	0.60	0.75
Sweden	0.79	0.77	0.70	0.49	0.60	0.61	0.62
Canada	0.75	0.83	0.79	0.85	0.86	0.79	0.80
Japan	0.75	0.70	0.71	0.70	0.75	0.76	0.76
Finland	0.90	0.90*	0.89	0.91	0.91	0.87	0.88
Spain	0.69	0.70*	0.71	0.67	0.65	0.62	0.55
Brazil	0.75	0.75	0.70	0.72	0.71	0.64	0.63*
South Korea	0.95*	0.93	0.89	0.84	0.87	0.84	0.82
Singapore	0.91	0.90*	0.90*	0.89	0.89	0.89	0.88
Average Gini scores	0.73	0.74	0.71	0.70	0.73	0.69	0.69

*Estimated by linear trend projection.

than has the PIC group. By itself this would indicate a greater dependence, and therefore vulnerability, of the PEC as opposed to the PIC. However, over time the Gini scores for both groups have declined, indicating that transactions in oil are becoming more evenly distributed for both blocs. It is also noteworthy that the difference between the two groups has been declining over time. That is, the PEC group is evening out its oil trade more rapidly than is the PIC group.

An additional dimension of each country in calculating bloc cohesion is the degree of oil trade concentration exhibited by each state's principal trading partner. This dimension is suggested by the original assumptions underlying our calculations and described above. In terms of principal trading partner, we will assume that the larger the percentage of dependence of a state on its principal trading partner, the more likely that state is to depart from the policies of its own bloc. To measure that dimension, we have employed the Gini index calculations described above along with analytical symbols from graph theory.

Consider Figure 7.6, which indicates that in 1964 the principal trading partner of the United States was Venezuela and the United States had an overall Gini score of .65. Figure 7.7 provides additional information by showing that in the same year Venezuela's principal trading partner was the United States and that Venezuela's overall Gini score was .86. The two states appear with arrows pointing to each other and enclosed in a box.

Figure 7.8 takes Figure 7.7 and adds three states (Indonesia, Qatar, and Saudi Arabia) in a semiclosed box. This structure indicates that these three states also had the United States as their principal trading partner, and indicates that their Gini concentration scores are .95, .83, and .75, respectively. Figure 7.8 also shows that Saudi Arabia is the principal supplier for India and Spain. To review the meaning of the symbols we have employed, a closed box [＿＿＿＿] indicates that the two states enclosed are principal trading partners in oil for each other. A semiclosed box [＿　＿] indicates that those in the box all share the same principal trading partner in oil. Arrows are used to indicate that the state from which the arrow originates is the principal oil trading partner for the state or states toward which the arrow is directed. Finally, the score beside the state is the Gini score of oil trade concentration for that state.

FIGURE 7.6

Display of U.S. Dependence on Venezuela for 1964

VEN ————————▶ US (.65)

FIGURE 7.7

Display of United States and Venezuela as Each Other's Principal Trading Partner for 1964

(.86) VEN ⇄ US (.65)

FIGURE 7.8

Partial Model of 1964 Trading Patterns in Oil

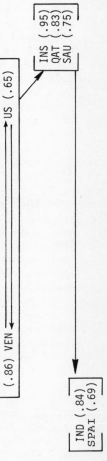

PRODUCERS

CONSUMERS

INS (.95)
QAT (.83)
SAU (.75)

(.86) VEN ⇄ US (.65)

IND (.84)
SPAI (.69)

215

With these definitions in mind, it is now possible to understand the entire graph representation for 1964 that is presented in Figure 7.9. The figure shows that in addition to Venezuela and the United States, Iraq and the United Kingdom were also principal trading partners of each other. The Gini scores can be interpreted to show degree of dependence on a particular trading partner. For example, the respective scores for Venezuela (.86) and the United States (.65) show that Venezuela more heavily concentrated its oil trade on the United States than the United States did on Venezuela. Other things being equal, we interpret this to mean that it would have been more difficult for Venezuela to alter its oil trade than it would have been for the United States to alter its oil trade in 1964. This sort of imbalance is even more noticeable in the case of the United Kingdom and Kuwait. To begin with, Kuwait had a higher Gini score than that of the United Kingdom (.77 compared with .53). In addition, there are five other states bracketed with Kuwait, which means that all five states looked to the United Kingdom as their principal market for oil. Hence, Kuwait was much more vulnerable than the United Kingdom in 1964.

Once these charts are formulated, it is possible to make comparisons across years to examine changes in trading patterns and, if our assumptions are correct, to discern the degree to which there are observable changes in the cohesion of either bloc. Because visual inspection of each of these charts from 1964 to 1970 would be difficult, it is necessary to dimensionalize the charts with a quantitative index. This can be done by combining the relative Gini scores and the number of other states that share the same chief trading partner into a single index of what might be termed "Resistance to Pressure" (RP) from the other bloc. The higher the RP for each state, the more difficult and more costly it would be for members of the other bloc to put pressure on that state by diverting oil trade. And the average RP for each bloc indicates the general RP that each bloc has relative to the other.

The RP index is computed by dividing the given state's Gini score into the Gini score of the state on which it is most dependent. This fraction is then multiplied by the proportion of other members of its bloc that do not share the same relationship with that principal trade partner. For Venezuela in 1964 this figure is .86 (Venezuela's Gini) divided into .65 (the United States' Gini) for a score of .76. Since all the other PEC countries are in different subgroupings, Venezuela's RP is .76. Kuwait's

FIGURE 7.9

Graphic Model of 1964 Global Oil-Trading Patterns

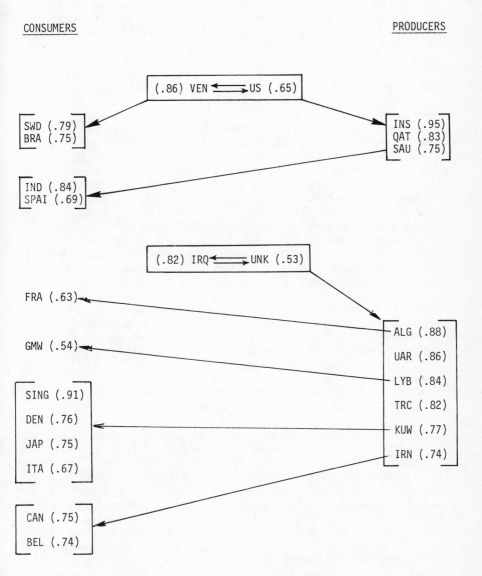

RP is found by first dividing .77 into .53, giving a score of .69. This number is then multiplied by the fraction of the PEC group not bracketed with Kuwait (.5). Kuwait's RP score is thus .35. The scores for all PIC and PEC states are computed in the same fashion and reported in Table 7.2.

This calculation makes even clearer than the Gini indexes alone the extent to which the potential bargaining strength of the two blocs has changed over time. In 1964 the PIC group had much higher RP scores than the PEC group, indicating that in the event of actual or potential disruption of oil flows, the estimated costs would be much greater for the PEC group. Over time, however, this one-sided relationship has markedly changed. While the scores of the PIC group have remained about the same, the PEC scores have greatly increased, indicating that the costs to the importers of substituting an exporter for bargaining or other reasons has greatly increased.

To illustrate how the graph model discussed above is related to the RP score, we have presented in Figure 7.10 the model for 1970. Comparing Figure 7.10 to Figure 7.9, we can see what the change in the RP score for the PEC states from .44 to .83 means graphically. The critical factor is that, in contrast to 1964, when each of the PEC countries had either the United States or the United Kingdom as its principal trading partner and therefore competed with one another, in 1970 only Indonesia and Saudi Arabia shared the same principal trading partner. As with the comparison of the RP averages for the two blocs, a comparison of the two figures illustrates that the PEC countries have become less open to pressure from the PIC states.

Cohesion Associated with Nonoil
Trade Patterns

In measuring the relative importance of trade in products other than petroleum, we were faced with somewhat different problems of measurement. Unlike oil flows, which are almost exclusively from one bloc to the other, trade is, at least potentially, a measure of both within- and between-bloc ties for each state under study. A further complication is that the magnitude of trade varies from one country to another largely as a function of size and level of development. The way in which we dealt with these problems was to create a single index indicating the extent to which trade led to within-bloc cohesion or cross-bloc pressure for each country under study. This index was

TABLE 7.2

Resistance-to-Pressure Scores for PEC and PIC States,
1964-70

	1964	1965	1966	1967	1968	1969	1970
Producers (PEC)							
Venezuela	0.76	0.89	0.94	0.97	0.93	1.10	0.95
Qatar	0.62	0.78	0.86	1.02	0.76	0.70	0.77
Indonesia	0.55	0.67	0.74	0.71	0.70	0.58	0.72
Saudi Arabia	0.69	1.20	0.89	0.69	0.85	0.76	0.96
Iraq	0.65	0.85	0.85	0.99	0.67	0.81	0.69
Kuwait	0.35	0.91	0.58	0.87	0.75	0.91	0.88
Trucial States	0.32	0.82	0.60	0.72	0.87	0.68	--
United Arab Re-							
public	0.31	--	0.65	0.80	0.83	0.72	0.87
Libya	0.32	0.80	0.64	0.72	0.84	0.84	0.75
Iran	0.36	0.93	0.93	1.10	1.23	1.04	0.97
Algeria	0.30	0.65	0.65	0.82	0.91	0.67	0.66
Nigeria	--	0.69	--	--	--	--	--
Average	0.44	0.83	0.83	1.00	0.78	0.84	0.82
Consumers (PIC)							
United States	1.32	1.13	1.07	0.95	1.07	0.91	1.19
Brazil	1.06	0.90	1.20	0.92	0.97	1.11	--
Sweden	1.00	0.88	1.13	1.36	1.15	1.09	1.13
India	0.82	0.93	--	0.78	--	--	--
Spain	1.15	--	--	1.13	1.06	1.07	--
Denmark	0.69	0.83	0.93	0.93	0.99	0.90	1.11
Italy	0.85	1.10	1.11	1.44	1.42	1.15	1.13
Japan	0.76	0.76	1.00	0.75	0.99	0.78	1.03
Singapore	0.62	--	--	0.65	0.67	0.80	--
West Germany	1.50	1.08	1.18	1.00	1.26	1.19	1.08
Belgium	0.92	1.00	0.99	0.94	1.30	1.15	--
Canada	0.91	0.82	0.97	0.84	0.80	0.91	1.05
France	1.40	1.54	1.17	1.46	1.35	1.24	1.52
United Kingdom	1.55	0.99	1.22	1.11	1.10	1.31	1.13
Netherlands	--	1.02	1.11	0.98	0.93	1.11	1.19
Philippines	--	1.04	1.05	--	--	0.86	--
South Korea	--	0.81	0.99	0.78	--	0.76	--
Australia	--	--	--	--	0.80	--	--
Finland	--	--	0.87	0.67	0.76	0.77	--
Average	1.04	0.99	1.07	0.98	1.04	1.01	1.04

FIGURE 7.10

Graphic Model of 1970 Global Oil-Trading Patterns

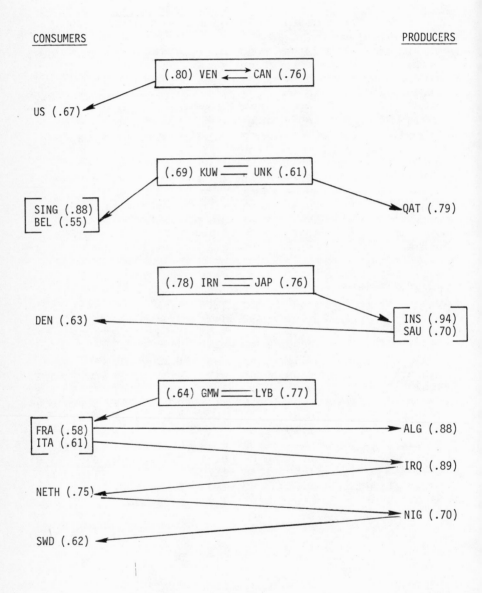

constructed by creating a ratio of the number of each
state's trading partners within its own bloc to the number
of its trading partners in the other bloc.

The logic behind this calculation is the assumption
that the more a state trades with members of a given bloc,
the greater the probability that that state will be open
to pressures from that bloc. We could have carried out a
set of calculations similar to the ones described in the
preceding section on oil trade patterns determining dependence. However, we chose number of trading partners to
illustrate how a simpler form of calculation could be employed. This index of relative bloc solidarity stemming
from trade contacts was constructed by taking the number
of trading partners within each bloc (PIC or PEC) for a
given country, and dividing that by the number of trading
partners for the country in the opposite bloc. Thus, the
United States in 1964 traded with 18 PIC countries and 12
PEC countries, for a ratio of 1.50, as shown in Table 7.3.
For both PEC and PIC in Table 7.3, the larger the ratio,
the greater the relative number of trading partners the
state has within its own trading group.

As would be expected, the PIC trade is much more
strongly turned inward than the PEC trade. Although the
exigencies of natural resource location forces the PIC
group to deal with the PEC for purposes of obtaining petroleum, this same relationship does not carry over into nonoil trade. The PEC group, on the other hand, tends to
deal with the PIC even on nonoil matters more than with
its own group. Insofar as trade is a valid indicator,
this is one measure that suggests a possible weakness of
the oil-producing group. There is relatively little within-
bloc PEC trade, certainly not as much as within the PIC
group. Table 7.3 also shows that although some individual
countries do change their ratio from one year to the next,
the bloc averages remain quite constant.

Cohesion Among States Associated
with Agreement on Nonoil
Political Issues

The first two procedures for transforming quantitative
data into measures of PIC and PEC cohesion dealt with economic data and involved a variety of analytic techniques
that are commonly used for such purposes. In this and the
following section, we will deal with variables used to measure the activities of states on political issues. Such

221

TABLE 7.3

Ratio of Within-Bloc to Between-Bloc Trading Patterns of PEC and PIC States, 1964-70

	1964	1965	1966	1967	1968	1969	1970
Producers (PEC)							
Venezuela	.11	.11	.05	.16	.13	.18	.20
Iran	.35	.37	.35	.35	.45	.44	.39
Iraq	.41	.39	.41	.35	.35	.44	.41
Kuwait	.12	.12	.19	.25	.24	.24	.18
Oman	.20	.17	.17	.20	.22	.33	.11
Saudi Arabia	.13	.13	.13	.17	.17	.22	.17
Trucial States	.33	.25	.25	.33	.20	.60	.20
United Arab Republic	.38	.33	.44	.44	.33	.62	.47
Indonesia	.12	.12	.12	.12	.06	.17	.12
Algeria	.29	.31	.21	.13	.13	.23	.23
Libya	.18	.20	.17	.45	.17	.08	.07
Nigeria	.27	.18	.24	.24	.11	.27	.13
Average	.24	.22	.23	.28	.21	.32	.22
Consumers (PIC)							
United States	1.50	1.50	1.58	1.58	1.58	1.58	1.58
United Kingdom	1.28	1.28	1.36	1.36	1.36	1.36	1.36
Belgium	1.38	1.38	1.46	1.46	1.46	1.46	1.46
Denmark	1.42	1.42	1.50	1.46	1.58	1.58	1.58
France	1.29	1.38	1.38	1.38	1.46	1.46	1.46
West Germany	1.38	1.38	1.38	1.38	1.46	1.46	1.46
Italy	1.38	1.38	1.46	1.38	1.46	1.46	1.46
Netherlands	1.38	1.38	1.46	1.46	1.46	1.46	1.46
Sweden	1.38	1.50	1.38	1.36	1.36	1.36	1.36
Canada	1.50	1.38	1.38	1.46	1.46	1.38	1.38
Japan	1.38	1.38	1.46	1.46	1.46	1.46	1.46
Finland	2.57	2.43	2.43	1.64	1.64	1.55	1.55
Spain	1.54	1.54	1.64	1.80	1.64	1.64	1.73
Australia	1.50	1.38	1.46	1.46	1.36	1.46	1.46
South Africa	16.00	15.00	16.00	15.00	15.00	16.00	16.00
Brazil	3.75	2.29	2.12	3.00	2.11	2.25	3.00
India	1.33	1.31	1.23	1.46	1.38	1.58	1.46
South Korea	7.00	7.50	5.00	8.50	8.00	8.00	3.75
Philippines	4.00	7.50	5.66	6.30	6.00	6.00	9.50
Average	2.79	2.86	2.70	2.89	2.80	2.87	2.87

activities are infrequently measured in quantitative terms. Therefore, the data sources become almost as important as the data transformation procedures.

The source for measuring national agreement and disagreement within and between the PIC and PEC blocs on nonoil issues is roll call voting in the UN General Assembly. While scholars have used such votes for similar purposes, there have been few policy-making uses of this technique.* The argument that the votes do not represent the true positions of the states should be raised at this point. Such an argument is frequently made by individuals knowledgeable in international relations, scholars and practitioners alike. While we would agree that in any given vote, there are likely to be random reasons for a given state voting a given way, we believe that when one looks at a large number of votes, the random factors should balance themselves out. Consequently, we have selected the entire set of roll calls in each General Assembly.

We are interested in such patterns of agreement and disagreement because it is a well-accepted characteristic of all political coalitions that basic relationships between two or more actors are based on their agreement or disagreement on the outstanding questions between them. This is particularly true as the interdependencies between states increase, since every facet of the social, economic, and political relationship between any two states in the modern world will create differences over policy outcomes.

Hence, under most conditions, any two states will have areas of agreement and disagreement. However, we also know that as conflict between two blocs of actors increases, there is a tendency for agreement to be higher across all issues within the bloc and for disagreement to be higher across all issues between members of different blocs. For our measure of bloc cohesion, we are interested in determining the level of agreement of states with other states within their own bloc and between their specific blocs. Without at present raising the question of whether high intrabloc agreement across all issues is a consequence of agreement on oil issues or whether the general agreements lead to a stronger coalition on oil issues, we will assume that as intrabloc issue agreement goes up, there is greater intrabloc cohesion.

---

*By using this broad range of issues, we hope to get an index of agreement in UN voting on nonoil issues that shows the general patterns of agreement and disagreement within and between the PEC and PIC blocs.

To measure the degree of agreement within and between the two blocs, we apply the analysis of a computer program called PROVOTE to roll call votes in the UN General Assembly. The program contains transformation procedures to generate a set of agreement scores between states and blocs of states. We will describe it briefly.

The PROVOTE program analyzes voting agreements by weighting them in accordance with how sharply divided an assembly is on each roll call. It calculates the number of voting agreements between each pair of voters, and between any specified blocs of members, which in this study we have identified as the oil-producing states on the one hand and the oil-consuming states on the other hand. Agreements are weighted so that if two states agree as part of a very large majority, their agreement counts less than if they agree as part of a small minority.

We have analyzed the votes on all issues in the General Assembly each year. Obviously, some of the issues voted on are much more important than others, for the PIC and PEC groups. However, in the absence of information about the relative importance of issues, we feel that a general voting agreement provides a general picture of the within- and between-group agreement. Table 7.4 shows these scores for each UN member that is either a principal oil producer or oil consumer. It shows, once again, a generally sharp distinction between the two groups. (In Table 7.4 the negative scores are the percentage of agreements less than the average agreement between all members in that voting body. Positive scores are agreement percentages in excess of the average level of agreement.)

Table 7.4 shows that all major producers except Venezuela are rather sharply in agreement with one another and in sharper disagreement with the PIC. The figure also shows that the PIC group has declined in its general agreement level, while the PEC group has slightly increased its general agreement on issues.

Bloc Cohesion Concerned with
Oil Issues

In measuring the implications of political issues with respect to oil questions for the cohesion of either bloc, we did not have available a data set similar to the roll call votes in the United Nations. Voting records in OPEC are not publicly available and there is no record of any intergovernmental organization's attention to oil is-

TABLE 7.4

Agreement Scores with PEC and PIC Bloc, 1965-70

	1965		1966		1967		1968		1969		1970	
	PIC	PEC	PIC	PEC	PIC	PEC	PIC	PEC	PIC	PEC	PIC	PEC
Producers (PEC)												
Iran	-.11	.12	-.13	.22	-.33	.31	-.17	.20	-.18	.30	-.07	.22
Venezuela	.09	.0	.11	-.16	-.10	.20	-.10	.10	-.11	.12	.05	.07
Saudi Arabia	-.31	.32	-.28	.26	-.39	.47	-.12	.28	-.23	.40	-.39	.24
Libya	-.24	.33	-.27	.31	-.37	.43	-.17	.33	-.27	.45	-.31	.36
Iraq	-.35	.37	-.30	.28	-.41	.44	-.36	.30	-.34	.38	-.40	.33
Indonesia	-.12	.30	-.28	.30	-.38	.40	-.11	.33	-.30	.39	-.18	.31
Egypt	-.37	.26	-.28	.29	-.38	.44	-.26	.32	-.32	.43	-.32	.36
Kuwait	-.24	.33	-.22	.22	-.50	.46	-.14	.30	-.31	.40	.29	.10
Nigeria	-.26	.31	-.23	.28	-.35	.37	-.13	.23	-.19	.33	-.37	.31
Algeria	-.39	.25	-.33	.26	-.46	.41	-.30	.30	-.34	.41	-.35	.28
Singapore	-.32	.27	.02	.26	-.33	.21	-.20	.16	-.17	.11	-.40	.30
Average	-.19	.14	.03	.13	-.31	.26	-.19	.15	-.23	.24	-.25	.19
Consumers (PIC)												
Australia	.26	-.25	.19	-.20	.17	-.55	.21	-.33	.18	-.41	.17	-.44
Brazil	.20	-.09	.08	-.03	-.05	-.07	-.07	-.10	.01	-.17	.07	-.25
India	-.18	.21	-.25	.23	-.42	.28	-.21	.26	-.22	.31	-.21	.26
Denmark	.32	-.24	.23	-.16	.17	-.48	.26	-.15	.24	-.30	.26	-.23
Finland	.21	-.21	.11	-.38	.08	-.45	.16	-.15	.09	0.24	.15	-.29
United States	.25	-.33	.13	-.11	.20	-.56	.19	-.40	.15	-.38	.11	-.47
Japan	.20	-.11	.06	-.47	.05	-.27	.21	-.21	.16	-.20	.16	-.16
United Kingdom	.16	-.35	.06	-.45	.16	-.54	.21	-.36	.17	-.37	.06	-.48
France	.06	-.37	.0	-.27	.02	-.47	.0	-.31	.02	-.45	.08	-.45
Italy	.34	-.29	.20	-.22	.15	-.44	.28	-.34	.19	-.34	.24	-.38
Canada	.35	-.24	.21	-.25	.21	-.44	.20	-.11	.21	-.33	.24	-.31
Netherlands	.35	-.30	.20	-.17	.21	-.45	.30	-.31	.27	-.34	.21	-.32
Sweden	.31	-.24	.20	-.22	.15	-.49	.25	-.19	.22	-.25	.22	-.24
Belgium	.32	-.32	.21	-.22	.27	-.45	.30	-.35	.27	-.33	.25	-.37
Luxembourg	.36	-.30	.26	-.09	.25	-.45	.30	-.35	.33	-.37	.26	-.36
Spain	.06	-.14	.06	.63	-.06	.14	-.07	-.08	-.11	.04	.10	-.06
South Africa	.17	-.57	.21	.11	-.15	-.60	.03	-.44	-.15	-.57	-.31	-.63
Philippines	.04	.16	.01	.13	-.08	.18	-.02	.20	-.04	.17	.02	-.11
Average	.15	-.19	-.19	.13	.01	-.31	.08	-.19	.06	-.23	.08	-.25

sues that could be used as a data set. Consequently, we
decided to apply procedures that have been developed in
other areas of the study of international relations, the
coding of events data from public sources. We decided to
code data on the number and type of actions taken by oil-
producing states with respect to oil companies. Most of
global oil issues are manifest at least in part by relations
between the oil-producing states and the companies operating within those states. Consequently, we systematically
coded from the Middle East Journal and from Deadline Data
the actions taken from 1964 through 1970 by the major PEC.
Since our purpose was to illustrate the possible utility
and the general feasibility of this particular source of
data, we did not use the extensive set of data sources that
would be available to the INR analyst. However, we believe
that our procedures and data sources were sufficient for
the minimum purposes we hoped to accomplish.

The data collected is summarized in Table 7.5. By
looking down the columns, we can see the countries that are
most active; by looking across the rows, we can see the
patterns of activity over years. Each act counted was
classified as to whether the act constituted a bilateral
agreement between a PEC and an oil company (A) or was a
unilateral act by a PEC (U); it was also classified as to
whether the issue involved was a question of revenue (R)
to the exporting country or ownership (O) of the company
operations.

Some interesting descriptive patterns emerge from the
data. First, while there were twice as many instances of
agreements as there were unilateral actions of the PEC,
there was an even division of activity between revenue and
ownership issues. Second, there were clear differences in
the patterns of PEC actions. Algeria, Libya, and Iran
were much more generally active than the other states. Algeria, Indonesia, and Iraq had more instances of unilateral
acts than acts involving agreements with the oil companies.
Finally, the patterns over time show a cyclical pattern
with frequencies of acts at a peak in 1967 and 1970, and at
low points in 1964, 1965, and 1969.

Several types of analysis could be performed on this
data to test generalizations about bargaining patterns between PIC and PEC. Time series analysis employing a variety of statistical techniques (as outlined in the case
study, "Predicting Violence in the Middle East") could be
undertaken to see if there are escalatory patterns. Alter-
natively, Markov chain process analyses could be carried
out (similar to those performed in the case study, "Ex-

TABLE 7.5

Actions of Oil-Producing States Toward Oil Companies, 1964-70

Country	1964 A	U	R	O	1965 A	U	R	O	1966 A	U	R	O	1967 A	U	R	O	1968 A	U	R	O	1969 A	U	R	O	1970 A	U	R	O	TOTAL A	U	R	O
Algeria	1	1			1		1				1	1		4	1	3	2	1	1	1	1		1	1	3	4	2	5	7	10	7	11
Indonesia						2		2									1			1									1	2	0	3
Iran	1	1	1	1					2		2		1	1	1	1	1		1		2		1	1	5		5		11	1	10	2
Iraq	1			1	1			1	1				1	1	1	1										1	1		2	4	4	2
Kuwait	1			1									3		3														4	0	3	1
Libya	1			1						3			2	3	3	2	1	2	1	2			1		5	4	9		13	9	14	8
Nigeria														1	1										2		2		2	1	3	0
Qatar	1			1					3			3	2			2					2			2					8	0	0	8
Saudi Arabia	1		1	1	1			1	3		2	1	1			1													6	0	3	3
U.A.R.		1	1	1	1			1	2	2		4	1			1													4	3	0	7
Venezuela															1										1	1	1	1	2	1	2	1
Total	7	2	3	6	6	3	2	7	10	4	6	8	11	9	10	10	5	3	3	5	5	1	2	4	16	10	20	6	61	31	46	46

Legend: A--Agreement   U--Unilateral Action   R--Revenue Change   O--Ownership Change

plaining Military Expenditures in Latin America") to determine whether there were discernible patterns of action by
the PEC over time. In addition to statistical analysis on
the events data set alone, we could determine whether there
were correlations between frequency and type of acts and
the measures developed on transaction data and UN voting.
These techniques were demonstrated in the case studies on
instability in black Africa and arms expenditures in Latin
America.

Conclusion

We have briefly identified data collection and analysis procedures that might be of use to the INR analyst in
discussing the bargaining behavior of states in the global
oil issue area. There are many ways in which the indexes
developed above could be used. They include descriptive
presentations of time series trends or cross-sectional
patterns (comparing oil-producing and oil-consuming states
at a given point in time) to buttress assumptions concerning increasing or decreasing strengths of either bloc.
The procedures described above are necessarily tentative;
thorough investigations into the implications of different
aggregating techniques would be required before they could
be used for analytical purposes. However, as we noted in
the first section of this chapter, INR analysts already
make some limited use of quantitative measures to support
their arguments about PEC bargaining behavior. By using
more sophisticated measures, they may be able to increase
the explanatory and predictive power of their analyses.
In the closing section, we will discuss the costs of developing such indicators. For now, it should be recognized
that there are many ways not only of attaching more meaning to the quantitative data now being used, but also of
adding other sources of quantitative data to INR analyses.

NONVERBAL REPRESENTATIONS OF THEORIES

Some scholars and practitioners argue that the former
deal in "theory" and the latter deal in "facts." However,
the truth of the matter is that both roles require theory.
The difference is that the scholar's theory is usually
more explicit, more aggregated, and less concrete than
the practitioner's theory. In any case, foreign affairs
analysts repeatedly make assertions about relationships

228

between concepts (frequently referred to as "factors") in offering explanations and predictions as part of their reports. In this section, we would like to demonstrate how assumptions or theories about the dynamics of global oil politics can be represented in a form that is less cumbersome and, therefore, easier to use and understand.

In this section, we will not be concerned with measurement and data collection. Those problems were explored in the preceding section of this chapter and in other case studies in this book. Our purpose is to show the use of nonverbal symbols for the kinds of theoretical viewpoints expressed by foreign affairs analysts concerning global oil politics.

It might be useful to begin this discussion by pointing out that even if reliable data on all of the factors considered to be important in global oil politics was available, we would not be able to use typical correlational procedures that we have described in other case studies. This is so because of the highly complex and interconnected nature of global oil politics. We need only mention two aspects of global oil politics that make standard correlational techniques either inappropriate or virtually impossible to use. The first is the nonlinear nature of the relationship between factors. In analyzing the relationship between nonoil issue agreement and PEC solidarity, for example, it is probably misleading to look for a constant coefficient that suggests the correlation between the two. It is probably the case that changes in issue agreement have no impact upon PEC bloc solidarity as long as the changes are within moderate ranges. But if, on the one hand, agreement becomes high enough to pass an upper threshold (as, for example, occurred during the 1967 June War) then this will have a major impact upon solidarity concerning oil questions. If, on the other hand, issue agreement falls below a threshold, this may have deleterious effects on PEC cohesion.

A second aspect of global oil politics that precludes the efficient use of correlational techniques is the presence of complex patterns of "feedback" among the factors of the system. To take the preceding example, we suppose not only that issue agreement affects PEC solidarity on oil questions but also that bloc solidarity will possibly alter agreement or disagreement on nonoil issues.

One useful analytical technique that can be employed to help clarify such complex assumptions about the relationships between variables is the development of simulation models. A simulation model can incorporate nonlinear relationships, threshold affects, feedback among variables, and whatever other complex relationships one believes might exist between components of the system. These relationships can be programmed, starting values can be entered for each component (such as issue agreement, oil transactions, and other components) and the program will produce results. The analyst can then alter starting values or estimated relationships between variables and compare the altered results with the earlier runs. In this way it is possible to estimate the effects of alternative policies within a given system, and also to see what impact upon the system will be produced if stipulated changes occur.

Hence, even if there were no data collection and measurement problems, the tasks of building and testing theory about the relationship among factors would make the development of a tested model for reliable forecasting purposes extremely difficult. Without such development, however, it is still possible to apply more formal procedures to articulating theories not only to help improve the INR analysts' predictive ability but also to increase his capacity to express his ideas to policy makers. To illustrate what we have in mind, we have employed some nonverbal symbols in articulating the theoretical ideas now found in discussions of global oil politics.

Let us start by taking some of the INR analysts' statements found in Figure 7.2 and supply symbolic representations. To begin, the statement "the tight oil market has enhanced the leverage of the Gulf states" can be represented as:

$$\frac{\text{Oil Demand}}{\text{Oil Supply}} \xrightarrow{\quad + \quad} \frac{\text{Power of PEC}}{\text{Power of PIC}}$$

Because the statement does not indicate the target of the leverage we have included control over both blocs' bargaining power in the representation. Another representation can be made of the following statement: "Whether a supply crisis would lead consumer countries to form a united front vis-à-vis the producing countries is not clear and is probably not a choice that will have to be made in the near future." This idea can be represented in the following manner:

$$\text{If } \frac{\text{Oil Demand}}{\text{Oil Supply}} \longrightarrow \begin{array}{c}\text{crisis}\\ \text{threshold}\\ \text{level}\end{array} \xrightarrow{\quad + \quad} \begin{array}{c}\text{Cohesion}\\ \text{of PIC}\end{array}$$

One more example is, "general opposition to U.S. foreign policy may affect oil policy pursued by Arab producing states." This can be represented as:

Nonoil   Cohesion Among
Issue   ⟶ +   Arab States on
Agreement   Oil Issues

While these quotations can be adequately represented in nonverbal symbols, it is unquestionably the case that isolated bivariate presentations fail to deal with the rich complexity of the global oil political system. To deal with this problem we adapted procedures developed for modeling physical systems and applied to a variety of social, economic, and political contexts, often called "dynamic modeling." The basic idea behind the procedure is to model feedback relationships between a set of variables. Figure 7.11 presents a series of assumptions about interrelationships among variables relevant to the coalition strength of the two blocs. The chart can be interpreted by assuming that each "+" denotes a positive relationship in the direction of the arrow, and each "-" a negative relationship. For purposes of simplification, we have omitted symbols indicating nonlinear or threshold relationship between variables. We have also left out coefficients of the degree of change.

The factors with the arrow indicate what are usually termed "exogenous" variables--that is, those factors outside the basic bargaining relationships between oil consumers and producers that have an impact on the relationships. To determine the effect of any one outside or exogenous factor, one can follow the arrows through the figure. For example, as perceived demand over supply for oil increases, PEC oil revenues go up. This, in turn, increases PIC cohesion and decreases PEC cohesion, leading to an eventual lessening of PEC revenues.

As with most feedback systems, the chief analytical problem arises from the fact that multiple external events can affect the within-system (or "endogenous") relationships. In this case, the bargaining relationship between the consumers and producers can be structurally altered by many different conditions. If, for example, intrabloc agreement for PIC went down, and perceived demand over supply increased, a major rise in oil revenue for PEC would take place. The equilibrium might be established some time later as the endogenous relationship between the two blocs balanced out. However, a substantial set

231

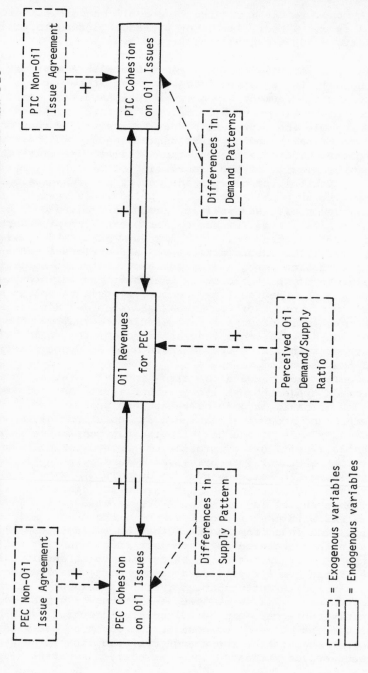

FIGURE 7.11

A Feedback System for Predicting Bargaining Outcomes Between PEC and PIC

$\begin{array}{l}\text{[ ]} = \text{Exogenous variables}\\ \square = \text{Endogenous variables}\end{array}$

of trends in the same direction could cause a system "blow-up" in which there would be no chance to reestablish the equilibrium.

Despite these remaining areas of uncertainty, we feel that a model like this can serve a useful analytical purpose even if it cannot be tested adequately with empirical data at the present time. Even in its present preliminary form it would serve to organize the kinds of theoretical questions that analysts must deal with. If such a model could be developed and shared among analysts, research findings and general arguments could be easily categorized in order to facilitate cumulative learning among analysts and communication between the policy making and academic communities.

To illustrate our point, we will discuss some general theoretical issues in the context of the model appearing in Figure 7.11. The first issue is whether the increased PIC commitment could counter PEC bargaining strength. In terms of the model, some argue that there is a high proba-bility of general equilibrium between PIC and PEC cohesion, resulting in a stabilization of prices based on the asser-tion that the oil companies are responsible for the absence of this equilibrium and for the rise in prices. The oil companies, in effect, depress the earning coefficient of the PIC states. This viewpoint could be expressed by re-moving the "+" sign between cohesion of states and PEC oil revenue. One might also place another variable, "activi-ties of oil companies," into the diagram with a positive arrow directed at "PEC Oil Revenues."

An opposing and widely held set of opinions on this question is that the most important relationship in the model is between the perceived demand/supply ratio and PEC oil revenues. Analysts maintaining this position tend either to see no clear pattern among any of the other vari-ables in the system or to posit critical threshold limits without specifying what those limits are for those varia-bles. In terms of the model they would remove all "+" signs and "-" signs in the system except for the "+" be-tween the demand/supply ratio and PEC revenues.

Of course the presentation of both of these positions is highly simplified and touches on only the surface of this policy argument. Nevertheless, showing how the two positions could be interpreted in terms of visual repre-sentation of the model can be useful for clarifying points of agreement and disagreement, and for ultimately leading to more cumulative research activity. If some such model were used as a medium of communication, separate research findings could be used to estimate the signs to be attached to arrows, the thresholds when such signs would apply, and also the magnitude of coefficients denoting the extent of expected change.

Moreover, debate over policy questions could be better organized and more fruitfully executed by using a heuristic model such as the one in Figure 7.11. For example, the question of the impact of an organization of petroleum-importing states would depend upon the magnitude and sign of the arrows between PEC and PIC cohesion (running through Oil Revenues for PEC). If those arrows and signs were con-sidered to be correct (as shown in Figure 7.11), the es-tablishment of an oil-importing organization could be viewed as raising the magnitude of the positive relation-ship between PEC revenues and PIC cohesion, and also the negative relationship between PIC cohesion and PEC revenues.

Another example might be the argument over whether the Middle East situation affects PEC cohesion and ulti-mately PEC revenues. We assume that PEC nonoil issue agree-ment usually goes up in years when there are Middle East flare-ups (recall that UN voting support among PEC was highest in 1967, the year of the Six-Day War). We might therefore conclude that actions resulting in such flare-ups ultimately lead to increases in prices. The theoretical question then becomes the magnitude of the degree to which PEC nonoil issue agreement is related to Middle East ques-tions and whether the sign between that factor and PEC co-hesion on oil issues is in fact as indicated in Figure 7.11.

In closing, we hope to have demonstrated how simple diagrams similar to that in Figure 7.11 can be used to represent complex theoretical ideas. If so, it can be of use to the foreign affairs analyst in sorting out the var-ious factors and relationships that he will need to esti-mate for explanation and forecasting purposes. As better and more complex measures are developed to test some of the relationships, models such as these could become more useful not only to the INR analyst in his attempt to dis-cover relationships among factors but also to the policy maker in forecasting political outcomes.

COSTS AND BENEFITS TO THE
INR ANALYST

In discussing the costs and benefits to the INR of the techniques described in this case study, we are faced with the dilemma that confronts any advocate of an under-

developed technology. Unlike most of the techniques described in other chapters, there is little firm record on
which to demonstrate how those techniques could be used to
improve the work of the INR analyst.

For the dynamic modeling techniques presented in this
case study, substantial development work is necessary before the INR can use the procedure in policy analysis.
Nevertheless, we believe that because the area of global
oil politics is so complex, quantitative techniques can
make a substantial, long-run contribution. As noted in
the other case studies, quantitative techniques can be
used to find common patterns across a wide variety of conditions. For example, our discussion in this case study
of the Relative Pressure index demonstrates the extent to
which quite sophisticated assumptions about the political
implications of economic patterns can be built into quantitative indexes. Using similar types of reasoning, quantitative techniques might be a major source of analytical
strength to the INR if sufficient developmental resources
are invested.

We will discuss the costs and benefits in terms of
(1) quantitative measures to aid the INR analyst in developing forecasts and (2) dynamic modeling to help bring order to competing ideas about the nature of global oil politics.

As far as quantitative measurement techniques go, we
feel that given the available quantitative data on oil and
nonoil transactions across national boundaries, a variety
of indicators that could shed light on political relationships should be developed. Such indicators could aid the
analyst in identifying trends in a policy realm where
short-range economic conditions affect political situations,
which in turn lead to longer-range economic conditions.
Measures such as Relative Pressure and the Gini score on
dependence patterns could help the analyst identify those
trends and help to improve their forecasts. Since the
data on such trends is available, the major resources required would be the time of the INR analyst and the efforts
of a computer programmer and statistician. Because a
great deal of exploratory work is necessary, however, the
use of outside consultants to develop political indicators
from economic data might be the most feasible course of
action. However, INR analysts in this area should be
closely involved in this work to make sure that the measures are useful and meaningful.

When we turn to data other than transactions, however,
we are faced with a serious deficiency in data. Except for

the computerized data on UN roll call votes, there are no
easily accessible measures of other kinds of national political positions. The kind of events data we have collected for demonstration purposes might be useful; the
costs for this procedure are relatively high, however.
Generally, we would repeat what we have suggested in the
case studies on European elections and Korean bargaining,
that is, that expert-generated data collected through questionnaires or through some system such as TAGS could be
used to gather data on the political positions of states
with respect to oil issues. However, to develop and utilize such systems would require substantial organizational
(although not financial) commitments. The costs of analysis would likewise be small in comparison with the costs of
collecting the data.

Turning from the use of quantitative indicators, we
should say a word about the use of nonverbal symbols for
theory explication. The style of the INR analyst is to
present a logical argument for a given interpretation, always allowing for sufficient qualifications to encompass
the latitude that is necessary in case the tentative conclusions prove wrong. The result is the long and sometimes
equivocal argument that characterizes much of the INR's
work.

Nonverbal symbols as those employed in Figure 7.11
can be used to express even highly complex theoretical arguments. If the INR analyst begins to use these nonverbal
symbols to deal with his own thoughts as well as to explore
the thoughts of others, we believe that he will be able
to distinguish between when he should and when he should
not equivocate. Ultimately, there may come a time when
the entire policy-making community will accept the presentation of competing arguments in the form of, for example,
whether a given sign should be a "+" or "-". But even in
the absence of such acceptance, the INR analyst will be
able to increase the cumulative nature of his own work by
developing a shared model with his colleagues in the policy-making structure as well as in the academic community.
This argument applies not just to global oil politics but
to all relatively self-contained areas of INR analysis.

To buttress the use of nonverbal symbols we might
point out the work of the economists. By agreeing upon a
set of critical variables and arguing about the exact relationship among those variables, economists have been able
to build models about economic processes that have aided
them substantially in advising governments. It is relatively easy to identify the points of contention among

economists because governmental and academic economists share the same basic concepts. This has come about only after years of development and substantial formalization of those concepts.

There is no question that models in such areas as global oil politics will be much more difficult to develop. However, from the vantage point of the history of the discipline of economics, that difficulty does not seem insurmountable. The data problems are much more severe and the lack of concerted cohesion among scholars is a serious roadblock. Nevertheless, if the economists were able to overcome their problems, political analysts should at least accept the challenge.

Even if these developments did not fully occur, however, we could still argue that presenting arguments about factors in global oil politics through nonverbal symbols similar to those in Figure 7.11 would lead to improved analysis. The INR analyst would find it less burdensome to classify competing interpretations, less difficult to communicate with government and academic colleagues, and ultimately less tiresome and confusing to present his research to various users. These benefits are relatively intangible. Their pertinence depends primarily on how the INR analyst feels about his work. Since their use will require little cost other than the willingness to spend small amounts of time developing somewhat formal models, the lack of concrete, direct, and immediate benefit should not be a substantial impediment.

RECOMMENDATIONS FOR THE USE OF QUANTITATIVE TECHNIQUES IN FOREIGN AFFAIRS ANALYSIS

8

EVALUATING THE USE OF QUANTITATIVE TECHNIQUES ON THE BASIS OF THE CASE STUDIES

Our aim in this part of the book is to present the conclusions we have reached as a result of our case studies, and to offer some recommendations based on these conclusions. The conclusions and recommendations focus on three of the general tasks performed by the INR analysts:

1. Information Gathering: Can quantitative techniques be employed to help the analyst gather and present reliable information on a more systematic and cost-effective basis?
2. Descriptive Analysis: Can quantitative techniques be employed to help the analyst assess the empirical validity of assumptions and hypotheses?
3. Forecasting: Can quantitative techniques be employed to help the analyst make precise and accurate forecasts?

Our discussion will focus on the twin questions of why we think quantitative techniques could help the analyst in his information gathering, descriptive analysis, and forecasting, and what we think ought to be done in the future to provide the opportunity for the analysis to apply quantitative techniques to those three tasks.

We will present evidence from the foregoing case studies on the utility of quantitative techniques to each of these tasks in turn. We will also point out where quantitative techniques were not able to improve on the methods of INR analysts.

INFORMATION GATHERING

The first advantage of quantitative techniques in the process of gathering information is that they tend to force clarity in the subject of analysis. Both the subject to be explained and the factors considered to be influential must be clearly defined before they can be measured, even if measurement entails only noting the absence or presence of a phenomenon.

This point is well illustrated by the case study on global oil politics (Chapter 7). INR analyses of the subject employ terms such as "cohesion," "unity," and "coalition." Without precise operational definitions of these terms, it is difficult to know whether they are talking about cohesion in terms of similar policy positions, unified bargaining procedures, collective action, or other types of unity. When the concept of cohesion was measured in the case study, it was necessary to specify exactly what was being referred to. Thus the case study talked of cohesion in terms of oil transfers, general trading relationships, agreement on nonoil issues, and coincidence of oil-related foreign policy acts. It is of course possible to conceive of other measures of cohesion. But it was at least clear in the study which of the meanings of cohesion were being used.

Further evidence for the advantage of quantitative techniques in terms of clarity was provided by the African case study (Chapter 2). One purpose of this analysis was to measure the phenomenon of political instability. In that study political instability was defined as: a condition affecting governments in which the established patterns of authority break down, and the expected compliance to the government is replaced by political violence. Given this definition of instability in terms of violence, it was then possible to measure the absence or presence of instability by recording the incidence of violence at the elite level (coups and plots) and at the communal level (civil war, rebellion, irredentism, and the ethnic violence). Again, there are many other conceivable, perhaps superior, ways of defining instability both quantitatively and qualitatively. But there is at least no doubt as to the meaning of political instability in this study.

A second advantage of quantitative techniques in the information-gathering task is that they facilitate the analysis of trends in a particular phenomenon. Using quantitative data displayed visually, the analyst can present a clear and concise picture of the course of a phenomenon over time.

This point is illustrated in several case studies, but perhaps most clearly in the Middle East case study (Chapter 6). In Figure 6.3 of that study, for example, the amount of violence between Israel and the Arab states, expressed in quantitative terms, is plotted for the period of January 1965 through December 1969. The reader can see at a glance when interactions became violent and when they were peaceful. The same information verbally presented would occupy several paragraphs.

The procedure used to gather information in the Middle East case study was content analysis. This technique, widely used by social scientists, requires a coding system that systematically identifies the frequencies of specified statements or actions in a set of documents. Content analysis coding schemes are frequently applied to newspapers and other public sources. These techniques can also be applied to cables and other government documents.

A system of collecting information over time and portraying trends could be implemented in a number of ways using existing procedures for collecting and disseminating information in the State Department. For example, the system of Traffic Analysis by Geography and Subject (TAGS), which uses classifications made by the sender of a cable, is one of the information sources that could be used for systematic monitoring and reporting of the frequencies of violent acts or other severe conflict between states. A computer-managed system, such as that described in the Middle East case study, could regularly furnish information through time series charts compiled on a daily basis. Graphic displays could be used to monitor potential and actual areas of conflict and provide the foreign affairs analyst with a quantitative aid to help better perform the early warning functions that his forecasts should provide. From the thousands of cues coming into the department each day, a technique such as the automatic provision of trend graphs could help to identify patterns in the cues that could foreshadow the major escalation of conflict. The analyst's interpretation of the importance of certain events will still be the critical factor in making such a forecast. But the availability of a set of information based on a monitoring system could be helpful in formulating and presenting his forecast.

Many types of data can be plotted over time to portray the trend of a condition or series of events. A series of issue positions, as generated in the Korean study (Chapter 5), could be graphed to show when a nation is becoming more or less amenable to change in the course of bargaining on an issue. Or, as in the Latin American case study, increases in arms expenditures over time would warn the analyst to look for comparable increases in other countries. Some aspects of the political history of a nation can be quickly appreciated by looking at a graph of the index of instability or other indicators, as developed in the African case study.

A third advantage of quantitative techniques is that they facilitate the comparison of events. The Korean case study provides an example of the use of quantitative techniques to facilitate comparison. In this case we were primarily interested in comparing issues, and not countries. The objective was to determine whether one issue is more likely to be resolved than another. To do this verbally it would be necessary to discuss at length the various factors favoring or opposing a quick settlement. But there would be no way to combine the verbal descriptions of these factors to make a systematic comparison of the likelihood of resolution of each issue in the bargaining. However, when the factors were presented in quantitative form, they could then be combined to produce a concise estimate of the likelihood of resolution, and these estimates could be compared for each issue.

Finally, the use of quantitative techniques presents the advantage of opening up many new data sources for the analyst. A substantial amount of quantitative data already exists in public sources, and much more is probably available from governmental documents not now being used for these purposes.

We have provided several examples of this final advantage of quantitative techniques. In the six case studies a wide variety of public sources was used, only a few of which were utilized in the 545 INR documents we analyzed. Chapter 6 used a foreign policy events data set (provided by Edward Azar) to measure the occurrence of violence in the Middle East. Chapter 7 used events data, UN votes, and trade data to measure cohesion among oil-producing and oil-consuming nations. Chapter 3 used election data, employment data, cost-of-living data, and events data to predict the outcome of elections in three European nations. Chapter 2 used events data (from Northwestern University) to measure political instability in Africa, and various types of social, economic, and political data to explain and predict that instability. Chapter 5 generated data using a systematic survey of State Department and academic experts to measure the issue positions of North and South Korea and an estimate of the outcome of bargaining. Finally, Chapter 4 used aggregate data from the Latin American Military Behavior (LAMB) Project of Syracuse University to analyze arms expenditures in Latin America.

The Korean case study deserves special mention with respect to the utilization of outside sources. In surveying documents it becomes apparent that a great deal of information from a wide variety of sources is studied by the analyst and then pieced together to form a coherent picture. For example, in studies of issues in North-South Korean bargaining, analysts take information from cables, newspaper reports, discussions with other Korean specialists, and other sources, not just within the State Department but also in other government agencies in Washington and elsewhere.

The Korean study developed a procedure for identifying issues and collecting information on factors relating to bargaining on these issues, including the policy positions of the two Koreas. A questionnaire on 10 of the issues in the bargaining was completed by 9 State Department officials and 16 academic specialists on Korea. There was a substantial amount of agreement on values assigned to the variables among governmental officials, but somewhat less agreement between the officials as a whole and the academics as a whole.

This technique appears to be a useful supplement to the INR analyst as an information-gathering procedure. If brief summaries of the viewpoints of experts were included in reports, readers would gain the advantage of receiving various perceptions of the situation.

Before closing this discussion of the use of quantitative techniques in the information-gathering task, let us introduce a note of caution. Not all types of information can or should be described with quantitative data. For example, in the case study on European elections (Chapter 3), it was pointed out that the description of issues and major parties in the election, as well as the long-term policy changes that result from an election, can best be described verbally. And even where quantitative techniques can be used to collect and present information on a subject, it should again be repeated that these techniques serve only as a supplement to the intensive verbal analysis of the INR analyst. If information is collected and presented in quantitative form only, it becomes a liability, for all subtlety of distinction and variety of detail are lost. But when quantitative techniques are used in conjunction with verbal information gathering and presentation, then they serve to highlight, to summarize, to enhance, and to clarify the analysis.

DESCRIPTIVE ANALYSIS

The major problem that we encountered in investigating the possible use of quantitative techniques for testing the assumptions and hypotheses of INR analysts was the many different factors and relationships considered to be important in the explanation of any topic covered by an INR analysis. Every statistical method--from the simplest to the most complex--requires an explicit statement of a limited number of the factors thought to influence a given phenomenon. As pointed out in the discussion of information gathering, this is one of the major advantages of quantitative techniques: it forces the user to be clear and explicit in his analysis.

The success of the case studies in testing hypotheses was not, to say the least, overwhelming. In many instances this can be attributed to the predisposition of the analyst (possibly for good and sufficient reason) not to limit or clearly identify those factors that have the most important effect on the subject of analysis. In other cases it is due to the inability to collect data on some factors or to the poor quality of the data in some instances. We will point out these shortcomings in the following discussion.

In a great many documents that were surveyed, analysts explained the occurrence of an event in a particular country by referring to past instances of a similar event in the same country. The prototype phrase is: "If previous experience is any guide . . . . " This historical factor was in many cases the sole explanation provided for an event. Quantitative techniques can be used to specify the forecasting power of the historical facts and thereby increase the clarity and power of the analyses.

In the case study on African instability, for example, the assumption of the analysts is that countries that have experienced instability in the past are more likely than others to experience instability again. This assumption can be tested simply by correlating a measure of instability in a past time period with a measure of instability in a later time period. By varying the time period, it can be determined how far back in history it is necessary to go to explain current instability. For example, to estimate the likelihood of instability at a given point in time is it most useful to study the previous six months, the previous year, or the previous five years? A correlation coefficient between time periods will help answer this question; the time periods that produce the highest correlation provide the best historical explanation. Thus in

the African case study a correlation of .97 was found between elite instability in 1960-64 and elite instability
in 1965-69. (A correlation coefficient ranges from -1, a
perfect negative or inverse relationship, through 0, an indication of no relationship, to +1, a perfect positive relationship.)

With this simple technique, the analyst can move beyond conjecture in his explanations. He can be more certain about those questions for which the past is a useful
guide. Using a simple measure of association, he can state
with more certainty whether or not past experience should
be considered, and how far back in history he should look
to explain the likelihood of an event's occurrence.

The African study showed a strong relationship between
elite instability at two different time periods. However,
it is not always satisfactory to find that history is our
best explanation of an event. Historical explanations are
of limited use to policy makers because historical events
cannot be the subject of policy activity. If this were
the sole factor affecting elite instability, then policy
makers would not be able to do anything about instability.
Therefore analysts naturally search for factors other than
the past occurrence of a phenomenon to explain present oc-
currences of that phenomenon.

In trying to explain the incidence of coups d'etat in
Africa by factors other than history, INR analysts generally
refer to two broad sets of factors. First, they talk of a
socioeconomic background that established an environment
in which a coup or other form of instability might take
place. Second, they talk of a set of political factors
that are considered to be more direct influences on the
occurrence of a coup, given an environment susceptible to
instability. The specific socioeconomic factors that were
identified from explicit or implicit references in INR materials were the size of a country, ethnic pluralism, social mobilization, urbanization, and national integration.
The political factors were interest group size, governmental economic performance, political party unity, and amount
of external support.

Several findings of the African case study, which relied on the application of regression analysis to the data,
might be of interest to foreign affairs analysts. First,
the study showed something about the relationship between
different forms of instability; there is little relationship between communal instability and elite instability.
(The correlation was .33.) Second, the study showed that
the explanatory factors have different influences on the

two types of instability. Third, the study also showed
the amount and direction of the effect that the factors
have on instability. For example, for every _increase_ of
one standard unit in our measure of national integration,
there is a _decrease_ of .17 standard units in communal instability. Finally, the study showed that some factors are
more important than others in the occurrence of instability,
and that some factors originally thought important appear
to be relatively unimportant.

The survey of INR reports on European elections (Chapter 3) showed that analysts were relatively explicit in
articulating the relationships between social, economic,
and political conditions and election results. Although
different assumptions were made concerning the relationships among factors in different countries, there did appear to be some basic ideas underlying the analysis of
elections in all countries. The most general way of conceiving of election results by INR analysts was in terms
of (1) percentage of vote gained by the prime minister's
party and (2) percentage of vote gained by the Communist
party. The factors most often cited as the major influences on election outcomes were voter turnout, unemployment, inflation, and dramatic external and internal events.

The study achieved mixed results in applying some simple quantitative techniques such as scattergrams and correlation coefficients. The study successfully tested the
impact of the three socioeconomic factors--turnout, unemployment, and inflation--on elections. That is, statistical tests showed the direction of the effect of each of
the factors on election results, a subject frequently dis-
puted by election analysts both inside and outside the
government. Among other noteworthy findings was that the
factors produced different results in different countries.
It would then appear to be more fruitful to conduct one-
country quantitative studies over time, rather than comparisons of different countries (as proved useful in the
African case study).

The study of the impact of major events on European
elections, while suggestive, did not produce notable results. This was partly because of the lack of an adequate
data base, and partly because of the absence of general
hypotheses with which to test the data.

Finally, in all of the tests, because of the small
number of election points over time for each country, we
could not acquire a large enough data set to satisfy standard statistical requirements. Thus to an appreciable extent the meager results of this case study are due to the
limitations inherent in the existing data base.

INR documents on Latin America (see Chapter 4) contained a great many implicit statements on the factors and relationships associated with arms spending. Several analyses were undertaken of the different explanatory factors. A major problem in this case study was "operationalization," or finding indicators to measure the explanatory factors. Such things as the role of the military in nonmilitary affairs, the intent of ruling elites to generate mass support, and the needs for external defense are extremely difficult variables to measure quantitatively.

The procedures employed in analyzing the factors were cross tabulation (contingency tables), correlation, and Markov chain processes. One important general finding was that the utility of quantitative techniques in descriptive analysis is directly related to the clarity of definition and precision of measurement of the factors employed in the explanation. Explanations involving GNP or military capabilities, for example, are easily tested with quantitative techniques, whereas factors related to "need" or "intent" are best tested with traditional verbal analysis. Generally, there were few systematic relationships found when the six major Latin American countries were treated together. However, when each country was treated separately over a long period of time, some strong correlations emerged.

The case study on violence in the Middle East (Chapter 6) presents what is perhaps the simplest use of quantitative techniques in descriptive analysis. It shows the close relationship between information gathering and presentation on the one hand, and descriptive analysis on the other. That is, the study shows that once information has been collected and presented in certain ways, it is but a short step to several alternative forms of quantitative analysis.

The case study analyzed the argument that a hard line by Israel deterred the Arabs from using violence. The pattern is familiar in the Middle East: Arab terrorism, followed by Israeli reprisals designed to discourage further Arab hostility. In the information-gathering task of the case study we had presented various time series graphs showing the trend of violent acts over different periods of time. In the descriptive analysis we had only to compare the graphs for Israel and the Arabs to determine first, if rises in Israeli violence preceded or followed rises in Arab violence, and second, if the instances of Israeli escalation following an Arab increase resulted in decreases in violence on the part of the Arabs. A pure

visual analysis of the combined graphs appears to support
the hypothesis of deterrence throughout part, but not all,
of the time period. However, a correlational analysis of
the monthly data disconfirms the hypothesis. More complex
analytical procedures such as time-lagged regression analysis and computer simulation are needed to resolve the con-
tradiction. However, the case study does show that simple
analysis of quantitatively presented information is a
straightforward method that can be used by foreign affairs
analysts to acquire some clues, if not definitive answers,
to relationships among variables.

The INR analyses of global oil politics (see Chapter
7) are extremely complex, since they involve relating di-
plomacy and economics. Some of the analyses attempted to
articulate assumptions about the likely behavior of the oil
producers and oil consumers under various conditions.
This case study included an attempt to abstract these assumptions. This was found to be an extremely difficult
task because of the complex conditions analyzed in the INR
documents. A variety of statistical and mathematical techniques were used to construct indexes to measure the dependence of both producers and consumers on trade in oil.
These indexes may be of some interest as ways of measuring
highly complex phenomena. However, the statistical analysis of these indexes failed to produce any meaningful correlations. Consequently, a less inductive approach was
tried. This involved transforming the models implicit in
the reports of INR analysts into explicit flowchart diagrams. This procedure helped to elucidate some, but by
no means all, of the factors that INR analysts saw as important.

FORECASTING

Each of the case studies developed a different tool
for making forecasts about the particular subject of analysis. This section will review those techniques and evaluate their utility for assisting the forecasting techniques
of foreign affairs analysts.

The following quotation from an INR report on the possibility of a coup in Africa is typical of forecasts in
many areas:

In the absence of an identifiable group strong
enough to challenge [General X], it would be pre-
mature to predict his early overthrow by a coup.

250

But the present power structure within the army is unstable enough to make a coup an ever-present danger, and it would not be surprising to see [General X] replaced by another army leader or group --thereby creating an even more unstable regime.

Two points can be made about this quotation. First, it is clear that the analyst felt that it was uncertain whether there would be a coup. Such uncertainty could have been more succinctly stated with a simple statement that there is a .5 probability of a coup over the next few months. With verbal, qualitative forecasting, ambiguity is almost inevitable, and there is a strong tendency to increase the number of words used to communicate uncertainty. Quantitative techniques help to avoid the ambiguity and to limit the length of the discussion while communicating more information. The African case study generated an index of a state's proneness to coups. Using the same statistical technique that banks use to determine credit risks, the case showed how probability estimates could be generated for forecasting the likely occurrence of coups. Estimates for the period 1970-72 were generated based on data from the period 1965-69. These estimates were compared with the actual occurrence of coups. The results were that 6 of the 12 states that were expected to have coups actually did experience them and that 19 of the 20 states that were expected not to have coups did not in fact experience coups. By using the index, the degree to which a coup was likely could be communicated precisely, quickly, and, as this case study showed, just as accurately.

This leads to the second point about the analyst's quotation. The analyst offers only one factor as the condition determining the coup. If a quantitative analysis had been used as a basis for the statement, the analyst would have been able to cite a set of several factors. He might have said, for example:

There is a .5 probability of a coup's occurring. On the one hand, the unrest in the army, the increase in inflation, and the lowering of exports are pressures favoring a coup. On the other hand, the absence of civil unrest in villages and towns, the lack of other coups in neighboring countries, and the increase in foreign aid minimize the chances of a coup.

251

Knowledge of the quantitative analysis of correlates of coups would allow the analyst to articulate more clearly both a forecast and the basis for it.

We can demonstrate a similar point by citing the Latin American case study. In that study, we developed a National Profile Scoresheet (NPS) for each of the six major countries studied. The NPS provided forecasting estimates of the likelihood of a country's increase or decrease in its annual defense expenditures. While the question of annual defense expenditures is not necessarily the most critical concern of INR analysts, there are similar topics (such as military spending on specific equipment) that may make the analytical technique worth considering.

The predictions of the NPS were compared with the actual changes in military spending from one year to the next. Of these 12 predictions, 8 were correct. Such a technique appears promising as an assist to analysts, particularly when it is used in conjunction with the checklist of factors that were found in the descriptive analysis to affect expenditures. The NPS and the list of explanatory factors can serve as an effective check on, and corroboration of, the intensive qualitative study of the foreign affairs analyst. In so doing, it can help the analyst express more precisely his forecasts while at the same time showing the range of factors that he has taken into consideration.

In addition to using correlation techniques to generate indexes for forecasting the likelihood of events, the INR analyst could use a range of quantitative techniques, usually classified as "trend analysis," to generate forecasts. The Middle East study demonstrated how trend analysis procedures might be applied. Using the analysis of daily reports of violence and other acts of conflict between Israel and the United Arab Republic, we applied techniques similar to those used by stock market analysts. We attempted to identify critical patterns of interactions that closely preceded the outbreak of major violence. Specifically, we found that if: (1) the running mean of the frequency of violent acts is increasing; (2) the running standard deviation around the mean is decreasing; and (3) the symmetry between the acts of the two nations is increasing, then there is a high likelihood of increased violence between the nations concerned. The predictions of changes in violence generated by this technique were compared with the actual changes for the time period and found to be correct in slightly better than three-fourths of the cases when predicting with a three-month time frame.

No attempt was made to predict the magnitude or outcome of violence, only the incidence of severe violence.
However, with more experience in using trend analysis techniques, analysts might be able to refine the tool so that
more precise predictions could be made. In addition, the
technique has two other advantages. The first is that instead of making forecasts for an unspecified future time,
the analyst will be able to forecast that a particular period of time in the future--for example, two weeks, or a
month--is likely to be most dangerous in terms of the estimated probability of escalation of violence. The other
advantage is that the predictions can be produced automatically by a computer program so that when the conditions
emerge that lead toward increased violence, the computer
can flag the situation as a warning for the analyst.

It must be admitted that trend analysis is far from
being a foolproof forecasting technique--as any stock market investor will attest. However, it is one more source
of information that foreign affairs analysts could prepare
and use in developing their forecasts. Its limitations
will become less constraining as analysts become more familiar with the use of trend analysis. Just as important,
as records are kept and analyzed over time, there could be
a basis for collective learning among analysts that would
in the long run help make trend analysis techniques even
more valuable.

A final application of quantitative techniques for
the task of forecasting is related to the general use of
experts both within and outside of government agencies.
The task of gathering and analyzing information that is
the most critical component of the INR analyst's activities
is highly labor-intensive. Consequently, there is a need
to establish a more systematic basis for both individual
work and cooperation among experts. In this endeavor the
analyst can be viewed as a critical source of analyzed information, and quantitative techniques can help to collect
and compare that information. We used experts to generate
two kinds of quantitative data: (1) predictions about the
likelihood of some event or condition in the future and
(2) information about current conditions that could be
used to make projections according to explicit forecasting
models.

The use of experts to generate predictions about future events has received extensive treatment in a number
of projects using one version or another of what is generally called the Delphi technique. These projects have
typically focused on making forecasts of long-term trends

(such as technological innovation or evolution in military strategy). Our plan was to illustrate a less complicated procedure that we called a "quick estimation questionnaire." In late February 1973 we attempted to collect from State Department analysts, journalists, and academics a prediction on the outcome of the French election of March 1973. The survey was conducted two weeks prior to the first round of balloting. The results of the survey were relatively accurate from each of the three sets of experts. However, the State Department analysts showed the most intragroup consensus of the three groups of experts and also provided the most accurate predictions.

We believe that the experiment demonstrates that such quick estimation procedures might generate useful information for analysts and their users. Even when one expert's viewpoint is considered especially authoritative, the knowledge of how a range of experts feel about the likelihood of a given event should be of some interest to analysts and possibly policy makers. Moreover, by acquiring data on the estimates made and comparing those estimates to the actual course of events, one might be able both to improve the individual analyst's ability to predict and also to discover patterns of expert opinions that might lead to a reconsideration of patterns of consulting and other estimating procedures.

On this latter point, the question of the degree of consensus among State Department analysts becomes important. In addition to providing information to analysts and policy makers, procedures for surveying experts may also be important as a self-correcting mechanism for the general process of intelligence analysis in the department. When, as will inevitably be the case, events turn out differently from predictions, it is important to know whether there was substantial disagreement among forecasting experts, or whether there was a clear-cut (but erroneous) consensus. In the former case one may well conclude that this was simply an example of the intractibility of the social world to analytical techniques; in the latter case, however, one might want to consider what should be done, such as engaging in a wider consultation, to help avoid such a consensus in the future.

In addition to using experts for generating predictions, quantitative techniques can be employed to survey experts about their perceptions of existing events and conditions. This procedure distinguishes sharply between the expert as a forecaster and the expert as an observer, synthesizer, and summarizer of reality. Unlike the Delphi procedure and the quick estimation questionnaire, where the expert plays the role of predictor, the use of the expert as observer yields quantitative data upon which many different kinds of quantitative forecasting techniques can be used. (We have already referred to several of these, including trend analysis, regression, and discriminant function analysis.) In the Korean case study, for example, we collected expert data on the position of the two Koreas on a set of 10 bilateral issues. We applied a computer simulation model to predict the likely outcome of those 10 issues. This procedure permitted all 10 issues to be easily and precisely compared as to the likelihood of their resolution.

As a method for generating data upon which forecasting can be based, the procedure applied in the Korean case study illustrates the potential for a significant breakthrough in the application of quantitative methods to policy forecasting. For a number of years, many people inside and outside the government, have advocated the use of probability estimates and forms of probability analysis such as Bayesian analysis. The Net Assessment project and the use of PARA are among the more significant attempts to get members of the State Department to assign quantitative values to events and conditions. However, the process by which these probability estimates have been generated has always been subject to the vicissitudes of social, political, and psychological factors operating at meetings in which the estimates were made. The use of a systematic questionnaire procedure such as the one presented in the Korean case study eliminates many of the outside factors that now sometimes arbitrarily shape the estimates of analysts.

This type of procedure could substantially improve the precision and ultimately the accuracy of forecasts by INR analysts. If experts on a particular set of political issues were to generate quantitative estimates of existing events and conditions on a regular basis, the data could be used to generate predictions. As experience with the data-generated technique and the use of the data increased, forecasting models could be developed that would yield more accurate predictions. Even if such models never developed, however, the process of collecting views among experts would help to improve their own thinking about events and would create more efficient flows of information within and between clusters of experts and policy makers.

CONCLUSION

The objective of this section is to illustrate how quantitative techniques could be used as an aid in some of the tasks of the foreign affairs analyst. In acquiring information, quantitative techniques help the analyst to amass a large amount of information in a systematic and organized fashion. In trying to piece together various pieces of information for analytical purposes, quantitative techniques help in several ways.

First, to use such techniques the analyst must be clear about his assumptions concerning the relationships among factors being studied. In using graphs, tables, or other forms of analysis, the writer must first articulate to himself his basic conception of the world. Quantitative techniques help force on the analyst a greater amount of self-awareness than is the case with purely qualitative analysis.

Second, in becoming more self-aware and more precise in articulating his assumptions, the analyst creates a structure for dialogue among others studying the same subject. This allows him to minimize the semantic problems that often interfere with the accumulation and sharing of knowledge. For example, the development of an index of "coup-proneness" would be a shared task with much more precise objectives than a general discussion of the factors leading to coups.

Third, quantitative methods can more directly aid the analyst in organizing information according to a variety of analytical structures. Tables and graphs visually portray relationships between variables that help the analyst see general patterns. Statistical methods go even further than visual techniques by determining the association of many different factors. At the most complex level, INR analysts can build models that systematically interrelate many factors into complex patterns. If the data is available, assumptions about relationships can be tested with quantitative techniques.

Finally, we should indicate that one of the most valuable payoffs from quantitative techniques is the kind of INR report it will help to generate. The usual INR product typically puts forth highly qualified forecasts with little precision as to time or scope. This format could be replaced by systematic presentation of alternative futures for specified conditions and periods of times. The tentativeness that has to be part of all prediction will still be present but in the form of probability estimates

256

and alternative trends rather than the often ambiguous verbal qualifications now frequently employed.

In addition to these operationally important consequences of increased use of quantitative techniques, their use will also have an impact on relationships among analysts interested in the same topic. One of the most important of these consequences is that the use of these techniques makes much more explicit the amount of agreement or dissent that exists among analysts concerned with a given question. The use of traditional modes of analysis permits dissenting views or extreme consensus to be minimized or ignored altogether. With quantitative techniques, analysts are forced to make explicit those factors they consider important, the way to measure these factors, and the nature of relationships among them.

There is consequently an almost automatic measurement of the extent of agreement among officials. For example, two of the case studies (on Western European elections and North-South Korean bargaining) showed that in comparison with academics, there was extremely high consensus on issues on which the State Department members were polled. The extent to which consensus in a decision-making group is desirable or undesirable is of course an open question, and unquestionably differs from issue to issue. But it is certainly important to be aware of the extent of agreement within an organization. Once this is known, it is then possible either to work to build up more agreement if consensus is judged to be too low, or to look for a wider variety of opinions if it is deemed that consensus has become so extensive as to produce narrowness of vision.

Finally, we would like to summarize the major conclusions:

- It is possible to apply quantitative techniques to a representative sampling of the analytical tasks performed by the foreign affairs analyst.
- The clearest evidence for the application of quantitative techniques is in the field of acquiring information by developing coding systems to collect data from written material and by developing expert-generated data systems to formalize the exchanges of views that now characterizes the information-gathering tasks of the INR analyst.
- There is some evidence that in areas such as political instability, international violence, and the international bargaining process, quantitative techniques can be used to generate predictions as well as identify those factors that the analysts should consider in making their predictions.

- Quantitative techniques could potentially be useful in testing the validity of the assumptions of the analysts. However, such application will be possible only after there is more standardization of the concepts used in the analyses.

ANALYSIS OF REPORTS FROM THE BUREAU
OF INTELLIGENCE RESEARCH,
U.S. DEPARTMENT OF STATE

The purpose of this coding scheme is to describe the
basic characteristics of documents surveyed in this study.
Coding will be done on scanning forms. Each "item"
on the scanning form contains numbered spaces that can be
blackened. The "10" in each item should be treated as a
"zero" by the coder. One item is used to code one-digit
numbers, two items for two-digit numbers, and so on. Note
what happens when there is more than one digit to code.
If you have space allotted for two digits but you are coding the value "1", then you should blacken the "zero" in
the first item and blacken the "one" in the second item.
Thus, you would have "01". If you wished to express the
value "1" when space for three digits is provided, then
you should blacken such that the form reads "001" across
those three items. Likewise, if you wish to code the value
"10" in two digit space, blacken the "1" in the first item
and the "zero" in the second item. If three spaces were
provided, you would blacken the "zero" in the first item,
the "1" in the second item, and the "zero" in the third
item.
The instructions for each category have been designed
to help you classify documents correctly. There are 13
general categories in the classification.

1. Document Identification Number (First three columns of
the "Student Number" box)
Each document to be coded should be assigned an identification number. This can be done by numbering consecutively each document as you code it, beginning with "1" on
up. For example, to code the first document you would
blacken the first three columns of the "Student Number"
box. The first column would have a "zero," and the third
column a "1". Thus, you would have "001" across the first
three columns. If it were document number ten, you would
have "010", and so on. Remember, you must make an entry
in each of the three columns provided.

2. Date (Last six columns of the "Student Number" box)
    Each document will have a date. Blacken the appropri-
ate number in each of the last six columns of "Student
Number." The six numbers should correspond to the month,
day, and year of the document. Thus, a document dated
August 4, 1971, would require you to blacken each number
in the last six columns such that the numbers "080471"
would appear in the columns.

3. Type of Document (Item 2)
    Documents may be classified as one of the following
four types. Blacken the space in item 2 on the scanning
sheet that corresponds to the number representing each
type of document.
    Research Study (RS)   1
    Intelligence Note (IN)   2
    Memo (MM)   3
    Other   4

4. Security Classification (Item 4)
    Documents will carry one of four security classifica-
tions. Blacken the one number in item 4 corresponding to
the level of classification.
    Unclassified   1
    Limited Official Use   2
    Confidential   3
    Secret   4

5. Origin (Items 6 through 7)
    "Origin" refers to the office from which the document
came. The first three letters of the four-letter document
code, located at the top right-hand corner of the document's
front page, indicate the office of origin. Blacken the
appropriate number in each item corresponding to the numbers given each office below.
    RAF - 01 - Office of Research and Analysis for Africa
    RAR - 02 - Office of Research and Analysis for Ameri-
                can Republics
    RAA - 03 - Combined Offices for Africa/American Re-
                publics
    REA - 04 - Office of Research and Analysis for East
                Asia and Pacific
    REU - 05 - Office of Research and Analysis for West-
                ern Europe
    RSE - 06 - Office of Research and Analysis for East
                Europe and the Soviet Union

```
     RES - 07 - Combined Office for Research and Analysis
                  for East Europe and the Soviet Union
     RNA - 08 - Office of Research and Analysis for Near
                  East and South Asia
     REC - 09 - Office of Economic Research and Analysis
     RSG - 10 - Office of Strategic and General Research
      SA - 11 - Office of Research on Science Affairs
Other DFR - 12 - Other Functional Research Offices other
                  than RSG and SA.  Or DFR itself.
Other DRR - 13 - Other Regional Research Offices besides
                  those listed above.  Or DRR itself.
 ____ - 14 - More than one office of origin.
```

6. Analyst (Items 9 through 11)
    As you code each document you should assign a number
to each analyst who writes each paper. Number them from
"1" up consecutively as you encounter them. When an analyst recurs, use the number you assigned to that analyst
when you first encountered him/her.

7. Number of Pages (Items 12 through 14)
    To calculate the number of pages in a document, exclude
the Abstract (if any). The number on the last page should
give you the correct page count; however, you should check
to see whether there are any unnumbered pages such as
charts, pictures, etc. and count them if they have not already been included. A document with 5 pages should be
coded "005" across the three spaces provided for page number. A document with 10 pages would be coded "010," and
so on.

8. Purpose (Item 15)
    Basically a document may be coded in one of three cate-
gories: (A) Current Intelligence, (B) Estimation or Forecasting, or (C) Both Current Intelligence and Forecasting.
    By "Current Intelligence" we mean that a document is
exclusively or almost exclusively a description analysis
of the past and present with little or no reference to the
future. Examples of current intelligence:

A document that says nothing about the future.

A document that contains only a concluding sentence or
short paragraph discussing the future.

A document in which the discussion of the future is
confined to phrases such as "Current trends expected
to continue," or "China will continue to supply arms
to North Vietnam."

Such documents should be coded "Current Intelligence." The general idea you should have in mind is that the _thrust_ of the document deals with the past and the present, not with the future.

By "Estimation or Forecasting" we mean that a document is exclusively or almost exclusively an estimated prediction of the future with but scant reference to the past and present, although there probably must be _some_ reference to past and current events. Examples:

A document that explicitly states forecasting or estimating as its purpose.

A document that makes little reference to the past or present, except as needed to base a prediction or forecast.

Again we emphasize that the above list contains some (but not all) of the possible "giveaways" of an Estimation/Forecasting document. Again it is the primary _thrust_ of the document we are after.

There will likely be cases where a document combines a discussion of the past and present with a discussion and prediction of the future. Examples:

A document that interlaces throughout a discussion of the past and present a discussion (estimation, forecasting) of the future in specific or detailed fashions.

A document that contains a lengthy final paragraph or several shorter paragraphs that give fairly developed, at least moderately specific and detailed, estimative or predictive discussions of the future.

A document containing at least one section entitled "PROSPECTS" or other similar title that truly does discuss the future.

The _thrust_ of such documents above is that they are not exclusively Current Intelligence or Forecasting, but are both.

Occasionally you will find a document in which the analyst recommends that a particular policy be adopted. He may state a particular goal and then review the alternatives and suggest the one that he feels would best fulfill that goal. These documents are called prescriptive, and you will find prescription occurring with one or both of the other purposes.

At times the Abstract of the document may help you out by explicitly stating the purpose of the paper, but before

coding the document according to this statement, check to be sure the document actually fulfills its stated purpose.
The codes are:

Current Intelligence	1
Estimation or Forecasting	2
Both	3
Prescription and Current Intelligence	4
Prescription and Estimation or Forecasting	5
All three	6

9. Time Span (Items 17 through 24)
   (A) Time Back (Items 17 through 20)

We are interested here in whether the document refers to past time and how it does so. It can do it in one of three ways: mention a specific date earlier than all others in the document, refer to the past in general terms, or not refer to the past at all. The codes for these three categories are as follows:

No Mention of Past	0000
Past Mentioned but Unspecified	9999
Month and Year of Earliest Date Mentioned	____

"No Mention of Past" means just that: no mention. "Past Mentioned but Unspecified" means that only general or vague references to the past are found. This entails the use of such phrases as "in the past," "formerly," "in the nineteenth century," and so on. All the references are general.

Month and Year of Earliest Date Mentioned" refers to cases where dates are at least as specific as a particular year or decade. For example, the mention of the date December 17, 1969, would cause the numbers "1269" to be blackened in the items. If only the year 1969 is mentioned, blacken as follows: "0069." If a general time period is referred to, code the earliest reasonable date. For example, a mention of a past decade, such as "the thirties" should be coded "0030."

263

(B) Time Forward (Items 21 through 24)

Here we want to know if and how the document refers to the future. As with the past there are three categories that are coded in the same manner:

No Mention of the Future   0000

Future Mentioned but Un-
specified   9999

Month and Year of Latest
Date Mentioned   _____

As with section (A), "No Mention of the Future" means just that: no mention. By "Future Mentioned but Unspecified" we mean a general reference to the future denoted by such phrases as "in the future," "present trends will continue," "in our generation," etc. References to a decade are considered unspecified when talking of the future because predictions become no more specific in that instance than when one talks about general trends continuing, etc. Referring to a decade in the future is not as specific in the future as it is in the past. "Month and Year of Latest Date Mentioned" follows the same rules as for the past, except that references to decades are coded not as specific but as unspecified dates.

10. Country Identification (Items 25 through 27, 29
    through 31, 33 through 35, and 37 through 39)

This variable category refers to the country or countries (or the region or regions) upon which the document primarily focuses. Up to four countries may be identified here, using the three-digit number assigned to each country.

To be coded under this item a country should not be just mentioned in passing but should be discussed at some length. For example, if a document talks about the relations between China and Latin America and if both China and Latin America are discussed in comparable detail, then the subjects of the document are these two countries and each should be coded under the country identification. This means blackening the country number for China in the first three items (25 through 27) and for Latin America in the next three items (29 through 31), and so on. If the document discusses the relations of one country, say Peru, with several other countries but each of the other countries receives only brief attention, then the subject of the document should be considered "Peru" and its three-digit code should be blackened in the first item.

The guiding rule for this section is to code only those countries that are treated as the subject of the document. It is possible that in terms of space allocated, time of discussion, attention, etc., more than one country may be considered the subject of the document. That is the reason why up to four countries may be coded in this category.

11. Issue (Items 41 through 64)
By "Issue" we refer to the policy questions that a document discusses. There are two components to code in this category: (A) Subject Matter and (B) Geographic Location.

(A) Subject Matter
By Issue Subject Matter we are referring to what we call the "type of issue"; that is, those specific topics of foreign and domestic policy such as diplomatic recognition, use of troops, forces, arms control/limitation, financial problems between states, and use of United Nations.

(B) Geographic Location
By Geographic Location we are referring to the physical location that the issue involves. If a document discusses a border dispute between two countries, those two countries would be coded under Geographic Location of the issue. For example, if the issue involved a border dispute between Mexico and the United States, both the United States and Mexican country numbers would be coded as the geographic location of that issue. Country codes are the same as those used for the country identification variable and will be found below. There need not necessarily be two geographic locations per issue. A discussion of France's domestic policies would have only one location connected with the issue--France. A discussion of Ghana's position on Viet Nam might have two locations coded (for both North and South Viet Nam) if the issue were the war or one location (North or South Viet Nam) depending upon which particular country the issue involved. Note that in this example Ghana is not coded here in the issue classification because Ghana is not the locus of the issue. Ghana would be coded in the Country Identification variable in #10 above. In summary, you should ask where the issue is taking place. Each issue will always have at least one location, even if the location has to be coded "980" for "unspecified." Bear in mind that the Country Identification number may, but need not necessarily, appear in the Geographic Location of the issue coding.

The space on the coding sheet allows you to code up to three issues per document, each issue having a Subject Matter and up to two Geographic Locations. The following is a breakdown of the items on the scanning form to be used for coding each issue. If you only use one location for an issue, leave the "Location 2" items blank.

Issue A
Subject Matter   (Items 41 through 42)
Location 1   (Items 43 through 45)
Location 2   (Items 46 through 48)

Issue B
Subject Matter   (Items 49 through 50)
Location 1   (Items 51 through 53)
Location 2   (Items 54 through 56)

Issue C
Subject Matter   (Items 57 through 58)
Location 1   (Items 59 through 61)
Location 2   (Items 62 through 64)

12. International Institutional Forum (Items 66 through 67)
    This classification refers to the setting in which interstate interactions described by the document take place. By setting we are referring to the most formal framework in which the interaction occurs. The UN General Assembly, the Security Council, the OAS, NATO, etc. are examples of institutional settings. One does not need to have a formal organization to have a setting. A forum of interaction could be diplomacy; that is, direct contact between states. Further interactions involving the negotiation within an institutional framework established by treaty means that we have another setting or forum, the treaty.
    Note that we are trying to tap the forum in which the interaction occurs. A document may refer to the countries of the EEC negotiating with their counterpart members in East Europe, COMECON. If the document indicates that the interaction is among individual countries that are members of the organizations, then the Institutional Forum is coded "diplomatic." If, on the other hand, the EEC as an organization deals with COMECON as an organization, then the forum would be coded "Non-UN Regional Intergovernmental Organizations." The distinction between an Intergovernmental Organization (IGO) and a Non-Governmental Organization (NGO) is that members of IGO are official representatives of national states. NGO members are private

citizens or groups of diverse nationalities. The coding
categories are listed below:

01 Diplomatic
02 Treaty
03 UN Security Council/General Assembly/Secretary General
04 Other UN (ECOSOC, Trusteeship Council, UNDP, etc.)
05 Specialized Agencies
06 Other non-UN Global Intergovernmental Organizations
   (for example, British Commonwealth)
07 Non-UN Regional Intergovernmental Organizations
   (NATO, SEATO, EEC, COMECON, ETC.)
08 Global Non-Governmental Organizations (Red Cross,
   Student Groups, Groups of Scientists, Technicians,
   etc.)
09 Regional Non-Governmental Organizations (groups similar to those listed in 08 above)
99 No International Institutional Forum

The basic difference between a specialized agency and
"other UN" agency is that the latter do not have budgets
independent of the UN Organization. They may be permanent
organs (for example, ECOSOC) or agencies (for example,
UNDP). The specialized agencies do have independent budgets and are generally not mentioned in the Charter. See
lists below in this codebook for guidance in classifying
organizations.

13. Use of Quantitative Data (Items 69 through 70)
    This category concerns if and how numbers are used in
a document. There are two parts to the coding here. The
first is a code for "Type of Data"; the second a code for
"Type of Data Organization."

    (A) Type of Data (Item 69)
    There are three general categories for Type of Data,
which can also be found in various combinations. Data can
be "Economic"; that is, involve the use of standard economic concepts and indicators such as GNP, inflation rate,
unemployment rate, balance of payments, and trade figures.
The second type is "Political" data, which may include such
figures as voting statistics, political party strengths,
strength of other governmental bureaucracies, and party
strength in legislatures. The third category is "Social,"
which could include figures on literacy/illiteracy rates,
media figures such as number of radios or newspapers, pub-

267

lic services, measures of urbanization, figures on composition and characteristics of social classes, rates of disease infections and other public health figures, or number of civil disorders. One applies the coding scheme for "Type of Data" when numbers are used, even if only one number is used. We code for this, since even one number could be used by an analyst in making inferences in his analysis of a particular situation. But if an analyst merely mentions a figure or figures and does not base an inference upon them or otherwise employ them in analysis, the coding in this category should be "9", None Used. The categories for "Type of Data" are listed below.

1 Economic
2 Political
3 Social
4 Both Economic and Political
5 Both Economic and Social
6 Both Political and Social
7 Economic, Political, and Social
9 None Used

Note that there should always be a code for this category. If a document uses no data, code for that by blackening the "9" in item 69.

(B) Type of Data Organization (Item 70)
This refers to the way in which the data mentioned is used. If an analyst employs figures in the text, drawing inferences from them but not attempting to organize them in any more formal fashion, then the document is coded "Textual" for type of organization in item 70. If the analyst organizes them into a table, the item should be coded "Tabular" in item 70. If he goes further and perhaps performs statistical analyses on them, item 70 should be coded as "Associative." Codes for the various categories and their combinations appear below.

1 Textual
2 Tabular
3 Associative
4 Both Textual and Tabular
5 Both Textual and Associative
6 Both Tabular and Associative
7 Textual, Tabular, and Associative
9 None Used

IDENTIFICATION NUMBERS FOR COUNTRIES

Western Hemisphere (002-199)

002 United States	070 Mexico	130 Ecuador
020 Canada	090 Guatemala	135 Peru
040 Cuba	091 Honduras	140 Brazil
041 Haiti	092 El Salvador	145 Bolivia
042 Dominican Re-	093 Nicaragua	150 Paraguay
public	094 Costa Rica	155 Chile
051 Jamaica	095 Panama	160 Argentina
052 Trinidad and	100 Colombia	165 Uruguay
Tobago	101 Venezuela	
053 Barbados	110 Guyana	

Europe (200-399)

200 United Kingdom	265 East Germany	345 Yugoslavia
205 Eire (Ireland)	(German Demo-	350 Greece
210 Netherlands	cratic Repub-	352 Cyprus
211 Belgium	lic)	355 Bulgaria
212 Luxembourg	290 Poland	360 Rumania
220 France	305 Austria	365 USSR
225 Switzerland	310 Hungary	375 Finland
230 Spain	315 Czechoslovakia	380 Sweden
235 Portugal	325 Italy	385 Norway
255 West Germany	328 Vatican City	390 Denmark
	338 Malta	395 Iceland
	339 Albania	

Africa (400-599)

420 Gambia	482 C.A.R.	520 Somalia
432 Mali	483 Chad	530 Ethiopia
433 Senegal	484 Congo, B.	551 Zambia
434 Dahomey	(Congo Repub-	552 Rhodesia
435 Mauritania	lic)	(Code as 200
436 Niger	490 Congo, K.	prior to
437 Ivory Coast	(Congo Demo-	11-11-65)
438 Guinea	cratic Repub-	553 Malawi
439 Upper Volta	lic)	560 South Africa
450 Liberia	500 Uganda	570 Lesotho
451 Sierra Leone	501 Kenya	571 Botswana
452 Ghana	510 Tanzania	572 Swaziland
461 Togo	511 Zanzibar	580 Malagasy Re-
471 Cameroun	(After 4/64	public (Mada-
475 Nigeria	code as 510)	gascar)
476 Biafra	516 Burundi	590 Mauritius
481 Gabon	517 Rwanda	

Middle East (600-699)

600 Morocco	640 Turkey	666 Israel
615 Algeria	645 Iraq	670 Saudi Arabia
616 Tunisia	651 UAR	678 Yemen
620 Libya	652 Syria	680 Southern Yemen
625 Sudan	660 Lebanon	690 Kuwait
630 Iran	663 Jordan	698 Muscat and Oman

Asia (700-920)

700 Afghanistan	732 South Korea	800 Thailand
710 China, Main-	740 Japan	811 Cambodia
land (Chinese	750 India	812 Laos
Peoples Repub-	770 Pakistan	816 North Vietnam
lic)	771 Bangla Desh	817 South Vietnam
712 Mongolia	775 Burma	820 Malaysia
713 Taiwan, For-	780 Ceylon	830 Singapore
mosa (Nation-	781 Maldive Is-	840 Philippines
alist China)	lands	850 Indonesia
731 North Korea	790 Nepal	900 Australia
		920 New Zealand

Special Areas (950-989)

950 Outer Space
951 Ocean Floor
952 High Seas
953 Airspace
980 Worldwide or not geographically specific
981 Western Europe (NATO)
982 Eastern Europe
983 Latin America
984 Caribbean
985 Middle East
986 Africa
987 South Asia
988 Southeast Asia
989 Far East

ISSUE-CODING SCHEME

10 Use of Troops, Bases, or Arms
11 Search for or Proposals for Peace
12 NATO, reorganization of, or other issues
13 Attempts at Unity or Détente

14 General Tensions between States
15 Balance of Tensions and Détente between States
20 Non-Military Intervention
30 General Arms Control and/or Limitation
31 Non-Proliferation Treaty
32 Underground Tests
33 Missile Limitations or Freeze
34 Force Cuts
35 Arms Expenditures
40 Territorial Rights including Border Disputes
41 Diplomatic Recognition and Independence
42 Espionage
43 Fishing Rights
50 Use of the United Nations
51 Use of other International Organizations
60 Cultural, including Sports and Student Exchanges
61 Scientific Research and Exploration
62 Joint Work on Construction Projects
63 Travel and Communications
64 Trade and Investments
65 Diplomatic
66 Economic/Technical Aid and Emergency Relief
67 Military Aid, including Arms Sales
68 News Media Personnel
70 Financial Problems between Countries
71 Pollution
72 Hijacking
73 Control of Common Waterway
74 Drug Control
80 Problems of Refugees
81 Asylum for Individuals or Groups
82 Extradition
83 Expulsion, Seizure, Arrest, Killing
84 Population Control and Management

Domestic/Internal Conditions

90 Internal Economic Condition (excluding Trade and
   Other External)
91 Political Unrest
92 Elite Maneuvering and Character
93 Elections
94 Interest-Group Activity
95 Political Parties (Non-Electoral Activities)
96 Legislative Behavior
97 Social Policies
99 More than 3 of any above subjects, whether Foreign
   Policy or Domestic Issue

CLASSIFICATION OF INTERNATIONAL
ORGANIZATIONS

United Nations Specialized Agencies

International Labor Organization (ILO)
Food and Agriculture Organization (FAO)
United Nations Educational, Scientific, and Cultural Or-
    ganization (UNESCO)
World Health Organization (WHO)
International Monetary Fund (IMF)
International Bank for Reconstruction and Development (IBRD)
International Development Association (IDA)
International Finance Corporation (IFC)
International Civil Aviation Organization (ICAO)
Universal Postal Union (UPU)
International Telecommunications Union (ITU)
World Meteorological Organization (WMO)
Intergovernmental Maritime Consultative Organization (IMCO)

Other United Nations Organizations

Economic and Social Council (ECOSOC)
Trusteeship Council
International Court of Justice (ICJ)
United Nations Conference on Trade and Development (UNCTAD)
United Nations High Commission for Refugees (UNHCR)
United Nations Children's Fund (UNICEF)
United Nations Development Program (UNDP)
Economic Commission for Africa (ECA)
Economic Commission for Asia and the Far East (ECAFE)
Economic Commission for Europe (ECE)
Economic Commission for Latin America (ECLA)

Selected Non-UN Global Intergovernmental Organizations

International Fisheries Commission
General Agreement on Tariffs and Trade (GATT)
International Atomic Energy Committee (IAEA)
Organization for Economic Cooperation and Development (OECD)
Consultative Committee on Cooperative Economic Development
    in South and Southeast Asia (Columbo Plan)
International Bureau for the Protection of Industrial and
    Intellectual Property (BIRPI)

EXPERT JUDGMENT QUESTIONNAIRE FORM
FOR NORTH AND SOUTH KOREAN
BARGAINING

Name_____

Date Questionnaire Completed_____

Office Address and Telephone_____

Actor to be Analyzed_____

_____

   This questionnaire is designed to generate data on
some variables related to international issues. Read it
over before you begin to supply any of the requested information. If you have any questions about the meaning of
terms or the procedures to be used, ask the administrator
before you begin.
   You are requested to rank the actor named above in
terms of several variables related to the set of issues
given to you on the accompanying index cards. These issues
do not include all of those facing the actor, or even the
most important facing him, but they are the ones with
which you will be concerned. Note that each issue on the
cards is stated in terms of a specific outcome that the
actor may oppose or approve. Also, note that each card has
a letter printed in the upper-left-hand corner. When you
fill in information, use only these identifying letters
and not the verbal descriptions of the issues.
   Remember that you are not to rank yourself on these
issues. Neither are you to "pretend" that you are the actor named on the first page. Rather, on the basis of your
past observations of that actor, you are to judge, to the
best of your ability, his scores on the variables. Please
proceed through the questionnaire in the order that it is
written.

1.0 Issue Importance

   After examining the set of issue cards, arrange them
in declining order of their importance to the actor, irrespective of whether the actor approves or disapproves of

the outcome stated. The most important issue should be placed first, the least important, last. Record the order that you have placed the cards in, using the identifying letters, in the spaces provided below.

Issue Importance (Relative Values)	Rank	Issue
	1	___
	2	___
	3	___
	4	___
	5	___
	6	___
	7	___
	8	___
	9	___
	10	___

Now you are asked to assign an importance score for the actor on each issue. Disregarding the rank of Issue A which you assigned above, circle the number below, from 0 to 10, which you think best represents the importance of Issue A to the actor. Consider 0 to represent a score of least importance and 10 to represent a score of maximum importance. You should continue to ignore whether the actor supports or opposes the issue outcome.

After circling the importance values, place parentheses around what you consider to be your confidence interval for the issue. By this term is meant the smallest range within which you are positive the importance value lies. For example, you may have judged, with some uncertainty, that the issue has an importance value of 6 for the actor. You are positive, however, that the importance value falls somewhere between 4 and 8. Therefore, the response you give will look like this:

0 1 2 3 (4 5 ⑥ 7 8) 9 10

The confidence interval need not be equal on both sides of the score; that is, parentheses can be placed, for example, one integer to the left and 3 to the right. Note that you will be supplying confidence intervals, in the same way, for all of the variables except issue position.

274

Perform this same operation for each of the issues in the space below.

Issue Importance (Absolute Values)	Issue	Value and Confidence Interval
	A	0 1 2 3 4 5 6 7 8 9 10
	B	0 1 2 3 4 5 6 7 8 9 10
	C	0 1 2 3 4 5 6 7 8 9 10
	D	0 1 2 3 4 5 6 7 8 9 10
	E	0 1 2 3 4 5 6 7 8 9 10
	F	0 1 2 3 4 5 6 7 8 9 10
	G	0 1 2 3 4 5 6 7 8 9 10
	H	0 1 2 3 4 5 6 7 8 9 10
	I	0 1 2 3 4 5 6 7 8 9 10
	J	0 1 2 3 4 5 6 7 8 9 10

2.0 Power

Regardless of whether an actor supports or opposes an issue outcome, he has power both to promote and obstruct that outcome, and these two types of power are not necessarily equal. Power is the capability you judge that the actor could reasonably exercise in support of or opposition to the set of issue outcomes.

2.1 Power to Support

Arrange the issue cards in declining order of the actor's power to support the stated outcomes. As before, the issue which the actor has the greatest power to support should be listed first. Record the order that you have placed the cards in, using the identifying letters, in the spaces provided below.

Power to Support (Relative Values)	Rank	Issue
	1	_____
	2	_____

3	____
4	____
5	____
6	____
7	____
8	____
9	____
10	____

Now you are asked to assign a value for the actor on his power to support each issue outcome. Proceed as you did for the issue importance values. For each issue circle the number on the 0 to 10 scale (least power to maximum power) that best represents the actor's power to support the outcome. Also, for each issue assign a confidence interval as you did before, using parentheses.

Power to Support (Absolute Values)	Issue	Value and Confidence Interval
	A	0 1 2 3 4 5 6 7 8 9 10
	B	0 1 2 3 4 5 6 7 8 9 10
	C	0 1 2 3 4 5 6 7 8 9 10
	D	0 1 2 3 4 5 6 7 8 9 10
	E	0 1 2 3 4 5 6 7 8 9 10
	F	0 1 2 3 4 5 6 7 8 9 10
	G	0 1 2 3 4 5 6 7 8 9 10
	H	0 1 2 3 4 5 6 7 8 9 10
	I	0 1 2 3 4 5 6 7 8 9 10
	J	0 1 2 3 4 5 6 7 8 9 10

2.2 Power to Oppose

In similar manner, you are to judge the capability that the actor could reasonably exercise in opposition to the issue outcomes, regardless of his actual position. Arrange the issue cards in declining order of the actor's power to oppose the stated outcomes. Record this ranking below.

Power to Oppose (Relative Values)	Rank	Issue
	1	_____
	2	_____
	3	_____
	4	_____
	5	_____
	6	_____
	7	_____
	8	_____
	9	_____
	10	_____

Now please assign a value for the actor's power to oppose each issue outcome, and do not forget to assign confidence intervals for each value.

Power to Oppose (Absolute Values)	Issue	Value and Confidence Interval
	A	0 1 2 3 4 5 6 7 8 9 10
	B	0 1 2 3 4 5 6 7 8 9 10
	C	0 1 2 3 4 5 6 7 8 9 10
	D	0 1 2 3 4 5 6 7 8 9 10
	E	0 1 2 3 4 5 6 7 8 9 10
	F	0 1 2 3 4 5 6 7 8 9 10
	G	0 1 2 3 4 5 6 7 8 9 10
	H	0 1 2 3 4 5 6 7 8 9 10
	I	0 1 2 3 4 5 6 7 8 9 10
	J	0 1 2 3 4 5 6 7 8 9 10

3.0 Issue Position

Now you are requested to decide what the actor's position is on each of the issue outcomes. Divide the issue cards into three piles--one comprised of those issue outcomes which the actor supports or favors, another for those issue outcomes toward which he shows neutrality or ambivalence, and a third for the issue outcomes he opposes. For each issue circle "S" if the actor supports the outcome, "N" if he is neutral, or "O" if he opposes the outcome.

Issue Position	Issue	Issue Position
	A	S N O
	B	S N O
	C	S N O
	D	S N O
	E	S N O
	F	S N O
	G	S N O
	H	S N O
	I	S N O
	J	S N O

4.0 Firmness

Recombine all of the issue cards. Disregarding issue position, you are now asked to judge the firmness with which the actor holds his issue position on each of the issues. Firmness is defined as the likelihood that an actor will change his issue position.

Arrange the issue cards in declining order of the actor's firmness of issue position. The issue on which the actor's position is most firm should be listed first. Record the order in which you have placed the cards, using the identifying letters, in the space below.

Firmness (Relative Values)	Rank	Issue
	1	_____
	2	_____
	3	_____
	4	_____
	5	_____
	6	_____

7	_____
8	_____
9	_____
10	_____

Now assign the actor a firmness score on each issue on a 0 to 10 scale (minimum firmness to maximum firmness). Also, assign a confidence interval that indicates the range within which you are certain the actor's firmness lies.

Firmness (Absolute Values)	Issue	Value and Confidence Interval
	A	0 1 2 3 4 5 6 7 8 9 10
	B	0 1 2 3 4 5 6 7 8 9 10
	C	0 1 2 3 4 5 6 7 8 9 10
	D	0 1 2 3 4 5 6 7 8 9 10
	E	0 1 2 3 4 5 6 7 8 9 10
	F	0 1 2 3 4 5 6 7 8 9 10
	G	0 1 2 3 4 5 6 7 8 9 10
	H	0 1 2 3 4 5 6 7 8 9 10
	I	0 1 2 3 4 5 6 7 8 9 10
	J	0 1 2 3 4 5 6 7 8 9 10

Please return the questionnaire to the administrator. Thank you very much for your cooperation.

APPENDIX C

RECOMMENDATIONS TO THE FOREIGN AFFAIRS
COMMUNITY FOR IMPROVING THE USE OF
QUANTITATIVE TECHNIQUES

In this appendix, we will outline suggestions based
on the conclusions appearing in Chapter 8. Our purpose is
first to suggest the kinds of quantitative analyses members
of the INR staff should be able to perform in the near future, and second to suggest how that capability may be developed within the INR.

KINDS OF TECHNIQUES THAT
SHOULD BE USED

Our basic recommendations are that quantitative techniques be used:

1. To improve information gathering;
2. To test assumptions;
3. To generate indexes that are considered predictors
of the kinds of political events and conditions foreign
affairs analysts seek to forecast.

We will briefly describe each of these analytical
tasks and the kinds of capabilities that they would require.

Information Gathering

By far the most important task that must be performed
if analysts are to use quantitative techniques for maximum
immediate payoff is to use quantitative techniques for
gathering information. This prescription, however, should
not be taken as an endorsement for an elaborate set of
computer data banks in which tremendous amounts of quantitative data are stored. There is admittedly a tendency to
think of the application of quantitative techniques to the
collection of data to mean the establishment of a large
computerized bank. Nevertheless, our recommendation is
that quantitative procedures be adopted on an ad hoc and

incremental basis in order to create "custom-made" data sets for those users who recognize the need for some specific data.

Basically, the case studies illustrated three kinds of information-gathering procedures: (1) collecting available aggregate statistics; (2) applying some kind of content analysis procedure to written information coming into the State Department; and (3) using expert-generated data questionnaire procedures. We do not recommend the use of broad mass and elite surveys because they are extremely costly and usually take many weeks or even months before their findings are available to analysts. We will describe specific projects that might be undertaken in each of these three areas.

As far as collecting available statistics goes, we suggest that for reports concerned with collecting information on social, economic, political, and military conditions within one or more countries, foreign affairs analysts learn to call for and use data sets. Scarcely any analysts use computerized information storage to generate tables and graphs of statistics. Although a few analysts occasionally had access to some print-outs, most of their data was collected and recorded by hand. One area in which there is existing data for use by analysts is computerized in UN voting records compiled by the staff in the administrative bureau. While these records have not yet been used in the State Department, they can eventually be a significant part of the research and decision making with respect to American policies in the United Nations.

The application of content analysis procedures to recorded information also is a possibility. However, we have concluded, partly on the basis of the enormous clerical costs of manual and automatic content analysis, that only specialized forms of propaganda analysis could be performed. Other than such specialized forms of analysis, content analysis as a method of creating quantitative data on events is excessively costly. Instead, we recommend taking advantage of methods already built into the system of information gathering and dissemination within the department. The TAGS system, for example, could be used to generate measures of internal and external conflict with respect to all states. Since it is based on mission reports and classified by the originator of the message, the TAGS system could be made to yield data similar to the content analysis procedures of academics at very little additional cost to the department.

Finally, we feel that expert-generated data collection methods are critical not only for the information-gathering process but for a wide variety of the tasks performed by INR analysts. At this time, the give-and-take among experts within the department, other governmental agencies, and experts in nongovernmental positions is so informal that a great deal of information is either lost or left extremely ambiguous. A formalization of this process could help analysts keep up with the increasing complexity of the phenomena with which they are dealing.

Testing Assumptions

The promise of quantitative techniques in this task is not as great as one might expect. On the one hand, the lack of standardization in the definition of terms and the lack of explicit assumptions about relationships among factors that is characteristic of the writings of the analyst preclude the efficient formulation of testable hypotheses. On the other hand, even if those assumptions could be identified in an explicit way, the multi-causal nature of the subjects of analysis would make it extremely difficult to generate meaningful tests. It is really the job of the academic outside of government to supply the validated findings that the intelligence analysts can then apply to their subject. However, academics usually do not deal with questions that relate to the kinds of assumptions that foreign affairs analysts have to make, while the analysts themselves are so pressured to meet their daily demands that they cannot establish effective interaction with the academics. It is not a matter of placing blame on either side. Rather, it is a question of discovering ways in which the academics can begin to build theoretical structures that can be used by the INR analysts. For this to happen, the scholars have to deal with less abstract and less highly aggregated variables, while the analysts must learn to formulate their concerns in a way that allows for testing and generalization.

Quantitative Forecasting

We have demonstrated several ways in which quantitative methods can be used to supplement the forecasting of foreign affairs analysts. We have identified four basic techniques:

1. Correlation studies can yield factors for creating a checklist helpful in writing qualitative descriptions and forecasts with respect to specific events and conditions.

2. Correlation and regression techniques can produce indicators of such things as coup-proneness or probabilities of change in arms expenditures.

3. Trend analysis procedures can project into the immediate future by summarizing trends in areas such as international violence.

4. Computer simulation models can use quantitative data to generate forecasts.

All of these techniques have been used in areas of policy analysis other than international relations, and could be applied to the tasks of the foreign affairs analyst. For such an application to take place, it would be necessary for the analyst to learn how to use the techniques and to acquire the kinds of quantitative data that the techniques require. At this time, neither condition prevails, so that the effort would be quite costly.

Unfortunately, academic research in the international relations and comparative politics fields has not been much help in providing guidelines for the analyst. As indicated in Chapter 1, scholars have been concerned not with producing analyses that lead to concrete predictions but rather with building theoretical structures that are designed to explain cause-and-effect relationships. This type of activity is relevant to the analysts' need to test their assumptions. But it provides little in the way of direct applications for forecasting. Although there are some works that aim at generating a predictive indicator through regression analysis, there are almost none that deal with trend analysis and computer simulation models.

COSTS OF USING QUANTITATIVE
TECHNIQUES

Before turning to specific recommendations, we should address the main types of costs that any attempts at change must anticipate and try to minimize. Up to this point, we have not discussed this question. To do so in specific terms in the context of this book would be neither feasible nor useful. However, it is necessary to indicate the kinds of costs that quantitative techniques might generate. Our discussion assumes that, on the one hand, the personnel and activities of the INR will remain relatively stable over the next few years and that, on the other hand, there will be no major breakthroughs in the development of quantitative techniques. Assuming both of these constraints, we can identify some costs that might be incurred if INR analysts were to apply quantitative techniques to some of their information gathering, descriptive analysis, and forecasting activities.

Under current conditions, we might identify four sources of costs:

1. Intellectual and analytical costs: Given the limited development of quantitative techniques, the need to generalize across a number of cases in order to apply such techniques may force the analyst to lose the detail he might need to complete his analysis or serve his user. For example, quantitative techniques tend to ignore the sequence of events because they lead to collapsing information over time periods. The sequencing of events, however, may be more important than the magnitude of all events. While quantitative techniques can be used to keep the information about sequencing, the efficiency usually provided by the techniques might be lost.

2. Resource costs: Given the fact that a substantial number of INR analysts are not well trained in quantitative techniques, the costs in time of staff, equipment, and technical assistance are important to consider.

3. Organizational costs: Given the general opposition to the use of quantitative techniques and the threat their use might pose, in addition to the redefinition of roles among analysts and between users and analysts, substantial costs might be incurred in the form of low morale, conflict among sections, and so on.

4. Communication costs: Analysts and users may have more trouble communicating with each other as the analysts become more involved in the application of quantitative techniques. Because of the formalism and special language required by the use of quantitative techniques, the process of translating from analyst to user could require additional time and effort.

Below we illustrate how each of the three major uses of quantitative methods is related to the four types of costs described. We have estimated each type of cost as being "High" or "Low" for each of the three basic analytical functions. We have ascribed the terms so that they are relative to each other within the domain of each of the four types of costs. One interesting point about the

	Type of Costs			
Type of Analysis	Intellectual Analytical	Resource	Organizational	Communication
Information gathering	Low	High	Low	Low
Testing assumptions	High	Low	High	High
Forecasting	High	Low	High	High

chart is that the resource cost is high where the other three costs are low, and vice versa. Our estimate is that only in the area of acquiring and storing information are there considerable costs in terms of manpower and machinery. In the other areas the costs are more intangible, but they certainly are real.

Even though we have said that the resource costs for information gathering are high relative to the resource costs for testing assumptions and for quantitative forecasting, it should be pointed out that many of the techniques we have discussed can be approached in a way to minimize cost. All of the case studies used data that was already in quantitative form or could be generated with small use of clerical and computer time. This position is contrary to the suggestions of many commentators who advocate large data banks. We feel that extensive data banks are not only costly but are of limited utility. Most analysts already have an information-overload problem. Providing greater access to huge data banks will not solve that problem unless there is both specific user demand and clear definition of the uses of a particular data set. Without the demand for a specific data set for a specific purpose, it would not be an efficient use of resources to generate computer data banks.

As far as the resource costs for testing assumptions and quantitative forecasting goes, the costs in terms of computer time and statistical staff time are small. This assumes, of course, that the INR analyst knows how to use the appropriate techniques. If not, training costs must be included. If so, the time necessary to test assumptions with quantitative data and generate forecasts is no greater than the time now required to come to the thoughtful analytical positions that most analysts now develop.

As far as the other three costs are concerned, the problems that generate these costs are beyond the scope of this book. Suffice to say, they will not be overcome because the resource costs are shown to be small relative to the benefits in information gathering, testing assumptions, and forecasting. A demonstration of resource costs is only part of a series of long-run development efforts that must take place to reduce the intellectual and analytical, organizational and communication costs that now accompany any attempt to use quantitative methods in the INR.

SOME SPECIFIC SUGGESTIONS FOR IMPLEMENTATION

Our suggestions in this section are based on the total experience we have had during this study. As such, they are based upon the following assumptions:

1. INR analysts now underutilize quantitative techniques.
2. Such techniques could aid some analysts in some of the tasks they perform, particularly in gathering information, checking assumptions, and making forecasts.
3. Existing contributions of quantitative work among academics is either too abstract or too underdeveloped to allow for immediate and massive translation to INR tasks.
4. Given the present configuration of staff and activities in the INR, on the one hand, and the limited utility of current applied quantitative techniques on the other, a conservative approach should be followed.

Our suggestions are based on these assumptions and are divided into two general categories: (1) training INR analysts and (2) conducting demonstration projects.

Training of Personnel

The first order of business should be to help bring interested members of the INR staff up to a level where they can feel comfortable using quantitative techniques. To do this it is necessary to identify the specific skills (and, by implication, attitudes) that are required. We have listed below six skills in the order of ascending level of sophistication and difficulty.

1. The ability to state explicitly a set of assumptions and to identify quantitative measures of the concepts in the assumptions so that the relationships can be checked.

2.   The ability to translate general descriptive statements into tables, matrixes, graphs, flowcharts, and probability statements.
3.   The ability to display graphically distributions
of one variable.
4.   The ability to display distributions of two variables.
5.   The ability to interpret the meanings of basic
correlation statistics.
6.   The ability to interpret the results of multiple
regression analysis.

There are, of course, more complex quantitative skills,
but they need not be listed here because most INR analysts
have only several or none of the six.
       The list of skills can be used in a variety of ways.
It can serve as a basis for developing training programs
and as a basis upon which INR analysts could diagnose their
own quantitative skills.   More important, the list can be
used to indicate to the potential user of quantitative
techniques whether he must be familiar with a given technique.   For example, for information-gathering purposes
the analyst would only need to have skills 1, 2, and 3,
whereas descriptive analysis and forecasting activities
would require all six skills.   The list might also be used
to judge whether a given technique should be taken seriously by INR analysts.   There is an unfortunate tendency
to bring in outside consultants versed in extremely complex techniques without first determining whether the
skill basis exists among a large enough group of analysts
to understand that technique.   At some time in the future,
the more complex techniques might be explored and made
available to analysts.   For the time being, consideration
should be given only to those techniques that can be understood by someone possessing at least some of the six skills.
       INR analysts can acquire these skills in many differ-
ent ways.   They might take a one-week course offered by
the Foreign Service Institute, or they might take a course
offered by one of the universities in the Washington area.
It is important to note that it is unnecessary to consider
leaves of absence or other major personnel investments.

Demonstration Studies

       We believe that the case studies have demonstrated
the potential utility of quantitative techniques in the

287

work of foreign affairs analysis. Any further demonstration studies should be planned in such a way that their results (directly and indirectly) can be applied to the day-to-day activities of the analyst. Unless potential users define the need and are willing to use the results of a particular demonstration study, evidence cannot be gained to assess the particular utility of a given technique.

To provide an idea of the kinds of studies that might be appropriate, we have listed below a few that have evolved out of our case studies.

1. The continuation of an expert-generated study on the bargaining between North and South Korea (or on some other appropriate topic). This study would generate information from government experts on a monthly basis. That data would be used to monitor conditions, to generate predictions, and to inform analysts of the degree of agreement or disagreement on the topic being analyzed.

2. The coding of TAGS data to monitor domestic and external trends that could lead to violence within and between selected states.

3. The development of small computerized access and analysis systems for those INR analysts who have data that they would like to use more fully. This might include data pertaining to global oil problems, to voting in the United Nations, to laws of the seas issues, or to social, economic, and political factors that might serve as predictive indicators.

4. The construction of predictive indicators in areas such as coup-proneness, that could provide a basis for making forecasts.

We think such demonstration studies are necessary for several reasons. First, they will provide experience for INR personnel and other State Department officials in applying general quantitative techniques to specific problems. Second, the studies will help to make the techniques developed by academics more relevant to the analyst's own needs. Third, they will provide an opportunity for pilot testing under operating conditions so that costs and benefits can be more concretely analyzed. In sum, the demonstration studies will have a training as well as a testing function as foreign policy analysts in the department attempt to come to grips with the application of quantitative techniques to their tasks.

Although we cannot at present spell out the exact types of demonstrations studies that might be undertaken, we can recommend for consideration a project that the INR, the Foreign Service Institute, or some other body might undertake. The follow-up to the case studies could be a one-year project in which individuals throughout the department are encouraged to pursue one of their information, descriptive analysis, or forecasting tasks using quantitative methods. For those individuals who make a proposal that appears to be feasible, outside contractors would provide a specific design and if possible provide assistance in the form of a student intern or computer and statistical analysis. The initiating officer should be expected to make the following commitments: (1) to initiate the proposal; (2) to work with the consultant to set up the project, making sure there is adequate access to data; and (3) to assess the results either by using them in his operational work or indicating why the results were not useful.

Two questions are raised by this proposal: (1) How do we get the officer who is probably already overburdened to make such a commitment and (2) What kinds of resources might be needed to support the services provided by the contractor? The following general remarks provide some answers to these two questions.

Officers from the INR and other bureaus in the department can be recruited through at least three channels. First, those individuals who have attended or will be attending the Foreign Service Institute's courses on computers and quantitative methods are likely recruits. As a follow-up to their experience, the opportunity for participating in a demonstration study could be offered to them. Some type of advanced certification by the institute might be granted, or if feasible, the university of the outside contractor could provide graduate credit. Second, individuals involved in the Senior Seminar or in other training programs might be offered the opportunity to perform such a demonstration study instead of the paper that is their frequent assignment. Third, a general announcement could be provided through regular communication channels and offered in conjunction with the publication of this book.

We estimate that there are at least 300 foreign service officers having the first three skills outlined above. Hence, there is a considerable base of trained personnel from which the demonstration project might draw. Our expectation is that at least 10 individuals or groups of individuals can be found to make the kind of commitments re-

quired for the project. They would submit their proposals
to a committee that would decide on which to support during
the first four months of the year in which the projects
were to take place.

Assuming that the recruits can be found, how can the
resources be delivered? The answer to this question will
depend upon the nature of the specific demonstration project, the kind of training of the individual making the
proposal, and the availability of support services to him.
Basically, however, the contractor would meet with each
project director and would develop a plan. He would periodically evaluate the work being performed under the plan.
In addition, where feasible a student assistant would be
assigned to the project and work either in Washington or
at the home base of the student. He would be responsible
for as much as the project director wished, including collecting and analyzing data, using the computer, and writing
draft reports.

Although the total amount of money required would vary
for each project, it is possible that costs could be kept
under $2,000 per demonstration project. The money would
pay for travel and consulting fee for the contractor, for
travel and maintenance living expenses of the student, and
in some cases for computer time and related materials.
The financial requirements would be so small because the
preparatory work and data-access problems would be taken
care of by the department official making the proposal.
The role of the outside contractor would be limited to design and to supervising the student, who would be working
on an apprentice basis.

We see these demonstration studies as an important
logical next step. Earlier studies involving outside quantitative contract work had the purpose of raising con-
sciousness. In the present period the concrete question
should be: Under what circumstances might quantitative
techniques be applied on a cost-effective basis? That the
State Department in general and the INR in particular has
moved to consider this question is an important milestone.
That further demonstration studies and hard evaluative activities should be undertaken to try to answer the question
seems an obvious conclusion.

MICHAEL K. O'LEARY is a professor of political science at Syracuse University. In addition to teaching courses on quantitative methodology and transnational policy analysis, he has served as a consultant to both governmental and nongovernmental groups in the area of systematic policy analysis. This book is the outgrowth of a major consulting project with the Department of State.

Professor O'Leary's past publications include <u>Congress in Crisis</u>, <u>The Politics of American Foreign Aid</u>, and (with Professor Coplin as coauthor) <u>Everyman's Prince</u>, <u>A Guide to Solving Your Political Problems</u>. He has also authored a series of papers and articles on comparative foreign policy making.

Professor O'Leary received his Ph.D. degree from Princeton University. In addition he has held postgraduate research and training fellowships at the University of Michigan, New York University, the North Atlantic Treaty Organization Headquarters in Belgium, and the Institute for Peace and Conflict Research, Denmark.

WILLIAM D. COPLIN is a professor of political science and Director of the International Relations Program, Syracuse University. He has taught graduate and undergraduate courses in international law and organization as well as served as a consultant to various local, federal, and international agencies. Professor Coplin's past publications include <u>The Functions of International Law</u> and <u>Introduction to International Relations</u>. He has also coauthored a book (with Professor O'Leary and Patrick J. McGowan), entitled <u>American Foreign Policy</u>.

Professor Coplin has received his Ph.D. degree from American University in international relations and has completed a year of postgraduate work on quantitative methods at the University of Michigan under a Science Faculty Fellowship from the National Science Foundation.

CRISIS DECISION-MAKING: Israel's Experience in 1967 and 1973
Abraham R. Wagner

THE ENERGY CRISIS AND U.S. FOREIGN POLICY
edited by Joseph S. Szyliowicz
and Bard E. O'Neill

THE LOGIC OF "MAOISM": Critiques and Explication
edited by James Chieh Hsiung

U.S. FOREIGN POLICY AND THE THIRD WORLD PEASANT: Land
Reform in Asia and Latin America
Gary L. Olson